CONTINGENCIES OF REINFORCEMENT

THE CENTURY PSYCHOLOGY SERIES

Richard M. Elliott, Kenneth MacCorquodale,
Gardner Lindzey, and Kenneth E. Clark

Editors

B. F. SKINNER

CONTINGENCIES OF REINFORCEMENT

a theoretical analysis

APPLETON-CENTURY-CROFTS

EDUCATIONAL DIVISION

New York   MEREDITH CORPORATION

BF
319.5
·0 6
659-1   S 55

Library of Congress Catalog Card Number: 78-90348

To LISA

Preface

In a paper published in 1950 (134) I asked the question "Are theories of learning necessary?" and suggested that the answer was "No." I soon found myself representing a position which has been described as a Grand Anti-Theory (165). Fortunately, I had defined my terms. The word "theory" was to mean "any explanation of an observed fact which appeals to events taking place somewhere else, at some other level of observation, described in different terms, and measured, if at all, in different dimensions"—events, for example, in the real nervous system, the conceptual system, or the mind. I argued that theories of this sort had not stimulated good research on learning and that they misrepresented the facts to be accounted for, gave false assurances about the state of our knowledge, and led to the continued use of methods which should be abandoned.

Near the end of the paper I referred to "the possibility of theory in another sense," as a critique of the methods, data, and concepts of a science of behavior. Parts of *The Behavior of Organisms* (129) were theoretical in that sense, as were six published papers,[1] in the last of which I insisted that "whether particular experimental psychologists

[1] "The Concept of the Reflex in the Description of Behavior" (124), "The Generic Nature of the Concepts of Stimulus and Response" (126), "Two Types of Conditioned Reflex and a Pseudo-Type" (125), "Two Types of Conditioned Reflex: A Reply to Konorski and Miller" (128), "The Operational Analysis of Psychological Terms" (130), and "Current Trends in Experimental Psychology" (131).

like it or not, experimental psychology is properly and inevitably committed to the construction of a theory of behavior. A theory is essential to the scientific understanding of behavior as a subject matter." Subsequently I was to discuss such a theory in three other papers[2] and in substantial parts of *Science and Human Behavior* (135) and *Verbal Behavior* (141).

Another kind of theory is also necessary. We know a great deal about human behavior, for we have observed it all our lives under a great variety of circumstances and have learned about it from others who have had similar experiences. We need to interpret familiar facts of this sort in the light of a scientific analysis. Much of *Verbal Behavior* is theoretical in that sense and so are discussions of other kinds of social behavior which have appeared in four papers[3] and in *Walden Two* (133). Similar issues arise in the practical application of a basic analysis, and I have discussed some of them in *The Technology of Teaching* (152).

That is not a bad record for a Grand Anti-Theoretician, and to it must now be added the present book. It is theoretical in several senses. Part I traces the emergence of the concept of contingencies of reinforcement and its use in the interpretation of cultural practices and in the prediction and control of human behavior. Part II takes up the nature and dimensions of behavior, the ontogenic and phylogenic variables of which it is a function, and the contingent relations among those variables.. Part III returns to theories which appeal to "events taking place somewhere else, at some other level of observation" and shows how they are replaced by an analysis of contingencies of reinforcement.

A reputation as an anti-theorist is easily acquired by anyone who neglects hypothetico-deductive methods. When a

[2] "A Critique of Psychoanalytic Concepts and Theories" (136), "What is Psychotic Behavior?" (138), and "The Flight from the Laboratory" (142).

[3] "Freedom and the Control of Men" (139), "The Control of Human Behavior" (137), "Some Issues Concerning the Control of Human Behavior" (140), and "The Design of Cultures" (145).

subject matter is very large (for example, the universe as a whole) or very small (for example, subatomic particles) or for any reason inaccessible, we cannot manipulate variables or observe effects as we should like to do. We therefore make tentative or hypothetical statements about them, deduce theorems which refer to accessible states of affairs, and by checking the theorems confirm or refute our hypotheses. The achievements of the hypothetico-deductive method, where appropriate, have been brilliant. Newton set the pattern in his *Principia,* and the great deductive theorists who followed him have been given a prominent place in the history of science.

Their significance has nevertheless probably been exaggerated, and in part for rather trivial reasons. Unlike direct observation and description, the construction of a hypothesis suggests mysterious intellectual activities. Like those who are said to be capable of extrasensory perception, the hypothesis-maker seems to display knowledge which he cannot have acquired through ordinary channels. That is not actually the case, but the resulting prestige is real enough, and it has had unfortunate consequences.

For one thing, the method tends to be used when it is not needed, when direct observation is not only possible but more effective. To guess who is calling when the phone rings seems somehow more admirable than to pick up the phone and find out, although one picks up the phone to confirm the guess. The more unlikely the caller, the more admirable the guess, although it is no more valuable. The extrasensory procedure is similar: to guess the pattern on a card and then turn the card over and look at the pattern is to make and confirm a hypothesis. Such performances command attention even when the results are trivial. Like those body-builders who flex their muscles in setting-up exercizes or hand-stands on the beach, the hypothesis-maker is admired even though his hypotheses are useless, just as the extrasensory perceiver is admired even though he never makes practical predictions of the movements of armies or fluctuations in the stock market. (Like that third specialist in unproductive behavior, the gambler, both are sustained by occasional hits—and by very rare hits, indeed, if they have been reinforced on a variable-ratio schedule favorably programmed.)

The hypothetico-deductive method and the mystery which surrounds it have been perhaps most harmful in misrepresenting ways in which people think. Scientific behavior is possibly the most complex subject matter ever submitted to scientific analysis, and we are still far from having an adequate account of it. Why does a scientist examine and explore a given subject? What rate of discovery will sustain his behavior in doing so? What precurrent behaviors improve his chances of success and extend the adequacy and scope of his descriptions? What steps does he take in moving from protocol to general statement? These are difficult questions, and there are many more like them. The scientist is under the control of very complex contingencies of reinforcement. Some of the more obvious ones have been analyzed and a few rules have been extracted (see Chapter 6), particularly by logicians, mathematicians, statisticians, and scientific methodologists. For a number of reasons these rules apply mainly to verbal behavior, including hypothesis-making and deduction. The student who learns to follow them no doubt behaves in effective and often indispensable ways, but we should not suppose that in doing so he displays the full range of scientific behavior. Nor should we teach such rules as if they exhausted scientific methods.[4]

---

[4] Nor should we promote hypothetico-deductive procedures in artificial ways. "Through the generosity of an anonymous donor" the American Association for the Advancement of Science offers an annual prize of one thousand dollars "intended to encourage studies and analyses of social behavior based on explicitly stated assumptions or postulates leading to conclusions or deductions that are verifiable by systematic empirical research; to encourage in social inquiry the development and application of the kind of dependable methodology that has proved so fruitful in the natural sciences."

Empirical surveys (for example, *An Introduction to Scientific Research* by E. Bright Wilson [168]) show a better balance in representing the contingencies under which scientists actually work, but a functional analysis which not only clarifies the nature of scientific inquiry but suggests how it may be most effectively imparted to young scientists still lies in the future.

Behavior is one of those subject matters which do not call for hypothetico-deductive methods. Both behavior itself and most of the variables of which it is a function are usually conspicuous. (Responses which are of very small magnitude or difficult to reach are notable exceptions, but the problems they pose are technical rather than methodological.) If hypotheses commonly appear in the study of behavior, it is only because the investigator has turned his attention to inaccessible events—some of them fictitious, others irrelevant. For Clark Hull (71) the science of behavior eventually became the study of central processes, mainly conceptual but often ascribed to the nervous system. The processes were not directly observed and seemed therefore to require hypotheses and deductions, but the facts were observable. Only so long as a generalization gradient, for example, remained a hypothetical feature of an inner process was it necessary to determine its shape by making hypotheses and confirming or disproving theorems derived from them. When gradients began to be directly observed, the hypothetico-deductive procedures became irrelevant.

Cognitive psychologists have promoted the survival of another inaccessible world to which deductive methods seem appropriate. An introspectionist may claim to observe some of the products and by-products of mental processes, but the processes themselves are not directly perceived, and statements about them are therefore hypothetical. The Freudian mental apparatus has also required a deductive approach, as have the traits, abilities, and factors derived from "mental measurements." We can avoid hypothetico-de-

ductive methods in all these fields by formulating the data
without reference to cognitive processes, mental apparatuses,
or traits. Many physiological explanations of behavior seem
at the moment to call for hypotheses, but the future lies with
techniques of direct observation which will make them unnecessary (see Chapter 9).

Some of the questions to which a different kind of theory
may be addressed are as follows: what aspects of behavior
are significant? Of what variables are changes in these aspects a function? How are the relations among behavior and
its controlling variables to be brought together in characterizing an organism as a system? What methods are appropriate in studying such a system experimentally? Under what
conditions does such an analysis yield a technology of behavior and what issues arise in its application? These are
not questions to which a hypothetico-deductive method is
appropriate. They are nevertheless important questions, for
the future of a science of behavior depends upon the answers.

B.F.S.

Contents

II An analysis of ontogenic and phylogenic contingencies

III A critique of alternative theories

I CONTINGENCIES OF REINFORCEMENT AND THE DESIGN OF CULTURES

1   The role of the environment

The environment was once thought of simply as the place in which animals and men lived and behaved. They may have behaved in different ways in different places, but not because the places were different. The environment was a necessary setting, which perhaps favored or hindered behavior but did not determine its occurrence or form. It was not until the seventeenth century that a more active role was suggested by Descartes in his anticipation of the reflex, and it was not until the nineteenth century that reflexes were isolated and studied. Physiologists then began to call the action of the environment a *stimulus*, the Latin for "goad." The term acquired further meaning as reflexes were discovered and studied, and its scope was extended when Pavlov showed how new stimuli could be conditioned. The discovery of tropisms lent support, particularly in the writings of Jacques Loeb, to the view that the environment somehow or other *forced* the organism to behave.

Such was the background against which stimulus-response psychology was born. John B. Watson adopted the principle of the conditioned reflex and added it to the older notion of habit. He contended that animals and men acquired new behavior through conditioning and then went on behaving as long as appropriate stimuli were active. The position was systematically developed by Clark Hull (71). E. B. Holt summarized it this way: "We are really prodded or lashed

3

through life" (70). But it was not easy to show that this was true of all behavior. Plausible stimuli could not be found for all responses, and some relevant environmental conditions, such as a shortage of food, did not act like stimuli. The original concept was soon replaced by something much less precise called the "total stimulus situation." Equally troublesome was the fact that many stimuli which obviously reached the surface of the organism seemed to have no effect. A new kind of stimulus was therefore invented; it was called a cue, and it had the curious property of being effective only when the organism needed it. (Ethologists solve a similar problem in the same way when they attribute unlearned behavior to "releasers," stimuli which act only when the organism is ready to respond.)

This was patchwork, designed to salvage the stimulus-response formula, and it had the effect of moving the determination of behavior back into the organism. When external stimuli could not be found, internal had to be invented. If a shortage of food was not itself a stimulus, it could at least generate a "drive" which prodded the organism from within. (Hunger pangs seemed to confirm this view, but comparable stimulation from swollen seminal vesicles, which Watson thought might explain sexual behavior, was less plausible.) Emotional variables led to the invention of other inner stimuli; fear, for example, became an acquired drive. Even instincts became stimuli, a view supported curiously enough by Freud.

Inner processes and mechanisms also had to be invented. If a conspicuous stimulus seemed to have no effect, it was because a central gatekeeper—a sort of Maxwell's demon—had refused to let it enter. When the organism seemed to behave appropriately with respect to stimuli which had long since disappeared, it was said to be responding to copies of those stimuli which it had stored in its memory. Many of these central activities were only thinly disguised versions of the mental processes which stimulus-response psychology had vowed to dispossess. Indeed, they continued to be called mental (or, as the fashion changed, cognitive) in a similar formulation derived from information theory. Let input stand for stimulus and output for response, and certain dimensional problems are simplified. This is promising but not promising enough, because central processes are still needed. Output follows input only when input has been "selected," "transformed," "stored," "retrieved," and so on.

Beyond stimulus and response

Every stimulus-response or input-output formulation of behavior suffers from a serious omission. No account of the interchange between organism and environment is complete until it includes the action of the environment upon the organism *after* a response has been made. The fact that behavior might have important consequences had not, of course, gone unnoticed. The philosophy of hedonism insisted that men worked to achieve pleasure and avoid pain, and utilitarianism tried to justify behavior in terms of its useful effects. Evolutionary theory pointed to the resulting adaptation or adjustment of the organism to the environment. Nevertheless, the full significance of consequences was only slowly recognized. Possibly there was some uneasiness about final causes (How could something which followed behavior have an effect on it?), but a major difficulty lay in the facts. There were embarrassing exceptions to all these rules. Men sometimes act in ways which bring pain and destroy pleasure, have a questionable net utility, and work against the survival of the species. Rewards and punishments do not always have predictable effects. Though we may know how much a person is paid, we cannot tell how hard he will work. Though we may know that the parents of one child respond to him with affection and those of another with the disciplinary measures of a martinet, we cannot tell which child will conform and which rebel. Though we may know that one government is tyrannical and another benevolent, we cannot predict which people will submit and which revolt. Many efforts have been made to explain failures of this sort—for example, by inventing other kinds of pleasures and pains—but they have never succeeded in preserving confidence in the basic principles.

A more reassuring order began to emerge when the temporal relation between behavior and its consequences was scrutinized. In Edward L. Thorndike's famous experiment, a hungry cat confined in a box could turn a latch and open a door; it could then escape from the box and reach food lying outside. Several features of this arrangement are worth noting. Escape from a box and access to food are more sharply specified than any net gain or ultimate advantage, and they follow immediately upon turning the latch. Indeed, they may coincide with traces of that response, in which case the issue of final causes can be avoided.

What Thorndike observed was that the behavior of turning the latch was, as he said, "stamped in." He could plot a learning curve showing how the cat came to turn the latch more and more quickly as the experiment was repeated. He did not need to assume that the response itself was in any way strengthened. It might have occurred more quickly just because other behavior in the box was "stamped out." A successful response could be selected by its consequences very much as a mutation was said to be selected by its contribution to survival in evolutionary theory. (This interpretation of the selective effect of consequences continued to be maintained by Edwin R. Guthrie.)

A further simplification of the experiment clarifies the process. A box in which a hungry rat depresses a lever and immediately obtains food is clearly in the Thorndike tradition. The response is simpler, however, and the consequence is immediately contingent upon it, at least if a conditioned reinforcer such as the sound of the food dispenser has been set up. But there is a more important feature: by thoroughly adapting the rat to the box before the lever is made available, most of the competing behavior can be "stamped out" before the response to be learned is ever emitted. Thorndike's learning curve, showing the gradual disappearance of unsuccessful behavior, then vanishes. In its place we are left with a conspicuous change in the successful response itself: an immediate, often quite abrupt, increase in rate (129).

By using rate of responding as a dependent variable, it has been possible to formulate the interaction between an organism and its environment more adequately. The kinds of consequences which increase the rate ("reinforcers") are positive or negative, depending upon whether they reinforce when they appear or when they disappear. The class of responses upon which a reinforcer is contingent is called an operant, to suggest the action on the environment followed by reinforcement. We construct an operant by making a reinforcer contingent on a response, but the important fact about the resulting unit is not its topography but its probability of occurrence, observed as rate of emission. Prior stimuli are not irrelevant. Any stimulus present when an operant is reinforced acquires control in the sense that the rate will be higher when it is present. Such a stimulus does not act as a goad; it does not elicit the response in the sense of forcing it to occur. It is simply an essential aspect of the occasion upon which a response is made and reinforced. The difference is made clear by calling it a discriminative stimulus (or S^D).

An adequate formulation of the interaction between an organism and its environment must always specify three things: (1) the occasion upon which a response occurs, (2) the response itself, and (3) the reinforcing consequences. The interrelationships among them are the "contingencies of reinforcement." The concept characterizes an aspect of the environment which Tolman and Brunswik may have been trying to identify when they spoke of its "causal texture" (160). The interrelationships are much more complex than those between a stimulus and a response, and they are much more productive in both theoretical and experimental analyses. The behavior generated by a given set of contingencies can be accounted for without appealing to hypothetical inner states or processes. If a conspicuous stimulus does not have an effect, it is not because the organism has not attended to it or because some central gatekeeper has screened it out, but because the stimulus plays no important role in the prevailing contingencies.[1] The other cognitive processes invoked to salvage an input-output formula can be disposed of in the same way.

In a laboratory for the study of operant behavior, contingencies of reinforcement are deliberately arranged and their effects observed. The experimental space contains various controllable stimuli, one or more operanda which report responses, and one or more means of reinforcement. Specific interrelations among these things are maintained by relays, timers, counters, rate analyzers, and so on. (The development of this equipment during the past twenty-five years is a fair record of the increasing complexity of the contingencies which have been submitted to analysis.) The behavior is usually recorded in a cumulative record because rate and changes in rate over substantial periods of time can then be seen at a glance, but further details are commonly clarified by analyzing interresponse times. Some contingencies require on-line computer processing of the behavior. With the help of such equipment, together with the experimental techniques for which it is designed, we have begun to *see* contingencies of reinforcement.

It is hard to see them in any other way. Suppose we ask an observer who knows nothing about the analysis of behavior to look into a typical experimental space when an experiment is in progress. He sees a pigeon, let us say, occasionally peck-

---

[1] A more active form of attention is analyzed as a sequence of contingencies; paying attention is precurrent behavior having the effect of changing stimuli. A pigeon will change the shape or color of a visual pattern if the contingencies under which it is reinforced are thereby improved.

ing one of several colored disks on a wall, and he may note that it pecks at different rates on different disks. The colors of the disks change from time to time, and a change is perhaps followed by a noticeable change in rate. A food dispenser occasionally operates and the pigeon eats, and our observer infers (possibly wrongly) that it has recently gone without food. The food dispenser usually operates just after a response has been made, but not necessarily after a response to a disk of a given color and in any case only very infrequently.

Our observer will find it hard to make any sense of these scattered facts. He has observed a behaving organism from what appears to be an almost ideal vantage point. Over a substantial period of time he has seen various stimuli, responses, and reinforcers appear and disappear. The fact remains that *direct observation, no matter how prolonged, tells him very little about what is going on.* He will be quite unprepared for the additional information to be found in a simple cumulative record, where for the first time he can estimate rate of responding accurately, compare different rates, and follow the accelerations which are now obvious. He has had, of course, none of the information about the recent history of the pigeon to be found in the log of the experiment. Above all, he could only vaguely have surmised the interdependencies among stimuli, responses, and reinforcers which he can now discover by examining the controlling equipment.

When we recall how long it took to recognize the causal action of the environment in the simple reflex, we should perhaps not be surprised that it has taken us much longer to see contingencies of reinforcement. The traditional homocentric view of human behavior discourages us from looking at the environment in this light, and the facts themselves are far from obvious. And now let us ask our observer to look at the environment at large, where animals and men are living and behaving under contingencies vastly more complex than any which have ever been submitted to experimental analysis.

If he could not see what was happening in a relatively simple experimental space, how can we expect him to understand the behavior he sees in the world around him? And everyone has been in his position until very recently!

It is only when we have analyzed behavior under known contingencies of reinforcement that we can begin to see what is happening in daily life. Things we once overlooked then begin to command our attention, and things which once attracted our attention we learn to discount or ignore. Topography of behavior, no matter how fascinating, then takes second place to evidences of probability. A stimulus is no longer merely the conspicuous onset or termination of an energy exchange, as in reflex physiology; it is any part of the occasion on which a response is emitted and reinforced. Reinforcement is much more than "being rewarded"; a prevailing probability of reinforcement, particularly under various intermittent schedules, is the important variable. In other words, we no longer look at behavior and environment as separate things or events but at the interrelations among them. We look at the contingencies of reinforcement. We can then interpret behavior more successfully.

The principles of hedonism, utilitarianism, and adaptation were not wrong, they were simply not precise. It is true that men work for money and affection and to avoid the whip and that they pursue happiness and seek relief from pain. At a comparable level, it is true that water boils when heated, freezes when chilled, runs down hill, and soaks into a sponge. These are all observed facts. They have their practical uses and are important in the early stages of a science, but science quickly moves on to a much more precise analysis, and an effective technology must do the same.

The interpretation of behavior

Verbal behavior is a field in which the concept of contingencies of reinforcement has proved particularly useful. The conspicuous thing in the field is the behavior of people speaking, or rather its audible products. Most linguists accept this as their subject matter: a language is the totality of the sentences spoken in it. Speech is said, noncommittally, to be a matter of "utterances." Samples can be obtained for study from anyone who speaks the language, possibly the linguist himself. The topography of the behavior is analyzed acoustically, phonetically, and phonemically and in those larger grammatical and syntactical structures called sentences. The environment is not ignored, of course. In fact, phonemes and acceptable sentences cannot be defined simply as features of topography because they involve effects upon a listener. The environment is what sentences are "about," but the relation alluded to with the word "about" is usually not analyzed beyond the level of meaning or reference. The meaning of an utterance is either some feature of the occasion upon which it is uttered or some effect upon a listener. The relation of speaker to listener is described in one of the simplest versions of an input-output formula, in which the speaker *transmits* information to the listener or *communicates* with him in the sense of making something common to them both.

Given these restrictions, it is not surprising that linguists and psycholinguists have failed to explain why men speak at all, say what they say, or say it in given ways. Nor is it surprising that they have turned to mental precursors. A speaker uses a word because he has the intention of expressing a meaning. He composes a sentence (in part by applying possibly innate syntactical rules) to express an idea or proposition. The structure of a language is said to reflect the structure of thought. This sort of psychologizing was wisely rejected by linguists in the early years of the century, but efforts to find a behavioral alternative, particularly by Leonard Bloomfield (21), failed because of the shortcomings of stimulus-response psychology. The result was either a pure structuralism or a return to mentalistic explanations such as those of generative grammarians.

The concept of contingencies of reinforcement leads to a much more useful formulation. A language is not the words or sentences "spoken in it"; it is the "it" in which they are spoken—the practices of the verbal community which shape and maintain the behavior of speakers. Verbal contingencies have the same status as contingencies maintained by laboratory equipment, but they involve the behavior of a second organism, the listener, and the behavior they generate therefore has many unusual characteristics. It is the contingencies which prevail in a given verbal community which "generate sentences." They shape and maintain the phonemic and syntactical properties of verbal behavior and account for a wide range of functional characteristics—from poetry to logic. They do so without the help of the mind of speaker or listener (141). No analysis of the mere structure of speech or language can do any of this, even when supplemented with an input-output formulation.

Structural linguistics is only one example of the movement in ethnology, anthropology, and sociology represented most clearly in the work of Claude Lévi-Strauss (89). It is concerned with the conspicuous thing about a culture: what the people in it are doing. Men have always been intrigued by customs and manners, especially in cultures which differ greatly from their own. They have reported the ways in which other people live—their family life, their kinship systems, their technologies, their social practices, and so on. They report such facts simply as such, or analyze their structure, or collect and compare different structures. Sartre has criticized the result as "static," but it is not movement which is lacking but function. Eventually we must ask why people behave in their respective ways. It is not enough to say that a custom is followed simply because it is customary to follow it. Nor is it enough to say that people behave as they do because of the ways in which they think. To understand the behavior of savages, we must do more than understand the "savage mind."

Malinowski was among the first to contend that customs are followed because of their consequences, and we can now formulate this functional position in a more comprehensive way. A culture is not the behavior of the people "living in it"; it is the "it" in which they live—the contingencies of social reinforcement which generate and sustain their behavior. (The contingencies are maintained by other members of the group, whose behavior in maintaining them is the product of earlier contingencies, just as the behavior of the listener in shaping and maintaining the behavior of the speaker is the product of earlier contingencies in the verbal community.) To record what the people in a culture *do* is an important step—but only a first step—in discovering why they do it. Rules which have been extracted from the contingencies, and used in maintaining them (see Chapter 6), are helpful to those who study a culture, but they usually represent only the more obvious contingencies. More subtle contingencies may go unsuspected for a long time. They are nevertheless the principal subject matter of anthropology and sociology.

A comparable movement in political science is called "behavioralism." It also represents an understandable reaction to premature psychologizing. The "behavioralist" confines himself to those aspects of the topography of political behavior which can be measured with empirical tools and techniques. It is not surprising that a symposium on "The limits of behavioralism in political science" (35) should complain of the neglect of subjective experience, ideas, motives, feelings, attitudes, and so on. They are indeed neglected, but it does not follow that the political scientist should return to them. It is true that political behavior cannot be understood simply in terms of its topography, as behavioralism seems to imply, but what is needed is not a mentalistic explanation but a further analysis of political contingencies of reinforcement.

The manipulation of behavior

When the variables discovered in an experimental analysis prove to be manipulable, we can move beyond interpretation to the control of behavior. Practical control is already a commonplace in the operant laboratory, where behavior is frequently manufactured to specifications and changed almost at will. Topography is shaped and maintained; rate of responding is increased or decreased; stimuli are brought into control; and complex patterns and sequences of response are constructed. Thus, if we are interested in vision, we set up contingencies which guarantee that an organism will look at a stimulus at a given time. If we are interested in emotion, we generate a standard baseline against which specific effects are likely to be seen. If we are interested in obesity, we arrange special contingencies under which an organism grossly overeats. If we are interested in sleep, we arrange contingencies which keep an organism awake for long periods of time, at the end of which it immediately sleeps. If we are interested in the nervous system, we set up standard patterns of behavior which are altered by lesions or central stimulation. If we are interested in new pharmaceutical compounds, we generate behavior which is affected by specific drugs in specific ways.

All these practices have a bearing on the control of human behavior in the world at large, which is, of course, vastly more important. Traditional techniques of control suffer from the shortcomings of the theories upon which they were based. They overemphasize conspicuous things—the topography of behavior rather than its probability and independent variables which have immediate and obvious effects. The concept of contingencies of reinforcement has led to a much more effective technology of behavior, a few examples of which may be cited.

Education. The topography of a student's behavior is the clearest evidence that he knows something, and it has always been overemphasized. In classical Greek and Chinese education boys were taught to recite long passages from great literary works, and when they could do so, there was no question that the teacher had been effective. We no longer require much literal recitation, but our concern for the right answer is in the same vein. Since the teacher is reinforced when the student responds correctly, he is likely to employ techniques which induce him to do so, but the probability that he will respond in similar ways in the future ("will use what he knows") is neglected (152).

Teachers have traditionally used only the most conspicuous environmental measures. The birch rod and the cane mark a long history of aversive control, which has not yet come to an end. Most students still study, recite, and take examinations primarily to avoid the consequences of not doing so. The consequences may have been moderated, but they are nevertheless aversive enough to have troublesome by-products. Simple permissiveness is not an effective alternative, and it is hard to make contrived positive reinforcers such as good marks, grades, diplomas, and prizes contingent on behavior in effective ways.

Teaching is the arrangement of contingencies of reinforcement which expedite learning. A student learns without being taught, but he learns more effectively under favorable conditions. Teachers have always arranged effective contingencies when they have taught successfully, but they are more likely to do so if they understand what they are doing. Programmed instruction is a technique taken directly from the operant laboratory, and it is designed to maximize the reinforcement associated with successful control of the environment. A program is a set of contingencies which shape topography of response and bring behavior under the control of stimuli in an expeditious way. An equally important advance is the arrangement of contingencies of reinforcement in the classroom which take over the function of "discipline."

Psychotherapy. The often bizarre behavior of the psychotic naturally attracts attention. Whether it is taken as the disorder to be treated or as the sympom of an underlying disorder of another kind, it is scrutinized for "significances." Meaning is sought in the gestures of the psychotic or in the self-destructive behavior of the autistic child. The important thing about a psychotic, however, is not what he is doing but what he is not doing. The behavior he exhibits is "abnormal" just because it is not characteristic of the situation. It might not be observed at all if normal behavior were stronger. The problem is not to find in the structure of the observed behavior some hint as to how it may be made to disappear, but rather to build up the behavior which is missing.

Traditional measures have been perhaps even more aversive than in education. Some of the more extreme forms arose from theories of demoniac possession; others were simply intensified versions of everyday practices in suppressing unwanted behavior. The by-products to be expected of aversive control have caused trouble, and many reforms have been proposed. Simple permissiveness is seldom feasible, and personal reinforcers, such as genuine or synthetic affection, are hard to make contingent on desired behavior.

When the psychotic shows an insensitivity to normal contingencies of reinforcement, an environment must be designed to which he is likely to respond. Ogden R. Lindsley has called such an environment "prosthetic" (92). In the "token economies" used in ward management, for example, special reinforcers are conditioned conspicuous contingencies. A token has a clear-cut physical status, it becomes a powerful conditioned reinforcer when exchanged for other reinforcers, and it can be made immediately contingent on desired behavior.

It is not always the psychotic's sensitivity to contingencies but the contingencies themselves which may be discovered to be defective. A well-known experiment in ward management by Ayllon and Haughton (7) shows how such contingencies can be improved. Several attendants had been needed to get thirty schizophrenic women into the dining room at mealtime, and it had taken them thirty minutes to do so. The contingencies were than changed. The attendants were not to make any effort to move the patients. Any patient who entered the dining room within half an hour after a bell had sounded could eat, but the others went without food, and no other food was available. At the first meal only a few patients reached the dining room, but eventually they all did so. The allowable time was then progressively shortened from a half hour to five minutes. At the end of the experiment all the patients went to the dining room within five minutes without help from the attendants.

The experiment illustrates several important points in the interpretation and manipulation of contingencies of reinforcement. In a ward of this sort the personal attention of an attendant is usually a strong reinforcer, but it is often contingent only on mild troublemaking. (Serious troublemaking is dealt with in other ways.) During most of the day, the attendant can avoid reinforcing patients when they make trouble by ignoring them, but this is not possible when he is responsible for getting them into the dining room. In effect, the dinner bell gave the patients a special power: they could now evoke reactions in the attendants by refusing to move, moving in the wrong direction, and so on. When the contingencies were changed, these behaviors were no longer reinforced, and a new reinforcer could then come into play. Institutional food is not always reinforcing, but it becomes so when the patient is hungry. The patients began to move toward the dining room not to avoid or escape from the mildly aversive action of the attendants, but because they were positively reinforced by food. Once it was established, the behavior did not require a special level of deprivation. It would be more likely to be classified as acceptable behavior in the culture at large. The experiment is not, of course, a solution to all the problems of ward management, but it shows how a change in contingencies can solve some problems and even lead to a sort of therapy.

Economics.   The behavior of an employee is important to the employer, who gains when the employee works industriously and carefully. How is he to be induced to do so? The standard answer was once physical force: men worked to avoid punishment or death. The by-products were troublesome, however, and economics is perhaps the first field in which an explicit change was made to positive reinforcement. Most men now work, as we say, "for money." But many problems survive, and they have parallels in the operant laboratory.

Money is not a natural reinforcer; it must be conditioned as such. Delayed reinforcement, as in a weekly wage, raises a special problem. No one works on Monday morning because he is reinforced by a paycheck on Friday afternoon. The employee who is paid by the week works during the week to avoid losing the standard of living which depends on a weekly wage. A supervisor who can discharge him is an essential part of the system. Rate of work is determined by the supervisor (with or without the pacing stimuli of a production line), and special aversive contingencies maintain quality. The pattern is therefore still aversive. It has often been pointed out that the attitude of the production-line worker toward his work differs conspicuously from that of the craftsman, who is envied by workers and industrial managers alike. One explanation is that the craftsman is reinforced by more than monetary consequences, but another important difference is that when a craftsman spends a week in completing a given object, each of the parts produced during the week is likely to be automatically reinforcing because of its place in the completed object.

Somewhat better contingencies are available under schedules of reinforcement based on counters rather than clocks. In piece-rate pay, the worker is paid for each item he produces. This is a so-called fixed-ratio schedule, and it generates a high level of activity. Piece-rate reinforcement is, indeed, so powerful that it has often been misused, and it is generally opposed by those concerned with the welfare of the worker (and by workers themselves when, for example, they set daily quotas). A salesman on salary and commission exemplifies a form of incentive wage which is a combination of schedules based on clocks and counters. Incentive wages are currently not in favor, possibly because they have also been misused, but they need to be investigated as promising alternatives to aversive control.

A particularly effective schedule is at the heart of all gambling devices. Consider a room full of people playing Bingo. The players sit quietly for many hours; they listen with great care as numbers and letters are called out; they arrange markers on cards rapidly and accurately; and they respond instantly when a particular pattern has been completed. What would industry not give for workers who behaved that way? And what would workers not give for work which absorbed them so completely? (The craftsman, by the way, is strongly under the control of ratio schedules.)

Other economic contingencies induce men to buy and sell, rent and hire, lend and borrow, prospect, invent, promote, and so on. The strength of a culture depends substantially upon the results, and it is no accident that we ask some basic questions about cultures in terms of their economic contingencies. Yet the distinguishing features of capitalism, socialism, communism, and other economic systems are more often traceable to geography, natural resources, forms of government, and political theories than to a technology based on a scientific analysis of economic behavior. The wealth of a culture depends upon the productive behavior of its members. It is a natural resource which is shamefully neglected because a true economic technology has yet to be devised. The basic principles are available in an experimental analysis of behavior.

Government. Governments are especially committed to aversive practices. At one time the State could be defined as the power to punish. The possibility of positive reinforcement was ignored. It is true that Gulliver found an exception in Lilliput, where "whoever can bring sufficient proof that he has strictly observed the laws of his country for seventy-three moons, hath a claim to certain privileges, according to his quality and condition of life, with a proportionable sum of money out of a fund appropriated for that use," but that was fiction—and it has not yet come true. Modern governments manipulate vast quantities of positive as well as negative reinforcers, but they seriously neglect the contingencies in both cases. The behavior to be reinforced is seldom defined, in either domestic or international affairs. Most governmental decisions still rest on historical analogies and personal experiences formulated in mentalistic ways. Wars, we are told by UNESCO, begin in the minds of men. A particularly unfortunate war is said to be the result of "misperception" (166). Violence in the streets is attributed to "frustration." This is dangerous psychologizing. It is no doubt difficult to arrange contingencies of reinforcement to solve problems of this magnitude, for decisions must often be made, here as elsewhere, without adequate information, but unscientific thinking is not the solution. Political action is always a matter of manipulating contingencies of reinforcement, and an understanding of contingencies and their effects could bring a dramatic improvement.

Daily life. The techniques of education, psychotherapy, economics, and government are all found in miniature in daily life. The members of a group teach each other, make each other's environments easier to live in, induce each other to work and exchange goods, and maintain ethical and moral sanctions which have the effect of governmental measures. They do so, of course, by arranging various contingencies of reinforcement, which are the proper subject matter of anthropology and sociology. It is a difficult field, in part because the practices are less likely to be codified than in other disciplines, and in part because there is no controlling figure—such as a teacher, therapist, employer, or governor whose behavior would make uncodified practices visible.

Daily life is sometimes explicitly designed, however. The religious communities in the Judeo-Christian tradition were based on sets of rules (e.g., the Rules of Benedict and Augustine) specifying contingencies of social reinforcement. Schools and colleges are to some extent communities in this sense and have their own rules. Institutions for the care of psychotics and retardates, orphanages, summer camps, and penal institutions are other examples. The techniques of control, codified or uncodified, are often aversive; but efforts have recently been made to design communities of these sorts using positive contingencies.

An experiment in the National Training School for Boys in Washington, D. C., the students of which are juvenile delinquents, is an example. The culture of that community was redesigned in the following way (38). Aversive control was minimized; no boy was required to do anything. A boy might, if he wished, "go on relief"; he could eat nutritious if uninteresting food, sleep on a pad in a dormitory, and spend each day sitting on a bench. He could greatly improve his way of life, however, by earning points exchangeable for more interesting food, a private room, a television set, admission to the game room, a trip away from the institution, and so on. Points could be earned by working in the kitchen or by performing janitorial services, *but most readily by studying and learning*. Right answers were worth points.

One result, important to management, was improved morale. The boys performed useful services and behaved well with respect to each other without aversive control and hence without its unwanted by-products. A more important result was related to the avowed purpose of the institution. Most juvenile delinquents have been conspicuous failures in school. They have been persuaded that they are dull or stupid. Under the powerful educational contingencies arranged in the training school, the boys discovered that they could learn and in many cases learn rapidly. In doing so, they acquired behavior which would prove useful when they left the school and which would therefore increase the chances that they would behave in acceptable rather than illegal ways.

Compared with education, psychotherapy, economics, and government, very little thought has been given to the explicit design of daily life. The exception is the so-called utopian literature. Utopian writers have been concerned with the social environment and with the possibility of redesigning it. Whether they have known it or not, they have been concerned with the contingencies of reinforcement under which men live. They have been limited by the theories of human conduct with which they were familiar; but as our understanding improves, it should be possible to suggest better versions. Basic science always leads eventually to an improved technology, and a science of behavior is no exception. It should supply a technology of behavior appropriate to the ultimate utopian goal: an effective culture.

Note 1.1   Some contingencies of reinforcement

A few contingencies which have been studied experimentally may be roughly described as follows. An experimental space contains one or more operanda such as a lever projecting from a wall which may be pressed by a rat or a translucent disk on the wall which may be pecked by a pigeon, various sources of stimuli such as sounds and lights, and reinforcing devices such as a food or water dispenser or a source of aversive stimulation such as a bright light or an electric grid to deliver shocks. Any stimulus arising from the space, the operandum, or special stimulating devices prior to a response is designated "S^D." A response, such as pressing the lever or pressing the disk, is "R." Food presented to a hungry organism is a positive reinforcer ("S^{rein}"), a bright light or shock a negative reinforcer. The interrelations among S^D, R, and S^{rein} compose the contingencies of reinforcement. All three terms must be specified.

(1) *Operant reinforcement.* A hungry rat presses the lever and receives food. (Frequency of pressing increases.) A pigeon pecks the disk and receives food. (Frequency of pecking increases.)

(2) *Escape.* The experimental space is brightly lighted. A rat presses the lever and reduces the intensity of the light. (The lever is then pressed more quickly when the light appears, or more often in sustained light.)

(3) *Avoidance.* A rat is shocked every twenty seconds except that a response to the lever postpones the next shock for twenty seconds. (Frequency of response increases and many shocks are avoided.)

(4) *Stimulus discrimination.* A rat presses the lever and obtains food when a light is on, but no food follows the response when the light is off. (Frequency of responding is higher in the presence of the light than in its absence—"S^Δ.")

(5) *Response differentiation.* Food appears only when the lever is depressed with a force above a given value. (Responses showing the required force appear more frequently.)

(6) *"Superstition."* The food dispenser operates every twenty seconds regardless of the behavior of the rat. (Any behavior occurring just before the appearance of the food is reinforced, and similar coincidences become more likely as the behavior is strengthened. The rat develops a "superstitious ritual.")

(7) *Chained operants.* Pecking a green disk changes the color to red, and pecking the red disk is followed by food. (The frequency of occurrence of the chain of responses increases.)

(8) *Observation.* A discrimination is set up under which a pigeon pecks a red disk but not a green. The color slowly fades,

however, until a discrimination becomes impossible. Pecking another disk reverses the fading. (The pigeon pecks the other disk to produce enough color to make a discrimination.)

(9) *Matching to sample.* Three disks are arranged in a row. The middle disk is either red or green, the other two unlighted. A response to the middle disk lights the side disks, one red and one green. A response to the matching disk is reinforced with food. (Responses to the matching disk increase in frequency.)

(10) *Delayed matching.* As in (9) but the middle disk is darkened before the side keys are illuminated. (If the side keys are presented immediately, the pigeon is able to match. A short delay makes matching impossible. "The pigeon cannot remember the color of the middle key.")

(11) *Mediated delayed matching.* There are five disks—one in the center and the others within easy reach at the four points of the compass. Center is either red or green. A response darkens it and projects white light on North and South. If Center was red, a response to North illuminates East and West, one red and one green. A response to the matching disk is reinforced. If Center was green, a response to South illuminates East and West, and a matching response is reinforced. Two chains are thus set up: (i) The pigeon pecks Center red, North white, and red on either East or West; (ii) The pigeon pecks Center green, South white, and green on East or West. The pigeon matches successfully because it responds to the red on East or West when it has just responded to North and to the green on East or West when it has just responded to South. Responding on North and South can then be protracted—for example, by requiring a number of responses to illuminate East and West. The number can be greatly increased. A long delayed matching response to East or West is mediated by the stimuli generated by responding to North or South.

(12) *Schedules of reinforcement.* Reinforcements may be scheduled in many ways. Each schedule, with given values of the parameters, generates a characteristic performance.

    a. Fixed interval. A response is reinforced only when it occurs after the passage of a period of time (for example, five minutes). Another period begins immediately after reinforcement.

    b. A fixed ratio. Every nth response is reinforced.

    c. Variable interval or ratio. The interval or number in

a. and *b.* need not be fixed but may vary over a given range around some average value.

    d. Multiple schedules. One schedule is in force in the presence of one stimulus, a different schedule in the presence of another stimulus. For example, a fixed interval prevails when the key is red, and a variable issue when the key is green. (A characteristic performance is obtained under each stimulus.)

    e. Differential reinforcement of rate of responding. A response is reinforced only if it follows the preceding response after a specified interval of time (DRL) or before the end of a given interval (DRH). In DRL the interval might be, for example, 3 minutes; in DRH, one half second.

    (13) *Multiple deprivation.* Pecking one disk is reinforced by food, pecking another disk is reinforced by water, pecking a third disk is reinforced with either food or water at random. Under different conditions of hunger and thirst the rate of responding on the third disk is the average of the rates on the first two.

Some contingencies in the field of verbal behavior are as follows:

    (14) *"Mand."* In the presence of a listener (S^D), the response *Water* is reinforced when the listener gives the speaker water.

    (15) *Echoic behavior.* When someone says *Water,* the speaker says *Water,* and reinforcement is contingent on the similarity of the two sounds.

    (16) *Textual behavior.* When looking at the printed word *Water,* the speaker is reinforced if he says *Water.*

    (17) *Intraverbal behavior.* Upon hearing or reading the word *Water,* the speaker is reinforced if he emits a thematically related response such as *Ice* or *Faucet.*

    (18) *"Tact."* In the presence of a glass of water, a river, rain, and so on, the speaker is reinforced when he says *Water.*

Note 1.2   From "stimulus and response" to "contingencies of reinforcement"

It was a long and difficult transition. The consequences of behavior were first treated simply as stimuli eliciting other responses. Complex acts were analyzed as chain reflexes. Each link was described as it occurred, to give some assurance of the physical status of the complete act. A stimulus was connected to a response which followed *via* the nervous system, and the response was connected with a subsequent stimulus *via* the environment. Beyond the presumption of reflex action, no effect on the probability of the response was implied (except by Guthrie, who argued that the second stimulus terminated the response, permitting it to form a stronger association with the first stimulus).

A possible effect of a stimulus upon the response which produced it was recognized in the theory of the circular reflex, defined by Warren (163) as "a reflex in which the response serves to renew the original stimulus." The function of this "reafferentation" was closer to guidance than to reinforcement, and guidance was later to assume a more important role in Wiener's cybernetics, where response-produced stimuli appear as "feedback," a term widely misused as a synonym for operant reinforcement. P. K. Anokhin (4) has recently attempted to analyze the effects of "the results of action" in terms of feedback or "inverse afferentation."[1]

In the experimental arrangement of Miller and Konorski (101) a consequence was explicitly added to a reflex. A tone was sounded, the leg of a hungry dog was flexed, reflexly or passively,

[1] His paper is an interesting demonstration of the power of Pavlov's influence in Russia. Anokhin writes:

"It seems strange that for so many years the results of action were never the subject of special physiological analysis, since they are the vital connecting link between the different stages of the behavioral act. This is even stranger if we think of the true nature of behavior. As a matter of fact, men and animals are always interested in the results of action. It is only because of them that often long chains of behavioral acts are embarked upon, for only failure to obtain the desired results acts as the stimulus for further acts until what is attained corresponds in some way to what is desired.

"In the classical 'reflex arc' there is no room for the evaluation of results. This is the most outstanding failing of the reflex theory, which showed the dualism of its creator and for a long time distracted physiologists from a materialist solution to the problem of purposiveness in human and animal behavior. In fact the very adaptation of the 'reflex arc' as the central model for explaining behavior for many years excluded all possibility of treating results as a motivating factor in the formation of variability of behavior. There was simply no place for results in the reflex model and so their physiological character or, more precisely, their decisive role in forming the functional systems of the organism remained outside physiologists' field of vision."

The passage is remarkable only for the fact that it was published in 1965.

and food was presented. Eventually, "the tone alone elicited the movement." Miller and Konorski offered the following explanation. The tone plus the complex of muscular and tactile stimuli generated by flexion becomes a compound conditioned stimulus which elicits salivation. Neither the tone nor the muscular and tactile stimuli will do so when presented separately, but given the tone the dog eventually flexes its leg to complete the compound stimulus. The dog flexes its leg in response to the tone "in order to form the complete conditioned complex" (*pour former ainsi le complex conditionnel total*).

The ultimate flexion in the experiment is no doubt an operant, but how is it related to the conditioned flexion? Konorski and Miller suggested a parallel with a rat pressing a lever and being reinforced with food. But what is at issue is not the nature of the behavior but the contingencies. If flexion is correlated with a shock, as in a reflex, and if food is mechanically contingent on flexion, then food is also contingent on the shock. An apparatus will have the Miller and Konorski effect if it simply administers a shock and then operates a food dispenser a second or two later, independently of the behavior. (The tone is unnecessary, so long as flexion is always followed by presentation of food.) Contingencies of this sort are rare, if not entirely lacking in the world at large. Operant behavior is observed only when there are "responses uncorrelated with observable stimuli."

Something similar to the Konorski and Miller arrangement survives (and unnecessarily complicates an experiment) when food is smeared on a lever to induce a rat to "press" it or when a child's hand is moved by the teacher to form a letter properly. Imitative and instructional stimuli used to evoke operant responses so that they can be reinforced do not fall in the same class because they do not elicit behavior. Even so, reinforcement is most effective when such stimuli are minimal.

My thesis (*The Concept of the Reflex in the Description of Behavior* [124]) was obviously close to reflex physiology, particularly in the work of Sherrington, Magnus, and Pavlov. The stimulus was still a prominent variable. Nevertheless, other variables were assigned a comparable role in the formula

$$R = f(S, A).$$

The example under discussion was "reflex fatigue," where the variable A represented, not a synaptic state as Sherrington contended, but time or number of elicited responses. Comparable formulations of conditioning, "emotion," and "drive" were suggested, in which a "third" variable—that is, a variable in addition to S and R—was to be invoked. My reply to Konorski and Miller (128) identified the contingency between a response and its consequence as the important variable in operant conditioning.

At first glance, Edward Tolman seems to have moved well beyond a stimulus-response formula. He made no use of eliciting stimuli, describing his rats as "docile." He turned from topography of response to goal-directedness, and used apparatus which emphasized purpose (represented spatially—see page 107). But he put the "third" variables inside the organism, where they "intervened" between stimulus and response. There was no reason to do this except to maintain something like the old reflex-arc pattern. His intervening variables quickly assumed the function of mental processes (as they were essentially designed to do), and it is not surprising that they have been warmly taken up by cognitive psychologists.

Clark Hull kept quite explicitly to the stimulus-response formula. In his *Principles of Behavior* (71) he emphasized topographical properties of a response as measures of its strength. He not only appealed to central processes; he made them the main object of inquiry. Two processes had no other function than to rescue a stimulus-response formula: "afferent neural interaction" converted physical stimuli into forms which seemed to be effective and "behavioral oscillation" accounted for discrepancies between predicted and observed responses. Other central processes were said to be the effect of variables other than stimuli and responses. The neurological character of all these central processes was increasingly emphasized.

2   Utopia as an experimental culture

Walden Two (133) describes an imaginary community of about a thousand people who are living a Good Life. They enjoy a pleasant rural setting and work only a few hours a day, without being compelled to do so. Their children are cared for and educated by specialists with due regard for the lives they are going to lead. Food is good and sanitation and medical care excellent. There is plenty of leisure and many ways of enjoying it. Art, music, and literature flourish, and scientific research is encouraged. Life in Walden Two is not only good, it seems feasible. It is within the reach of intelligent men of goodwill who will apply the principles which are now emerging from the scientific study of human behavior to the design of culture. Some readers may take the book as written with tongue in cheek, but it was actually a quite serious proposal.

The book was violently attacked as soon as it appeared. *Life* magazine (91) called it a "slander on some old notions of the 'good life' . . . Such a triumph of mortmain, or the 'dead hand', [as] has not been envisaged since the days of Sparta . . . a slur upon a name, a corruption of an impulse." In *The Quest for Utopia* (104) Negley and Patrick, while agreeing that sooner or later "the principle of psychological conditioning would be made the basis of the serious construction of utopia . . .," found they were quite unprepared for "the shocking horror of the idea when positively presented. Of all the

29

dictatorships espoused by utopists," they continued, "this is the most profound, and incipient dictators might well find in this utopia a guide book of political practice." And Joseph Wood Krutch soon devoted a substantial part of *The Measure of Man* (87) to an attack on what he called an "ignoble utopia." The controversy grows more violent and puzzling as the years pass.

There is clearly a renewal of interest in utopian speculation. A pattern is probably not set when, as two psychoanalysts have suggested, "in need of and in despair for the absent breast, the infant hallucinates the fulfillment and thus postpones momentarily the overwhelming panic of prolonged frustration" (42), but there are other possibilities. For many people a utopia serves as an alternative to a kind of political dream which is still suppressed by vestiges of political witchhunting. For some it may show dissatisfaction with our international stance; an experimental community is a sort of domestic Peace Corps. Whatever the explanation, there is no doubt that many people are now inclined to scrutinize the way of life in which they find themselves, to question its justification, and to consider alternatives.

But this is also an anti-utopian age. The modern classics—Aldous Huxley's *Brave New World* (72) and George Orwell's *Nineteen Eighty Four* (108) describe ways of life we must be sure to avoid. George Kateb has analysed the issue in *Utopia and Its Enemies* (77), a title obviously based on Karl Popper's *The Open Society and Its Enemies* (114), which was itself an early skirmish in the war against utopia. The strange thing in all this is the violence. One of Plato's characters calls his *Republic* "a city of pigs," but never before have dreams of a better world raised such a storm. Possibly one explanation is that now, for the first time, the dream must be taken seriously. Utopias are science fiction, and we have learned that science fiction has a way of coming true.

Utopian techniques

We can take a step toward explaining why Utopia only now seems within reach by looking at some classical examples. In his *Republic* and in parts of other dialogues, Plato portrayed a well-managed society patterned on the Greek city-state. He suggested features which would presumably contribute to its success, but he put his faith in a wise ruler— a philosopher-king who, as philosopher, would know what to do and, as king, would be able to do it. It is an old and not very honorable strategy: when you do not know what should be done, assume that there is someone who does. The philosopher-king was to patch up a defective governmental design as the need arose, but it was not clear how he was to do so.

There are those—among them theologians—who argue that the next great utopian vision was the Christian heaven. St. Augustine developed the theme in his *City of God.* It was certainly a good life based on the highest authority, but important details were missing. Everyone who went to heaven was to be happy, but it was not clear just why. No one, in fact, has ever portrayed a very interesting heaven. St. Augustine's mundane version set the pattern for the monastic communities of early Christianity, but it would be hard to defend it as a good life. The monastery was a transitory state to which men turned with assurance that it was to be followed by a better life in a world to come.

Plato hoped to find the good life *sub homine,* and St. Augustine sought it *sub deo.* It remained for Thomas More to propose that it might be found *sub lege.* More was a lawyer, and history had begun to show the importance of charters, constitutions, and other agreements which men might make among themselves in order to live peacefully together. The title of his book, *Utopia,* which gave the name to this kind of speculation, has an ambiguous etymology. The Greek root of Utopia denotes a place, but the prefix means either good or nonexistent—or possibly, and cynically, both. Within a century another lawyer, Francis Bacon, had extended More's appeal to reason in his fragmentary utopia, *The New Atlantis,* in which he also looked to government and law for a solution —although he suggested that scientists might be called on as advisers. (The scientific institution he described—Solomon's House—was in fact the model on which the Royal Society was soon founded.)

But was law and order the answer? Erasmus thought not. He supported More's utopian vision, but with reservations. Reason might contribute to the good life, but it was a mistake to overlook other things. Erasmus was amused by the fact that More's name was the Latin root for "fool," and he whimsically defended his friend by writing *The Praise of Folly.* Government, he said, is all very well, but were it not for the folly of sex, no one would be born, and were it not for the folly of appetite, no one would survive, to be governed.

It was not long before further doubt was cast on the necessity or sufficiency of law and order. Round-the-world voyagers returning from the South Seas brought back stories of a good life which flourished without benefit of civilization on the European pattern. Men were peaceful and happy although completely ignorant of western morals and with little or no visible government. Diderot developed the theme in his *Supplement to the Voyage of Bougainville*—for example, in the amusing scene in which a Catholic priest and a Tahitian chief discuss sexual morality. Jean-Jacques Rousseau took a stronger line: government was not only unnecessary, it was inimical to the good life. Natural man—the noble savage—was wise and good; government corrupted him. Here were the beginnings of a philosophy of anarchy which still finds a place in utopian speculation.

(The South Seas proved that natural man was not only good but self-sufficient. Governments made men dependent upon other men, but the shipwrecked sailor, aided by the abundant resources of a tropical isle, could be master of all he surveyed. A special kind of utopian writing began to take shape when Robinson Crusoe put the solitary good life to the test. Frontier America offered many opportunities to the individual *coureur de bois,* and the theme was still strong in the middle of the nineteenth century when Henry David Thoreau built his own tropical island on the shores of Walden Pond.)

Exaggerated reports of life in the South Seas led to a rash of idyllic utopias, many of them set in the tropics. And now, for the first time, such a world seemed feasible. It is true that the Greeks dreamed of Arcadia, which was a real place, and proposals to found a utopia were occasionally made (according to Gibbon [53] the Emperor Gallienus was on the point of offering the philosopher Plotinus a captured city so that he might try Plato's experiment when, perhaps fortunately for Plotinus, he was called away on emergencies of state), but More and Bacon were not drawing blueprints; they were simply describing societies with which contemporary life might be compared. The South Seas were real, and life on that pattern could therefore be taken seriously. Etienne Cabet's *Voyage en Icarie* (34) was one of the most popular of the idyllic utopias, and Cabet actually came to America in the 1850's planning to set up Icaria on the Red River in Texas. He died in St. Louis, Missouri, but a community on the Icarian principle survived for some time in the Middle West.

It was the idyllic utopia which Karl Marx attacked. To portray a good life was one thing, to bring it about quite another. In this sense Marx was anti-utopian, but he had his own vision, and it was not entirely unrelated to the South Sea idyll. It was possible that human happiness might be traced not so much to the absence of government as to an abundance of goods. Nature could not always be counted on to supply what man needed to be happy in the style of the South Seas, but man would provide for himself if he were able. A Utopia hinged on economic principles.

The notion had been developing for a long time. Goods were essential to the good life, but where were they to be found? Bacon had argued that science was power, and the technology which he advocated and which began to emerge in the seventeenth century seemed a possible answer. If men were not producing the wealth they needed to be happy, it was because they did not know how. Science must come to the rescue. The great encyclopedia of Diderot and D'Alembert was to have this effect. Many recipes, formulae, and systems for the production of wealth which had been trade, guild, or family secrets had only to be made public and men would go busily to work.

Marx thought he saw another reason why men were not producing the wealth they needed for happiness: the means of production were being sequestered by selfish people. The good life would follow when the necessary tools were made available to everyone. This was the solution emphasized in nineteenth-century utopias, exemplified in England by William Morris's *News From Nowhere* (102) and in the United States by Edward Bellamy's *Looking Backward* (13). The doctrine that the good life will follow when each has been supplied "according to his need" is scriptural: it is St. Augustine, not St. Karl. It has remained, of course, a strong utopian theme: technology is to solve our problems by making everyone affluent. A few years ago Mr. Khrushchev announced that before long all food, clothing, and housing in Russia would be free. The good life was just round the corner.

An irritating problem survived. Given both the skills and the means, men may still not produce wealth. Nineteenth-century theorists found it necessary to appeal to a natural compulsion to work. William Morris describes a man looking for work, not to earn money but simply to express a need. A Russian economist when asked why men will work when all food, clothing, and housing are free, replied with a confident smile, "For the common good," but that is by no means certain. "To each according to his need" must be balanced by "from each according to his ability," and that is an assignment which has so far proved to be beyond the reach of economics. And there are other kinds of goods which physical technology has not yet been able to supply. A more comprehensive behavioral science is needed.

Behavioral Utopias

Rousseau knew that natural man would not solve all his problems, and Marx knew that economic principles would not suffice, and both took other characteristics of human behavior into account. A thoroughgoing behavioral utopia, however, was to wait for the twentieth century. The two leading figures of behavioral science in that century are Freud and Pavlov. Curiously enough, no utopian novel seems to have been written on Freudian principles. Pavlov was drawn into utopian speculation by accident. In 1917 the Russians needed the principle of the conditioned reflex to support their ideology, and they made Pavlov a national hero. If men were neither productive nor happy, it was the fault of their environments, and with the help of Pavlovian principles the Russian government would change the world and thus change men. But by the early nineteen-thirties the position had become embarrassing, as Bauer (11) has noted. The government had had its chance, and Russians were not yet conspicuously productive or happy. Pavlov went out of favor, and for twenty years Russian research on conditioned reflexes was confined to physiological processes not closely related to behavior. When the Second World War restored Russia's confidence, Pavlov returned as an intellectual hero, and the conditioned reflex was given another chance to build the good life.

Meanwhile, Aldous Huxley had explored the utopian implications of Pavlov's work in *Brave New World*. The book is, of course, a satire, heralding the threat rather than the promise of the conditioned reflex. There is nothing really new about conditioning, and Huxley seems to have known it.

When Miranda in *The Tempest* exclaims, "Oh, brave new world that has such creatures in it," she is talking about creatures washed up on the shores of her utopian island who have come from the contemporary world.[1] For Huxley the conditioned reflex was a means of determining what the citizens of his brave new world would call good. It was important, for example, that certain kinds of workers should not be distracted by literature or nature, and babies who were destined to be workers of that sort were therefore appropriately conditioned. They were put on the floor of a laboratory near a few attractive books and bouquets. As they moved toward them and touched them, they were electrically shocked or frightened by loud noises. When they tried again, the treatment was repeated. Soon they were safe: they would never again take an interest in literature or nature. Pavlov had something to say about changing what is good about the good life because he had studied responses which have to do with what one feels. The good life which Huxley portrayed (with contempt, of course) *felt* good. It is no accident that it included an art form called the "feelies" and drugs which produced or changed feelings.

The good things in life have other effects, however. One is the satisfaction of needs in the simple sense of the relief of distress. We sometimes eat to escape from the pangs of hunger and take pills to allay pain, and out of compassion we feed the hungry and heal the sick. For such purposes we design a culture which provides for each "according to his need." But satisfaction is a limited objective; we are not necessarily happy because we have everything we want. The word *sated* is related to the word *sad*. Simple abundance, whether in an affluent society, a benevolent climate, or a wel-

---

[1] The title of the French translation—*Le meilleur des mondes*—makes the same point. Pangloss assures Candide that it is *this* world, in spite of its diseases, earthquakes, and famines, which is the best of all possible worlds. Nor were Huxley's economics part of any world of the future; they were early Keynesian or Rooseveltian. His psychedelic drug "soma," though it anticipated LSD, was used like mescalin or alcohol.

fare state, is not enough. When people are supplied according to their needs, *regardless of what they are doing*, they remain inactive. The abundant life is a candy-mountain land or Cockaigne. It is the *Schlaraffenland*—the idler's land—of Hans Sachs, and idleness is the goal only of those who have been compulsively or anxiously busy.

Heavens are usually described by listing the good things to be found in them, but no one has ever designed a really interesting heaven on that principle. The important thing about the good things in life is what people are doing when they get them. "Goods" are reinforcers, and a way of life is a set of contingencies of reinforcement. In utopian literature, the arrangements of contingencies have seldom been explicit. As we have seen, contingencies of reinforcement are not the most conspicuous aspects of life, and the experimental analysis which has revealed their nature and their effects is of recent origin. There is probably a better reason, however, why they have been overlooked. The very reinforcers which figure in utopian writing exert too powerful an effect upon the writer. If we ask someone to describe the kind of world in which he would like to live, he will probably begin to list the reinforcers he would want to find in it. He will go straight to the things which make life good, and probably simply because he will be reinforced for doing so. Food, sex, security, the approval of one's fellow men, works of art, music, and literature—these are the things men want and act to get and therefore the things they mention when they are asked to describe a world in which they would like to live. The significant fact is that *they seldom mention what they are to do to get them.* They specify a better world simply as they wish for it, dream of it, or pray for it, giving no thought to the manner of their getting it.

A much more interesting possibility arises when we recognize the role of contingencies of reinforcement, for we can then apply something like the "behavioral engineering" of *Walden Two* to cultural design. A utopian community is a pilot experiment, like the pilot plant in industry or the pilot experiment in science, where principles are tested on a small scale to avoid the risks and inconvenience of size. Utopias have usually been isolated geographically because border problems can then be neglected, and they have usually implied a break with tradition (symbolized in religious communities, for example, by a ritual of rebirth) because problems raised by conflicting cultures are then minimized. A new practice can be put into effect more easily in a small community than in the world at large, and the results more easily seen. Given these helpful simplifications and the demonstrated power of a behavioral technology, a successful utopia is not too hard to imagine. The necessary physical environment is being analyzed in the field of urban design. The micro-rayons in Russia, the Newtownes of Great Britain, and many urban experiments in the United States, while still largely concerned with physical aspects, have also been designed with some attention to the basic principle that a city or a building is meaningful only as an environment in which people live and must rest upon an understanding of the interaction between behavior and the environment. It is true that the special communities represented by hospitals for psychotics, homes for retardates, training schools for delinquents, camps, and standard classrooms are not typical communities because the population at large is not properly represented, but the problems which arise in designing communities of that sort are not far from those in communities in the utopian sense. As solutions to those problems grow more successful, the plausibility of a utopian design increases. To most people "utopian" still means "impossible," but that usage may have to be changed.

Liking a way of life

A common objection to *Walden Two* (and no doubt to other utopias) goes like this: "I shouldn't like to live there. I don't mind doing the things the author is at pains to save me from doing, I don't like to do some of the things I should be expected to do, and I like to do things I could not do. Granted that life there meets many traditional specifications of the Good Life and compares favorably with existing cultures, it is still a world designed to please the author, and he is bound by his own culture, not mine. *He* would like to live there, of course, but he must not expect me to join him."

We "like" a way of life to the extent that we are reinforced by it. We like a world in which both natural and social reinforcers are abundant and easily achieved and in which aversive stimuli are either rare or easily avoided. Unfortunately, however, it is a fact about man's genetic endowment and the world in which he lives that immediate rewards are often offset by deferred punishments, and that punishments must often be taken for the sake of deferred rewards. To maximize net gains we must do things we do not like to do and forgo things we like. A culture cannot change these facts, but it can induce us to deal with them effectively. Indeed, this is its most important function.

It is not too often successful. A common practice, for example, is to extract rules from the prevailing contingencies, natural or social, and to make positive and negative reinforcers contingent upon the behavior of following them (see Chapter 6). The rule-following contingencies are often unskillfully designed, and members of a culture seldom take net consequences into account. On the contrary, they resist control of this sort. They object to what they are asked to do and either drop out of the culture—as hermits, hobos, or hippies—or remain in it while challenging its principles.

Contingencies of reinforcement which maximize net gains need to be much more effective. Conditioned reinforcers can be used to bridge the gap between behavior and its remoter consequences, and supplementary reinforcers can be arranged to serve until remote reinforcers can be brought into play. An important point is that effective contingencies need to be programmed—that is, they are effective only when a person has passed through a series of intermediate contingencies. Those who have reached the terminal contingencies will be productive, creative, and happy—in a word, maximally effective. The outsider confronted with the terminal contingencies for the first time may not like them or be able to imagine liking them.

The designer must take something else into account which is still more difficult to bring to bear on the individual member. Will the culture *work*? It is a question which is clarified by the concept of a community as an experiment. A community is a thing, having a life of its own. It will survive or perish, and the designer must keep that fact in mind. The problem is that survival is often furthered by behavior which is not only not reinforced but may have punishing (even lethal) consequences. Phylogenic contingencies of survival (see Chapter 6) supply examples. When a member of a herd of grazing animals spots the approach of a predator and utters a warning cry, the group is more likely to escape and survive, but the member who emits the cry calls attention to himself and may perish. Ontogenic contingencies of reinforcement work in the same way: a culture induces a hero to die for his country or a martyr for his religion.

Contingencies which promote survival are also usually badly designed. Something seems to be gained if the culture can be identified with a race, nation, or religious group, but this leads to jingoistic excesses. Contrived sanctions, positive and negative, are often spurious. The result is a different kind of dropout, who objects to taking the survival of a culture as a "value." The protest sometimes takes this form: "Why should I care whether my way of life survives or contributes to the way of life of the future?" An honest answer would seem to be, "There is no good reason, but if your culture has not convinced you that there is, so much the worse for your culture." The thoughtful person may inquire further. Why should the *culture* care whether it survives? Survival for what? How do we know that a culture is evolving in the right direction? Questions of this sort show a misunderstanding of the nature of evolution, biological and cultural. The processes of mutation and selection do not require, and may not provide, any advance plan of the state toward which they lead.

A well-designed culture is a set of contingencies of reinforcement under which members behave in ways which maintain the culture, enable it to meet emergencies, and change it in such a way that it will do these things even more effectively in the future. Personal sacrifice may be a dramatic example of the conflict of interests between the group and its members, but it is the product of a bad design. Under better contingencies behavior which strengthens the culture may be highly reinforcing. A jingoistic nationalism may be an easy way of underlining the good of a group, but the survival of a culture regarded simply as a set of practices, quite apart from those who practice them, can also be made the basis for a design. (It is significant that current discussions of survival are likely to speak of competition between ways of life rather than between nations or religions.) Here again effective contingencies must be programmed, and the terminal contingencies will not necessarily be "liked" by those who confront them for the first time.

The problem, in short, is not to design a way of life which will be liked by men *as they now are*, but a way of life which will be liked by those who live it. Whether those who are not part of a culture like it may have a bearing on whether they join and therefore on the promotion of a new culture and possibly on the design of early features intended to attract outsiders or prevent the defection of new members. It has no bearing on the ultimate goodness of the design. It is nevertheless in its effects on human nature—on the genetic endowment of the species—that any environment, physical or social, is to be evaluated.

The man who insists upon judging a culture in terms of whether or not he likes it is the true immoralist. Just as he refuses to follow rules designed to maximize his own net gain because they conflict with immediate gratification, so he rejects contingencies designed to strengthen the group because they conflict with his "rights as an individual." He sets himself up as a standard of human nature, implying or insisting that the culture which produced him is the only good or natural culture. He wants the world he wants and is unwilling to ask why he wants it. He is so completely the product of his own culture that he fears the influence of any other. He is like the child who said: "I'm glad I don't like broccoli because if I liked it, I'd eat a lot of it, and I hate it."

Objections to a designed culture

Many of those who like a given way of life may still object to it if it has been deliberately designed. Suppose one of the critics of *Walden Two* were to happen upon a small isolated community where—to repeat the first paragraph of this chapter—people were working only a few hours a day and without compulsion, children were being cared for and educated by specialists with due regard for the lives they were going to lead, food was good and sanitation and medical care excellent, and art, music, literature, and science flourished. Would he not exclaim, "Here is the good life!" But then let him discover that the community was explicitly designed, and the spectre of the designer would spoil it all. Why?

Design implies control, and there are many reasons why we fear it. The very techniques are often objectionable, for control passes first to those who have the power to treat others aversively. The state is still identified with the power to punish, some religious agencies still claim to mediate supernatural punishments, and schoolboys are still caned. This is "control through fear," and we naturally fear it. There is historical evidence that men have slowly turned to nonaversive methods. They have thereby escaped from some aversive stimuli, but they have not necessarily made other kinds of control acceptable. Even when a wealthy government can reinforce the behavior it wants instead of punishing the behavior it does not want—the result may still be exploitation.

The archetype of a nonexploiting controller is the benevolent dictator. We suspect him because we cannot imagine why he should control benevolently. Yet in some of the special communities we have noted the contingencies which control the designer do not conflict with those he uses in his design. When contingencies are well arranged in a hospital for psychotics, for example, the fact that patients make fewer demands on the staff and yet display as much dignity and happiness as their pathology permits is enough to explain the behavior of the designer. In a home for retarded children, if aversive control is minimal and happiness and dignity therefore maximal, and if some of the children learn enough to be able to move into the world at large, these effects will be among the important reinforcers of those who have designed the community. If juvenile delinquents behave well in a training school and at the same time acquire skills which permit them to lead nondelinquent lives after they leave it, the design can be explained. In each of these communities a way of life is designed both for the good of those who live it and for the good of the designer, and the two goods do not conflict. Nevertheless, technologies of this sort are often opposed just because control is exerted.

Democracy is an effort to solve the problem by letting the people design the contingencies under which they are to live or—to put it another way—by insisting that the designer himself live under the contingencies he designs. It is reasonable to suppose that he will not use aversive techniques if he himself will be affected by them or positive techniques which lead to exploitation if he himself will be exploited. But specialization is almost inevitable (minorities readily understand how difficult it is to keep the controller and the controllee in the same skin), and specialization implies special contingencies which are still open to suspicion.

One safeguard against exploitation is to make sure that the designer never controls; he refuses to put his design into effect himself or is forbidden to do so or—better still—dies. In *Walden Two* the protagonist, Frazier, has simply abdicated. (As an additional assurance that he exerts no current control, he was given what might be called negative charisma.) But he may still be feared because a particularly subtle kind of exploitation survives. No matter how benevolent he may be, or how far from the exercise of power, the designer gets credit for the achievements of the community, and the credit is taken from those who live in it. A ruler who discovers a better way of inducing people to behave well gets credit for an orderly society but at the expense of those who live in it, who would be more admired if they behaved well in a disorderly society. A man who designs a better way of teaching gets credit for the benefits of improved education but at the expense of the students, who would be more admired if they learned when badly taught or not taught at all. The industrialist who designs a better way of producing goods gets credit for increased production but at the expense of the workers, who would get more credit for being efficient and enterprising under another system. A utopia as a completely managed culture seems to work a wholesale despoliation of this sort. Its citizens are *automatically* good, wise, and productive, and we have no reason to admire them or give them credit. Some critics have gone so far as to say that they have been robbed of their very humanity. Mr. Krutch has accused me of dehumanizing men, and C. S. Lewis entitled a book on this theme *The Abolition of Man* (90).

We admire people and give them credit for what they do in order to induce them to behave in admirable ways (149). We are particularly likely to do so when no other kind of control is available, as I have shown elsewhere. When alternative practices are invented, or when the world changes so that the behavior at issue is no longer necessary, the practice of admiration is dropped. (It is a temporary measure, the weakness of which is suggested by the fact that we do not admire those who are obviously behaving well simply because they have been admired for doing so.) Admiration often supplements aversive control (we admire those who meet their responsibilities and hence need not be punished), and it may indeed represent an early form of an alternative practice, but it must eventually yield to other alternatives. As we come to understand human behavior and its role in the evolution of cultures, and particularly the contingencies which induce men to design cultures, we must dispense with the practice of giving personal credit. But that step is disturbing for other reasons.

Man and his destiny

The notion of personal credit is incompatible with the hypothesis that human behavior is wholly determined by genetic and environmental forces. The hypothesis is sometimes said to imply that man is a helpless victim, but we must not overlook the extent to which he controls the things which control him. Man is largely responsible for the environment in which he lives. He has changed the physical world to minimize aversive properties and maximize positive reinforcements, and he has constructed governmental, religious, educational, economic, and psychotherapeutic systems which promote satisfying personal contacts and make him more skillful, informed, productive, and happy. He is engaged in a gigantic exercise in self-control, as the result of which he has come to realize more and more of his genetic potential.

He has reached a very special point in that story. He is the product of an evolutionary process in which essentially accidental changes in genetic endowment have been differentially selected by accidental features of the environment, but he has now reached the point at which he can examine that process and do something about it. He can change the course of his own evolution through selective breeding, and in the not too distant future he will quite possibly change it by changing his chromosomes. The "value judgments" which will then be demanded are beginning to attract attention. The point is that *we have long since reached a comparable stage in the evolution of cultures.* We produce cultural "mutations" when we invent new social practices, and we change the conditions under which they are selected when we change the environments in which men live.

To refuse to do either of these things is to leave further changes in our culture to accident, and accident is the tyrant really to be feared. Adventitious arrangements of both genetic and environmental variables have brought man to his present position and are responsible for its faults as well as its virtues. The very misuse of personal control to which we object so violently is the product of accidents which have made the weak subject to the strong, the dull to the sharp, the well-intentioned to the selfish. We can do better than that. By accepting the fact that human behavior is controlled—by things if not by men—we take a big step forward, for we can then stop trying to avoid control and begin to look for the most effective kinds.

Whether we like it or not, survival is the value by which we shall be judged. The culture which takes its survival into account is most likely to survive. To recognize the fact is not, unfortunately, to resolve all our difficulties. It is hard to say what kinds of human behavior will prove most valuable in a future which cannot be clearly foreseen. Nor is it easy to identify the practices which will generate the kinds of behavior needed, but here at least we have made some progress. The design of behavior to specification is the very essence of a technology derived from an experimental analysis.

The authors of the classical utopian literature proposed to achieve the good life they described in ways which are now seen to be inadequate, but the value of utopian thinking must not, therefore, be underestimated. In a curious way it has always taken cultural evolution into account. It has scrutinized the sources of social practices, examined their consequences, and proposed alternatives which should have more desirable consequences—and all in the experimental spirit characteristic of science.

In the long run, of course, we must dispense with utopian simplifications, for the real test of a culture is the world at large. (The anti-utopians, of course, are talking about that world too; they would scarcely be so violent about a community of a few hundred people.) And the persistent question about that test is this: Is it to be *our* culture which survives and contributes most to the culture of the future? We can point to certain reassuring features. We enjoy the advantages which flow from the very practice of changing practice; until recently we have been perhaps unique in our disposition to try new ways of doing things. We give thought to consequences. Our practice of asking whether something works or whether something else would work better is often criticized as a crude pragmatism, but it may prove to have been an important cultural mutation. We readily change practices because we are not greatly restrained by revelation or immutable decrees, and for similar reasons we are free to pursue a science of behavior. Above all, we have recognized the need for the explicit design of a way of life.

But not all signs are propitious. The contingencies of reinforcement which shape and maintain the behavior of the cultural designer are not yet very clear. Obvious economic contingencies bring yearly improvements in automobiles, for example, but there are no comparable forces at work to improve governmental and ethical practices, education, housing, or psychotherapy. The survival of the culture has not yet been brought to bear in a very effective way on those who are engaged in government in the broadest sense.

Another danger signal is anti-utopianism itself (the clarification of which may be one of the most important contributions of utopian thinking). Anti-utopian arguments are the utopian arguments of an earlier era; that is why we call them reactionary. At one stage in the evolution of a culture, for example, aversive control may be effectively centralized in a despotic government. The appropriate philosophy or literature which supports it may outlive its usefulness without losing its power and will continue to support those who oppose any change—say, to democratic practices. Something of the same sort is now happening with respect to the doctrine of individual freedom. In undermining despotic control it is important to convince the individual that he is the source of the power to govern, that he can free himself of restraining forces, that he can make unique contributions, and so on. This is done by calling him free and responsible, admiring him for meeting his responsibilities, and punishing him for failing to do so. The supporting philosophy and literature have remained effective and are responsible for much of current anti-utopianism.

A scientific analysis of human behavior and of genetic and cultural evolution cannot make individual freedom the goal of cultural design. The individual is not an origin or source. He does not initiate anything. Nor is it he who survives. (The doctrine of survival after death is a source of personal reinforcers appropriate only to an earlier design.) What survives are the species and the culture. They lie "beyond the individual" in the sense that they are responsible for him and outlive him. Nevertheless, a species has no existence apart from its members or a culture apart from the people who practice it. It is only through effects on individuals that practices are selected or designed. If by "man" we mean a member of the human species with its unique genetic endowment, its human nature, then man is still the measure of all things. But it is a measure we can use effectively only if we accept it for what it is, as this is revealed in a scientific analysis rather than in some earlier conception, no matter how convincing that conception may have seemed or how effective it may have proved to be in another culture.[2]

It has been argued that it was the well-governed city-state which suggested to the Greeks that the universe itself might show law and order and that in their search for the laws which governed it, they laid the foundations of modern science. The problems of government have grown more difficult, and no modern state is likely to be taken as the model of a lawful system. It is possible that science may now repay its debt and restore order to human affairs.

[2] A more detailed analysis of the concept of freedom and dignity from this point of view is in preparation (153).

3   The environmental solution

The world in which man lives has been changing much faster than man himself. In a few hundred generations, highly beneficial characteristics of the human body have become troublesome. One of these is the extent to which human behavior is strengthened by certain kinds of reinforcing consequences.

It was once important, for example, that men should learn to identify nutritious food and remember where they found it, that they should learn and remember how to catch fish and kill game and cultivate plants, and that they should eat as much as possible whenever food was available. Those who were most powerfully reinforced by certain kinds of oral stimulation were most likely to do all this and to survive—hence man's extraordinary susceptibility to reinforcement by sugar and other foodstuffs, a sensitivity which, under modern conditions of agriculture and food storage, leads to dangerous overeating.

A similar process of selection presumably explains the reinforcing power of sexual contact. At a time when the human race was periodically decimated by pestilence, famine, and war and steadily attenuated by endemic ills and an unsanitary and dangerous environment, it was important that procreative behavior should be maximized. Those for whom sexual reinforcement was most powerful should have most quickly achieved copulation and should have continued to copulate most frequently. The breeders selected by sexual competition must have been not only the most powerful and skillful members of the species but those for whom sexual contact was most reinforcing. In a safer environment the same susceptibility leads to serious overpopulation with its attendant ills.

The principle also holds for aggressive behavior. At a time when men were often plundered and killed, by animals and other men, it was important that any behavior which harmed or frightened predators should be quickly learned and long sustained. Those who were most strongly reinforced by evidences of damage to others should have been most likely to survive. Now, under better forms of government, supported by ethical and moral practices which protect person and property, the reinforcing power of successful aggression leads to personal illness, neurotic and otherwise, and to war—if not total destruction.

Such discrepancies between man's sensitivity to reinforcement and the contribution which the reinforced behaviors make to his current welfare raise an important problem in the design of a culture. How are we to keep from overeating, from overpopulating the world, and from destroying each other? How can we make sure that these properties of the human organism, once necessary for survival, shall not now prove lethal?

Three traditional solutions

One solution to the problem might be called the voluptuary or sybaritic. Reinforcement is maximized while the unfortunate consequences are either disregarded—on the principle of eat, drink, and be merry for tomorrow we die—or prevented. Romans avoided some of the consequences of overeating, as an occasional neurotic may do today, by using the vomitorium. A modern solution is nonnutritious food. Artificial sweeteners have an effect on the tongue similar to that of ripe fruit, and we can now be reinforced for eating things which have fewer harmful effects. The sybaritic solution to the problem of sexual reinforcement is either irresponsible intercourse or the prevention of consequences through contraception or nonprocreative forms of sex. Aggressive behavior is enjoyed without respect to the consequences in the donnybrook. Some consequences are avoided by being aggressive towards animals, as in bearbaiting and other blood sports, or vicariously aggressive toward both men and animals, as in the Roman circus or in modern body sports and games. (Broadcasters of professional football and prize fights have used special microphones to pick up the thud of body against body.)

It is not difficult to promote the sybaritic solution. Men readily subscribe to a way of life in which primary reinforcers are abundant, for the simple reason that subscribing is a form of behavior susceptible to reinforcement. In such a world one may most effectively pursue happiness (or, to use a less frivolous expression, fulfill one's nature), and the pursuit is easily rationalized: "Nothing but the best, the richest and fullest experience possible, is good enough for man." In these forms, however, the pursuit of happiness is either dangerously irresponsible or deliberately nonproductive and wasteful. Satiation may release a man for productive behavior, but in a relatively unproductive condition.

A second solution might be called, with strict attention to etymology, the puritanical. Reinforcement is offset by punishment. Gluttony, lust, and violence are classified as bad or wrong (and punished by the ethical group), as illegal (and punished by the government), as sinful (and punished by religious authorities), or as maladjusted (and punished by those therapists who use punishment). The puritanical solution is never easy to "sell," and it is not always successful. Punishment does not merely cancel reinforcement; it leads to a struggle for self-control which is often violent and time consuming. Whether one is wrestling with the devil or a cruel superego, there are neurotic by-products. It is possible that punishment sometimes successfully "represses" behavior and the human energies can then be redirected into science, art, and literature, but the metaphor of redirection of energy raises a question to which we must return. In any event the puritanical solution has many unwanted by-products, and we may well explore other ways of generating the acceptable behaviors attributed to it.

A third solution is to bring the body up to date. Reinforcing effects could conceivably be made commensurate with current requirements for survival. Genetic changes could be accelerated through selective breeding or possibly through direct action on the germ plasm, but certain chemical or surgical measures are at the moment more feasible. The appetite-suppressing drugs now available often have undesirable side effects, but a drug which would make food less reinforcing and therefore weaken food-reinforced behavior would be widely used. The possibility is not being overlooked by drug manufacturers. Drugs to reduce the effects of sexual reinforcement—such as those said to be used, whether effectively or not, by penal institutions and the armed services —may not be in great demand, but they would have their uses and might prove surprisingly popular. The semistarvation recommended in some religious regimens as a means of weakening sexual behavior presumably acts through chemical changes. The chemical control of aggressive behavior—by tranquilizers—is already well advanced.

A physiological reduction in sensitivity to reinforcement is not likely to be acceptable to the sybarite. Curiously enough, the puritan would also find it objectionable because certain admirable forms of self-control would not be exhibited. Paraphrasing La Rochefoucauld, we might say that we should not give a man credit for being tranquil if his aggressive inclinations have been suppressed by a tranquilizer.

A practical difficulty at the moment is that measures of this sort are not specific and probably undercut desirable reinforcing effects.

A fourth solution

A more direct solution is suggested by the experimental analysis of behavior. One may deal with problems generated by a powerful reinforcer simply by changing the contingencies of reinforcement. An environment may be designed in which reinforcers which ordinarily generate unwanted behavior simply do not do so. The solution seems reasonable enough when the reinforcers are of no special significance. A student once defended the use of punishment with the following story. A young mother had come to call on his family, bringing her five-year-old son. The boy immediately climbed onto the piano bench and began to pound the keys. Conversation was almost impossible and the visit a failure. The student argued for the puritanical solution: he would have punished the child—rather violently, he implied. He was overlooking the nature of pianos. For more than two hundred years talented and skillful men have worked to create a device which will powerfully reinforce the behavior of pressing keys. (The piano, is, indeed, an "eighty-eight lever box." It exists solely to reinforce the pressing of levers—or the encouraging of others to press them.) The child's behavior simply testified to the success of the piano industry. It is bad design to bring child and piano together and then punish the behavior which naturally follows.

A comparable solution is not so obvious when the reinforcers have strong biological significance because the problem is misunderstood. We do not say that a child possesses a basic need to play the piano. It is obvious that the behavior has arisen from a history of reinforcement. In the case of food, sex, and violence, however, traditional formulations have emphasized supposed internal needs or drives. A man who cannot keep from overeating suffers from strong internal stimulation which he easily mistakes for the cause (rather than a collateral effect) of his uncontrollable behavior, and which he tries to reduce in order to solve his problem. He cannot go directly to the inner stimulation, but only to some of the conditions responsible for it—conditions which, as he puts it, "make him feel hungry." These happen also to be conditions which "make him eat." The easiest way to reduce both the internal stimulation and the strength of the behavior is simply to eat, but that does not solve the problem. In concentrating on other ways of changing needs or drives, we overlook a solution to the behavioral problem.

What a man must control to avoid the troublesome consequences of oral reinforcement is the behavior reinforced. He must stop buying and eating candy bars, ordering and eating extra pieces of cake, eating at odd times of the day, and so on. It is not some inner state called hunger but overeating which presents a problem. The behavior can be weakened by making sure that it is not reinforced. In an environment in which only simple foods have been available a man eats sensibly—not because he must, but because no other behavior has ever been strengthened. The normal environment is of a very different sort. In an affluent society most people are prodigiously reinforced with food. Susceptibility to reinforcement leads men to specialize in raising particularly delicious foods and to process and cook them in ways which make them as reinforcing as possible. Overanxious parents offer especially delicious food to encourage children to eat. Powerful reinforcers (called "candy") are used to obtain favors, to allay emotional disturbances, and to strengthen personal relations. It is as if the environment had been designed to build the very behaviors which later prove troublesome. The child it produces has no greater "need for food" than one for whom food has never been particularly reinforcing.

Similarly, it is not some "sexuality" or "sex drive" which has troublesome consequences but sexual behavior itself, much of which can be traced to contingencies of reinforcement. The conditions under which a young person is first sexually reinforced determine the extent as well as the form of later sexual activity. Nor is the problem of aggression raised by a "death instinct" or "a fundamental drive in human beings to hurt one another" but rather by an environment in which human beings are reinforced when they hurt one another. To say that there is "something suicidal in man that makes him enjoy war" is to reverse the causal order; man's capacity to enjoy war leads to a form of suicide. In a world in which a child seldom if ever successfully attacks others, aggressive behavior is not strong. But the world is usually quite different. Either through simple neglect or in the belief that innate needs must be expressed, children are allowed and even encouraged to attack each other in various ways. Aggressive behavior is condoned in activities proposed as "a moral equivalent of war." It may be that wars have been won on the playing fields of Eton, but they have also been started there, for a playing field is an arena for the reinforcement of aggressive action, and the behaviors there reinforced will sooner or later cause trouble.

The distinction between need and reinforcement is clarified by a current problem. Many of those who are trying to stop smoking cigarettes will testify to a basic drive or need as powerful as those of hunger, sex, and aggression. (For those who have a genuine drug addiction, smoking is reinforced in part by the alleviation of withdrawal symptoms, but most smokers can shift to nicotine-free cigarettes without too much trouble. They are still unable to control the powerful repertoire of responses which compose smoking.) It is clear that the troublesome pattern of behavior—"the cigarette habit"—can be traced, not to a need, but to a history of reinforcement because there was no problem before the discovery of tobacco or before the invention of the cigarette as an especially reinforcing form in which tobacco may be smoked.

Whatever their other needs may have been, our ancestors had no need to smoke cigarettes, and no one has the need today if, like them, he has never been reinforced for smoking.

The problem of cigarette smoking has been approached in the other ways we have examined. Some advertising appeals to the irresponsible sybarite: buy the cigarette that tastes good and inhale like a man. Other sybaritic smokers try to avoid the consequences; the filter is the contraceptive of the tobacco industry. The puritanical solution has also been tried. Cigarettes may be treated so that the smoker is automatically punished by nausea. Natural aversive consequences —a rough throat, a hoarse voice, a cigarette cough, or serious illness—may be made more punishing. The American Cancer Society has tried to condition aversive consequences with a film, in color, showing the removal of a cancerous lung. As is often the case with the puritanical solution, aversive stimuli are indeed conditioned—they are felt as "guilt"—but smoking is not greatly reduced. A true nicotine addiction might be controlled by taking nicotine or a similar drug in other ways, but a drug which would be closer to the chemical solution promised by anti-appetite, anti-sex, and anti-aggression drugs would specifically reduce the effect of other reinforcers in smoking. All these measures are much more difficult than controlling the contingencies of reinforcement.

(That there is no need to smoke cigarettes may be denied by those who argue that it is actually composed of several other kinds of needs, all of them present in nonsmokers. But this is simply to say that cigarette smoking is reinforced by several distinguishable effects—by odor, taste, oral stimulation, vasoconstriction in the lungs, "something to do with the hands," appearing to resemble admired figures, and so on. A nonsmoker has not come under the control of a particular combination of these reinforcers. If any one should cause trouble on its own or in some other combination, it could be analyzed in the same way.)

Making contingencies less effective

The problems raised by man's extraordinary sensitivity to reinforcement by food, sexual contact, and aggressive damage cannot be solved, as the example of cigarette smoking might suggest, simply by removing these things from the environment. It would be impossible to change the world that much, and in any case the reinforcers serve useful functions. (One important function is simply to encourage support for a culture. A way of life in which food, sex, and aggression were kept to a bare minimum would not strongly reinforce those who adopted it nor discourage defections from it.) The problem is not to eliminate reinforcers but to moderate their effects. Several possible methods are suggested by recent work in the experimental analysis of behavior. The mere frequency with which a reinforcer occurs is much less important than the contingencies of which it is a part.

We can minimize some unwanted consequences by preventing the discovery of reinforcing effects. The first step in "hooking" a potential heroin addict is to give him heroin. The reinforcer is not at first contingent on any particular form of behavior; but when its effect has been felt (and, particularly, when withdrawal symptoms have developed), it can be made contingent on paying for the drug. Addiction is prevented simply by making sure that the effect is never felt. The reinforcing effects of alcohol, caffeine, and nicotine must be discovered in a similar way, and methods of preventing addiction take the same form. The process underlies the practice of giving free samples in food markets; customers are induced to eat small quantities of a new food so that larger quantities may be made contingent on surrendering money. Similar practices are to be found in sexual seduction and in teaching the pleasures of violence.

Reinforcers are made effective in other ways. Stimuli are conditioned so that they become reinforcing; aversive properties are weakened through adaptation so that reinforcing properties emerge with greater power (a "taste" is thus acquired); and so on. Processes of this sort have played their part in man's slow discovery of reinforcing things. It has been, perhaps, a history of the discovery of human potentialities, but among these we must recognize the potentiality for getting into trouble. In any case, the processes which make things reinforcing need to be closely scrutinized.

The excessive consummation which leads to overweight, overpopulation, and war is only one result of man's sensitivity to reinforcement. Another, often equally troublesome, is an exhausting preoccupation with behavior which is only infrequently consummated. A single reinforcement may generate and maintain a great deal of behavior when it comes at the end of a sequence or chain of responses. Chains of indefinite length are constructed in the laboratory by conditioning intermediate reinforcers. Teachers and others use the same method for many practical purposes. We may assume that something of the sort has occurred whenever we observe long chains. The dedicated horticulturalist is ultimately reinforced, say, by a final perfect bloom, but all the behavior leading up to it is not thereby explained; intermediate stages in progressing toward a final bloom must in some way have become reinforcing. In order for early man to have discovered agriculture, certain early stages of cultivation must first have been reinforced by accident or at least under conditions irrelevant to the eventual achievement.

The reinforcers we are considering generate many sequences of this sort with troublesome results. Ultimate reinforcement is often ridiculously out of proportion to the activity it sustains. Many hours of careful labor on the part of a cook lead at last to brief stimulation from a delicious food. A good wine reinforces months or years of dedicated care. Brief sexual reinforcement follows a protracted campaign of seduction (see, for example, Choderlos de Laclos's *Les liaisons dangereuses* [88] or Kierkegaard's *Diary of a Seducer*

[81].) The campaign of the dedicated aggressor, domestic or international, is often similarly protracted and suggests a long history in which a chain has been built up. Problems of this sort can be solved simply by breaking up the conditions under which long chains are formed.

Another kind of exhausting preoccupation is due to intermittent reinforcement. A single form of response is repeated again and again, often at a very high rate, even though only infrequently reinforced. Activities such as reading magazines and books, going to the theatre, and watching television are examples. Such behavior is often maintained by very infrequent reinforcement provided the schedules have been carefully programmed. Reinforcement is at first relatively frequent, but the behavior remains strong as the frequency is reduced. Thus, a television program grows less and less reinforcing as the writer runs out of themes or as the viewer no longer finds the same themes interesting, but one who has followed a program from the beginning may continue to watch it long after reinforcements have become quite rare. The dishonest gambler prepares his victim by steadily "stretching" the mean ratio in a variable ratio schedule. Eventually the victim continues to play during a very long period without reinforcement.

There are many natural systems which stretch ratios. As addiction develops, the addict must take more and more of a drug (and presumably work harder and harder to get it) for a given effect. To the extent that novelty is important, all reinforcers grow less effective with time. The gourmet is less often reinforced as familiar foods begin to cloy. The ratio schedule of sexual reinforcement is automatically stretched by satiation. The enormities suffered by the heroine in de Sade's *Justine* suggest that her many persecutors were being reinforced on ratio schedules severely strained by both aging and sexual exhaustion. Frank Harris has suggested, in his biography of Oscar Wilde (60), that the word "lead" in "lead us not into temptation" is an unconscious recognition of the progression through which more and more trouble-some forms of behavior are approached. Unwanted conse-quences are averted in all such cases by breaking up the pro-grams through which infrequent reinforcement comes to sustain large quantities of behavior.

Arranging useful contingencies

We are usually interested—for example, in education—in getting the greatest possible effect from weak reinforcers in short supply. The problem here is just the reverse—we are to minimize the effect of reinforcers which are all too abundant and powerful. Hence, instead of systematically building up long chains of responses, we prevent their formation, and in-stead of constructing programs which make strained sched-ules effective we break them up. We can use the same pro-cedures in the more familiar direction, however, in another solution to our problem. Reinforcers can be made contingent on productive behavior to which they were not originally related. Soldiers have often been induced to fight skillfully and energetically by arranging that victory will be followed by the opportunity to plunder, rape, and slaughter. It has always been particularly easy for the barbarian to mount an attack on a more advanced civilization which emphasizes the delectations of food and sex. It has been said, for ex-ample, that the wines of Italy (and presumably her well-groomed and beautiful women) made Rome particularly vul-nerable. All governments make aggressive damage to an enemy especially reinforcing to their soldiers with stories of atrocities. Religious visions of another world have been made reinforcing in the same modes. Many of the offerings to the gods portrayed in Egyptian temples are edible, and Greek and Roman gods were distinguished by their taste for am-brosia and nectar, although less advanced civilizations have looked forward only to a happy hunting ground. Sex has its place in the Muslim heaven where men may expect to enjoy the attention of beautiful virgin Huris, and some theologians have argued that one of the attractions of the Christian heaven is the spectacle of sinners being tormented in hell— a spectacle which, as portrayed, for example, in the *Inferno,* competes successfully with the Roman circus at its most violent.

Marriage is often described as a system in which unlimited sexual contact with a selected partner is contingent on non-sexual behavior useful to the culture—such as supporting and managing a household and family and, following St. Paul's famous principle, forsaking sexual activity elsewhere. Women have often raised moral standards with practices which were merely carried to an extreme by Lysistrata. Educators use the basic reinforcers rather timidly. Erasmus advocated cherries and cakes in place of the cane in teaching children Greek and Latin, but he was the exception rather than the rule. Homosexual reinforcement was explicit in Greek education, however, and a sadistic or masochistic violence has supported corporal punishment and competitive arrangements among students down to modern times (152). Economic transactions characteristically involve food, sex, and aggression since money as a generalized reinforcer derives much of its power when exchanged for them. In the nineteenth century it was expected that wages would be exchanged primarily for food, and charity was opposed on the grounds that the industrial system needed a hungry labor force. Better working conditions have made other reinforcers effective, but many of them are still related to sex and aggression.

Reinforcers have, of course, a special place in art, music, and literature. Their place in science is not always obvious. Max Weber has argued, indeed, that the scientist is a product of the puritanical solution—profiting, for example, from the scrupulous or meticulous concern for exact detail generated by aversive consequences (the etymologies of *scrupulous* and *meticulous* show punitive origins). Feuer (47) has recently shown, however, that almost all outstanding men in science have followed a "hedonist ethic."

A solution to our problem in which food, sex, and aggression are made contingent on useful forms of behavior to which they are not naturally related has much to recommend it. It should be acceptable to the sybarite because he will not lack reinforcement. It should also assuage the puritan, not only because objectionable consequences which seem to call for punishment have been attenuated but because a man must work for the reinforcers he receives. It should not require any change in human behavior through chemical, surgical, or even genetic means, since a natural sensitivity to reinforcement is now useful rather than troublesome.

The solution has not yet been satisfactorily worked out, however. The contingencies of positive reinforcement arranged by governmental and religious agencies are primitive, and the agencies continue to lean heavily on the puritanical solution. Economic reinforcement might seem to represent an environmental solution, but it is badly programmed and the results are unsatisfactory for both the employer (since not much is done) and the employee (since work is still work). Education and the management of retardates and psychotics are still largely aversive. In short, as we have seen, the most powerful forces bearing on human behavior are not being effectively used.

The concept of drive or need is particularly at fault. We neglect contingencies of reinforcement because we seek solutions to our problems in the satisfaction of needs. "To each according to his need" is the avowed goal of both an affluent society and a welfare state. If those who seem to have everything are still not happy, we are forced to conclude that there must be less obvious needs which are unsatisfied. Men must have spiritual as well as material needs—for example, they must need someone or something beyond themselves to believe in—and it is because these needs are unfulfilled that life seems so often empty and man so often rootless. This desperate move to preserve the concept of need is unnecessary because a much more interesting and fruitful design is possible.

Men are happy in an environment in which active, productive, and creative behavior is reinforced in effective ways. The trouble with both affluent and welfare societies is that reinforcers are not contingent on behavior. Men who are not reinforced for doing anything do little or nothing. This is the "contentment" of the Arcadian idyll and of the retired businessman. It may represent a satisfaction of needs, but it raises other problems. Only when we stop using reinforcers to allay needs can we begin to use them to "fulfill man's nature" in a much more important sense.

Note 3.1 Needs

We say that an organism needs food, a plant needs water, a candle flame needs oxygen, and a flashlight needs a battery. There is a common element in all four expressions: Because something is lacking, a process cannot proceed or an effect be achieved. But with animals and plants the need leads to action. A hungry animal explores its environment in ways which increase its chances of finding food or in ways which have previously been reinforced by food. Its need is not only a shortage but a condition in which certain behavior is likely to occur.

The two are presumably related through contingencies of survival (see Chapter 7). The young infant responds to tactile stimulation near its mouth, makes contact with its mother's breast, and actively nurses. It is well that the behavior should be strong when the infant lacks nourishment, but it would be wasteful and even dangerous at other times. There are similar reasons why food is particularly reinforcing when an organism is hungry and why behavior reinforced by food is then particularly strong.

Do we need the gustatory stimulation associated with nutritious food? The Roman soldier under the Republic is said to have eaten a cereal porridge and not much else. Was the porridge as reinforcing as occasional sweets or roast meat, or were the spoils of war therefore so much the more powerful in reinforcing the behavior of making war, as some historians have claimed?

"Comfort" raises a comparable question: We escape from and avoid aversive stimulation, but have we a need to do so? The question is important in the design of a culture. Although the physical environment will no doubt continue to operate by shaping and maintaining responses which are basically avoidance or escape even when its aversive properties have been minimized, aversive social control may disappear. Will men then suffer from a need for aversive stimulation or a need to behave in ways which reduce it? After all, much of the behavioral endowment of the human organism has been acquired in the process of avoiding climatic extremes, predators, and enemies. What happens to this endowment in a nonaversive environment? Perhaps the question is of the same order of importance as what happens to the physiological processes which restore a broken bone if one never breaks a bone.

Is there another kind of need for aggression? Can we say that man's capacity to be reinforced by damage to others is out of line with his condition in the world today when we have violence in our streets and enemies abroad? These are indeed the kinds of conditions which evoke aggressive behavior, and any change in our culture which would make such behavior less effective may appear to be threatening. But problems which seem to call for solutions through remedial aggression often have aggressive origins, and to moderate aggression is perhaps a necessary step in discovering other solutions. A reduction in aversive practices in education, for example, has proved to be the first step toward the discovery of effective alternatives. It may be that men make war as a form of thrill-seeking. To go sailing when storm warnings are up or to climb the most dangerous face of a mountain is to create aversive stimuli in order to be reinforced by escaping from them. The behavior does not mean that aversive stimulation is needed but only that escape from it is reinforcing. Chefs and confectioners have been busily at work for centuries creating particularly effective gustatory stimuli, but this does not mean that such stimuli are needed, but only that they are reinforcing.

Man is not "in bondage" to his needs; he is not "driven by greed or lust." If such statements can be paraphrased at all, he is in bondage to the things which gratify his needs. But the term bondage goes too far; the trouble is in the contingencies. The greedy or lustful man is not suffering from deprivation (we do not call a starving man greedy); he is suffering from a particularly effective schedule of reinforcement. Don Giovanni is a classical example. Although an inherited or pathological condition may make a person "oversexed," a Don Giovanni is more likely to be the product of a particularly effective schedule. A moderate susceptibility to sexual reinforcement should be enough to make every attractive girl the occasion for attempted seduction if early successes are favorably programmed. An effective variable-ratio schedule should maintain the behavior at a high level even in a person who is sexually below normal, in which case it might be tempting to argue that the above-normal behavior shows "compensation."

Cotton Mather and many other Puritan divines spent much time "wrestling with the devil." Whether or not they took that metaphor seriously (see Chapter 9), they were struggling to keep from behaving in ways classified by their cultures as sinful. Their religion taught them puritan techniques for the suppression of sexual, gluttonous, and aggressive behaviors; but it is possible that a slight change in a few cubic millimeters of tissue in the hypothalamus would have permitted them to spend their time in more profitable and enjoyable ways. We can easily imagine making such a change with the help of drugs, and electrical or surgical measures may not be far off. But have the great spiritual triumphs been nothing more than slight physiological rectifications? Certainly those who value moral struggle will deny it. Yet it is quite possible that the devil who is eventually vanquished is no more than a troublesome bit of nerve tissue.

The environmental solution contrasts less sharply with the puritan. It is characteristic of the puritan solution that it leads to a time-consuming and wasteful struggle against which a biological solution seems extraordinarily efficient. An environmental solution avoids the problem altogether; it leaves no room for struggle because conflicts never arise. At the moment an environmental solution may seem to be as far out of reach as a chemical, but the environment need not be drastically changed. An important part of that solution is to teach techniques of self-control in which the devil could be said to be tricked rather than vanquished.

Note 3.2   The problem of leisure

It might have been argued in Chapter 2 that, thanks to progress and technology, men do less and less to get the things they want and that contingencies of reinforcement are therefore less and less important in the design of a culture. Food, shelter, and protection from predators and enemies were once secured only through long hours of exhausting and often dangerous labor; but the invention of clothing, housing, agriculture, and weapons has changed all that (the acts of invention having been reinforced by the change). It may eventually be unnecessary to do more than push a button (an almost effortless electronic button at that) and since that will be little more than wishing, contingencies can then, indeed, be ignored. But that day is not yet here, nor are all contingencies so easily disposed of. Social reinforcers, for example, are particularly hard to analyse and arrange (and in part just because they have been misused in solving the simpler problem; men have avoided hard or dangerous work by getting others to work for them, just as they have got some of the good things in life by stealing them). And in any case, we still have to face the problem of what men do, and enjoy doing, when it is not necessary to do anything.

What do they in fact do? Possibly little or nothing. Once satiated and free from aversive stimulation man, like many other species, becomes inactive and goes to sleep. But only for a while. Sleep and inaction, with or without the support of drugs, will not take up all the slack.

Some leisure-time behavior can be traced to reinforcers which remain effective although there is no current deprivation. The gourmand continues to eat although he no longer needs food in a physiological sense, and the aggressive person damages others although he is not threatened. The survival value of sexual reinforcement concerns the species rather than the individual, and consummation makes no lasting change in the strength of the behavior. The man who is "at leisure," therefore, may continue to fight, attack others, and copulate, and to engage in the pre-current behaviors leading up to such activities.

Contingencies which do not involve consummation may also be effective. The play of animals resembles serious behavior and is often said to have survival value as a kind of practice. Some forms of human play may have a comparable significance. Men hunt and fish for food which they do not eat, but they are then presumably more skillful when they grow hungry. The capacity to be reinforced by the successful manipulation of a medium, as in the arts and crafts, may have survival value because it leads to behavior which is effective when more specific contingencies arise. Nonconsummatory behavior is also shown by listeners, readers, and spectators. There are probably both phylogenic and ontogenic reasons why men are reinforced as they watch others engage in serious behavior—for example, in the aggressive and sexual displays of the Roman circus and the modern theatre and cinema.

Nonconsummatory behavior may also be traced to generalized reinforcers which are not followed by the primary reinforcers upon which they are based. Money is the archetypal generalized reinforcer, and men are reinforced by it even when they do not exchange it for other things. The possibility of a generalized negative reinforcement must also be considered; much of what is called irrational or compulsive behavior has the form of avoidance or escape in the absence of aversive stimuli.

Many drugs, of which alcohol is probably the best example, have reinforcing consequences; and drug-taking is also common when the serious business of life can be neglected. Some drugs simulate the consequences of serious behavior, as in reducing aversive stimulation, and may do so in a particularly powerful way when addiction has developed.

It does not help to call these forms of leisure-time behavior substitutes for, or sublimations of, behavior having a clearer biological significance. It simply happens that when the environment has been altered so that major reinforcers are no longer powerful, lesser reinforcers take over. A further principle then comes into play: Weak reinforcers become powerful when they are intermittently scheduled. The principle explains many puzzling aspects of the behavior of men at leisure. It may seem far-fetched to say that a man is reinforced when playing solitaire by the fact that he is successfully controlling his environment. The control which is shown when a game "comes out" or when the play of a single card makes that outcome more probable is far from earthshaking. Nevertheless, such consequences maintain behavior, often for hours, and they do so primarily because they occur on the variable-ratio schedule determined by the rules of the game. All systems of gambling employ variable-ratio schedules, and it is not surprising that gambling rivals the consumption of alcohol as the outstanding feature of cultures which have achieved a good deal of leisure. Intermittent reinforcement also explains the extent to which the other reinforcers mentioned above take over when men do not "need to do anything."

The design of leisure. It is not too difficult to explain why men have discovered and elaborated leisure-time activities. The reinforcements which explain excessive consummation of food explain as well the invention of new kinds of food by chefs and confectioners. Drugs which reinforce behavior are presumably discovered or created just because they reinforce search or invention. Games of skill are invented because they sharpen the contingencies of winning and losing, and games of chance because they arrange effective variable-ratio schedules. Spectacles are designed to please the spectators; and new forms of art, literature, and music evolve because they reinforce the producer on the one hand and the viewer, reader, or listener on the other.

More surprising is the fact that cultures have from time to time *suppressed* the nonessential behaviors which would otherwise dominate leisure time. Excessive consummation has been tabooed, drugs proscribed, and gambling made illegal. Simple games of chance, dancing, and sports have been forbidden. Plato dispensed with music and drama in his Republic. Curiosity about nature and the resulting knowledge have been branded as sins. The principle has been generalized; any behavior has been called wrong if it leads to pleasure. Even essential behavior is not to be enjoyed; one may hunt and kill if one is hungry, but it is wrong to enjoy doing so.

Cultural restrictions upon what a man does at his leisure may be explained if they prevent aversive consequences. Excessive consummation and drugs are dangerous to health and have injurious effects upon others. The gambler almost always loses in the long run. Ethical and moral sanctions are involved; the devil always has things for idle hands to do. Among them is simply doing nothing. "Raising the wages of day laborers is wrong," said Dr. Johnson (25), "for it does not make them live better, but only makes them idler, and idleness is a very bad thing for human nature." We recognize some of these reasons when we sacrifice the pleasures of leisure in wartime or during periods of austerity which are imposed to promote the common good.

But a culture which proscribes activities of this sort runs the risk of disaffection. By definition, the suppression of any positively reinforced behavior makes a way of life less reinforcing. To interfere with the pursuit of pleasure is particularly resented. Why should a man not be permitted to be a drunkard or a drug addict if he hurts no one but himself? Why should he not gamble away his fortune if he pleases? The more trivial the reinforcer, the greater the resentment; innocent activities like card playing or dancing or simply doing nothing should certainly be left to the individual.

But the question is: *Can* they be left to him? Are they not instead left to contingencies which are either accidental or contrived by enterprising people who stand to gain from them? When productive contingencies become so efficient that a great deal of time is left for nonessentials, the strength of a culture depends upon what happens in that time. Leisure-time activities do not by definition give the culture much current support, but they have a bearing upon its further development and upon its ability to meet emergencies. A culture is not strengthened when its members do nothing, consume excessively, use stultifying drugs, engage in the repetitive behaviors of gambling, or merely watch others engaging in serious behavior. The culture suffers in particular when these contingencies prove inadequate and men then turn to the strong reinforcers of aggression. The culture is clearly strengthened, however, when its members turn to other kinds of leisure behavior. Arts, crafts, and games develop important skills. Scientific exploration and research (encouraged when governments, foundations, and universities make it unnecessary for men to do other things in order to survive) make an obvious contribution. The nonscientific study of human behavior, as in history and literature, promotes a useful understanding. (All these uses of leisure are embodied in the concept of a liberal education.) Education can do much more than it now does in this direction. It can teach the skills exhibited by artists, musicians, and craftsmen. It can build a sustained interest in literature as well as in the arts and music. It can teach techniques of self-management (now largely abandoned by religious and ethical agencies) which help the individual to avoid drugs and excessive consummation and to resist the special contingencies arranged by gambling systems. It can also teach the skills and build the interests which will make productive work reinforcing. Economic agencies may reduce aversive labor to a minimum or reduce the aversive by-products of labor, as by substituting positive inducement for coercive control, or making it possible for men to earn their living by doing what they would do anyway if support were forthcoming from other quarters.

The problem of leisure appears in a particularly acute form in designing a way of life for the incarcerated, including those who are forcedly incarcerated because they would otherwise harm themselves or others (psychotics, retardates, and criminals), the chronically ill, and those who work in isolated quarters such as remote weather stations or interplanetary space ships. For all such people the physical environment is necessarily limited, and the social environment, if any, likely to suffer from the same limitations. What contingencies can be designed which will provide "something to do" during most of the waking hours? These are all challenging problems for the specialist in contingency management.

II   AN ANALYSIS OF ONTOGENIC
AND PHYLOGENIC CONTINGENCIES

4 The experimental analysis of behavior

A natural datum in a science of behavior is the probability that a given bit of behavior will occur at a given time. An experimental analysis deals with that probability in terms of frequency or rate of responding. Like probability, rate of responding would be a meaningless concept if it were not possible to specify topography of response in such a way that separate instances of an operant can be counted. The specification is usually made with the help of a part of the apparatus—the "operandum"—which senses occurrences of a response. In practice, responses so defined show a considerable uniformity as the organism moves about in a framework set by its own anatomy and the immediate environment.

An emphasis on rate of occurrence of repeated instances of an operant distinguishes the experimental analysis of behavior from kinds of psychology which observe one or more of the following practices.

(1) Behavior is taken merely as the sign or symptom of inner activities, mental or physiological, which are regarded as the principal subject matter. Rate of responding is significant only because it permits us to follow a process (such as learning or maturation), or to determine a state or condition (such as an excitatory tendency or alertness or wakefulness), to detect available psychic energy or the strength of a drive or emotion, and so on. The observed behavior is not expected to be very orderly. It is only a rather noisy "performance,"

from which presumably more stable states and processes are to be inferred with the help of statistical procedures. These practices have discouraged a careful specification of behavior, and the data obtained with them are seldom helpful in evaluating probability of response as such.

(2) Behavior is held to be significant only in meeting certain standards or criteria. An organism is described as "adjusting to a situation," "solving a problem," or "adapting to the environment." With respect to normative criteria its behavior may improve or deteriorate; with respect to developmental criteria it may be arrested or accelerated.

In reporting these aspects of behavior the experimenter may not specify what the organism is actually doing, and a rate of responding cannot be satisfactorily inferred.

(3) Changes in probability of response are treated as if they were responses or acts. The organism is said to "discriminate," to "form concepts," to "remember," to "learn what to do" and, as a result, "know what to do," and so on. These are not, however, modes of response. To discriminate is not to respond but to respond differently to two or more stimuli. To say that an organism has learned to discriminate between two stimuli is to report a possibly useful fact, but it is not to say what the organism is actually doing.

(4) The dimensions studied, though quantifiable, are not related in any simple way to probability of response. The force with which a response is executed and the time which elapses between stimulus and response—called, often inaccurately, latency or reaction time—are popular measures. When they change under differential reinforcement, they are relevant to an experimental analysis, but they may not throw much light on probability. Other common measures, such as the time required to complete a task—to get through a maze, to solve a problem, or to cross out all letters of a given kind on a page—or the number of errors made or the number of trials taken in meeting a criterion are still less useful. "Amount remembered," an aspect of behavior first empha-

sized by Ebbinghaus, has recently enjoyed a renewed popularity. The experimenter may want to know, for example, how a set of responses come under the control of a corresponding set of stimuli, but instead of following the change in probability he measures the number of responses correctly emitted in recall at a later time.

An experiment is often designed so that the important result is a ratio between two such measures, when the arbitrariness or irrelevance of the aspects measured seems to cancel out. A ratio is still of little help in an experimental analysis. Such measures are chosen primarily because they are quantifiable—force of response can be accurately recorded, number of trials exactly counted, and elapsed time measured on the most accurate of clocks—but quantifiability is not enough. Rate of responding is a basic dimension, not simply because responses can be accurately counted, but because rate is relevant to the central concern of a science of behavior.

(5) The inner entities of which behavior is said to be a sign or symptom include the traits, abilities, attitudes, faculties, and so on, for which various techniques of psychological measurement have been designed. But even the most impeccable statistical techniques and the most cautious operational definitions will not alter the fact that the "tests" from which the data are obtained are very loosely controlled experimental spaces and that the "scores" taken as measures have some of the arbitrary features just mentioned. The important issues to which these techniques have been directed —for example, the covariation in probability of groups of responses—must be studied in other ways before the results will be useful in an experimental analysis.

(6) Instead of observing behavior, the experimenter records and studies a subject's statement of what he would do under a given set of circumstances, or his estimate of his chances of success, or his impression of a prevailing set of contingencies of reinforcement, or his evaluation of the magnitude of current variables. The observation of behavior

cannot be circumvented in this way, because a subject cannot correctly describe either the probability that he will respond or the variables affecting such a probability. If he could, he could draw a cumulative record appropriate to a given set of circumstances, but this appears to be out of the question (see page 116).

The independent variables

One task of an experimental analysis is to discover all the variables of which probability of response is a function. It is not an easy assignment, but it is at least an explicit one. It distinguishes an experimental analysis of behavior from other approaches at many points.

(1) The stimulus is, of course, an important independent variable. An early association with the concept of the reflex gave it, as we have seen, the character of a goad, something which forced an organism to respond. That was perhaps as wrong as the traditional view that the organism forced the environment to stimulate—to become visible, audible, and so on. The position of an experimental analysis differs from that of traditional stimulus-response psychologies or conditioned reflex formulations in which the stimulus retains the character of an inexorable force. It does not follow, however, that the organism acts upon the environment in the manner suggested by terms like *detect, identify, perceive, experience, classify,* and *judge,* or by terms which appear to describe later responses to stimuli, such as *recall how something looked* or *remember what happened.* Such terms, like expressions borrowed from computer technology which describe the organism as processing information, do not specify what the organism is actually doing. The concept of the discriminative stimulus (the well known "S^D") and the related notion of stimulus control assign to stimuli a more reasonable role as independent variables.

An experimental analysis describes stimuli in the language

of physics. The experimenter does not ask whether a stimulus looks the same to the organism as it does to him. In studying a generalization gradient with respect to wave length of light, for example, lights are sometimes matched for brightness, so that the gradient will represent a reaction to color only; but this is an unwarranted intrusion into the data. To guess what an organism sees when a stimulus is presented and to suppose that what is guessed is what is being presented would be to abandon all that physics has to offer by way of specifying environmental events. The importance of certain classical problems is not thereby denied. Stimuli are often difficult to specify in physical terms. Different stimuli may appear to have the same effect and the same stimulus different effects under different conditions. But it is no solution to fall back upon the response of an experimenter to achieve some sort of invariance. Similarly, any reference to "parameters relating to the complexity of a task" or to "frustrating" or "anxiety-generating" properties of a situation is also objectionable, whether the subject or the experimenter serves as indicator of the complexity or the emotion.

(2) Other independent variables are found in the classical fields of motivation and emotion. The experimental analyst does not manipulate inner states as such. He manipulates, not hunger, but the intake of food; not fear as an acquired drive, but aversive stimuli; not anxiety, but preaversive stimuli. He administers a drug, not the physiological effects of a drug. He takes the age of an organism, not a level of maturation, as a variable. He sometimes uses a collateral dependent variable—but not as a measure. He may use weight, for example, in lieu of a history of deprivation, but it is simply another effect of deprivation, not a measure of hunger as a state.

(3) Contingencies of reinforcement are an important feature of the independent variables studied in an experimental analysis, but many psychologists are unaware of the complexity of the contingencies now commonly studied. In addition

to many standard schedules of reinforcement, reinforcement may be contingent on rate of responding, rate of change in rate, or specific patterns of rate changes detected by on-line computer analyses. Contingencies may involve several stimuli and responses interrelated in various ways. Considerable skill may be needed to design programs of instructional contingencies which will bring behavior under the control of complex terminal contingencies of this sort. The importance of programming is, indeed, often completely overlooked. For example, the statement that a given type of organism or an organism of a given age "cannot solve a given kind of problem" is meaningless until the speaker has specified the programs which have been tried and considered the possibility that better ones may be designed.

Describing a set of contingencies in instructions to the subject is no substitute for exposing the subject to the contingencies, particularly when they need to be programmed. Instructions have effects, of course, depending in part on the verbal history of the subject, but the behavior of a subject to whom an experimenter has explained how a piece of apparatus works will not necessarily resemble one who has come under the control of the terminal contingencies established by that apparatus.

Contingencies of reinforcement have been analyzed formally in theories of probability, decision-making, and games, but the theorist often has no way of knowing, aside from observation of his own behavior, what effects a given set of contingencies will have or what kind of program may be needed to make it effective. Certain assumptions—for example, that an organism will behave rationally—are sometimes used in lieu of observations to complete a statement of contingencies. Formal statements of contingencies, like instructions, have their effects and if detailed enough may supply rules which function as prior stimuli to control behavior resembling that which would be generated by prolonged exposure to the contingencies themselves. The two cases must, however, be clearly distinguished. When an organism is brought under the control of complex contingencies, it is not necessarily "applying the rule" which describes them (see Chapter 6).

Treatment of relationships among variables

The behavioral processes studied in an experimental analysis usually consist of changes in probability (or rate of response) as a function of manipulated variables. The changes are followed in real time rather than from "trial to trial"—a practice derived from accidental features of early psychological research. An emphasis on real time is another reason why cumulative records are useful. (A cumulative record is sometimes used to "smooth" other kinds of data—for example, the errors made during repeated trials in learning a maze or in solving a problem—and it is often implied that a cumulative record of responses in time also gains an unwarranted smoothness of the same sort. The important difference is that the slope of a cumulative curve in real time represents a meaningful state of behavior.)

Relations among dependent and independent variables are seldom explored according to a prior "experimental design," as R. A. Fisher used that term. The null hypothesis finds itself in the null class. Research which is not designed to test hypotheses—physiological, mentalistic, or conceptual—may seem puzzling to those who identify statistics with scientific method, though it appears perfectly reasonable to physicists, chemists, and most biologists. The usual practice is to construct an experimental space in which stimuli, responses, and reinforcements are interrelated in a set of contingencies. The contingencies depend in part on the behavior which the organism brings to the experiment. Provision is usually made for changing the apparatus as the behavior changes, but seldom according to a predetermined plan. The experimental control of variables is emphasized rather than a later evaluation of their presumed importance through statistical analyses. The number of organisms studied is usually much smaller than in statistical designs, but the length of time during which any one organism is observed is usually much greater.

It is often said to be impossible to distinguish between significant and insignificant facts without a hypothesis or theory, but the experimental analysis of behavior does not seem to bear this out. It has progressed by building upon its past. Improved formulations and techniques have led to more precise and reproducible data over a much greater range, but not to the outright rejection of earlier work. (For one thing, few data have become useless because a theory they were designed to test has been discarded.) In retrospect there appears to have been little random or aimless exploration. Such a field as the systematic analysis of contingencies of reinforcement, for example, does not require a theory. A study of schedules of reinforcement (46) can proceed in a rather Baconian fashion, as a table of the possibilities generated by combinations of clocks, counters, and speedometers, fixed and variable sequences, and so on is completed. Most of the contingencies examined in theories of probability, decision-making, and games can be generated in a similar way—the "theory," if any, being concerned with what organisms will do under the contingencies analyzed. The experimental analysis of behavior dispenses with theories of that sort by proceeding to find out.

In addition to the systematic manipulation of contingencies, the interpretation of human affairs is a rich source of suggestions for experiments. Do conditions detected in some episode in daily life actually have the effects observed when more carefully controlled? Can a certain history of reinforcement be shown to be responsible for a current performance? What changes in contingencies will have different and possibly more acceptable results? The guesses and hunches with which the experimenter proceeds to answer questions of this sort are not the formal hypotheses of scientific method; they are simply tentative statements for which further support is sought. The philosopher of science may still want to reconstruct the behavior so that it fits a hypothetico-deductive model, but efforts in that direction grow less impressive—particularly as an alternative formulation of the behavior of Man Thinking is glimpsed as one of the more distant reaches of an experimental analysis.

Research which enlarges an established corpus of facts or simplifies an effective formulation is usually less dramatic than research which topples hypotheses or confirms broad theories, but it has its compensations. For those so inclined, theoretical activities are by no means ruled out, even though scientific methodologists have usually been hesitant in accepting the position adopted in an experimental analysis. Quite aside from testing hypotheses, one may look for simplifying uniformities. For example, one may develop a theory as to why schedules of reinforcement have the effects they have, seeking certain simplifying relations among the many performances generated by different schedules. The conditions which prevail at the precise moment of reinforcement are important, but a better theory in this sense is no doubt possible and desirable.

In representing the relationships discovered by an experimental analysis of behavior, little use is made of metaphors or analogies drawn from other sciences. Reports seldom contain expressions like *encode, read out from storage, reverberating circuits, overloaded channels, gating, pressure, flow, drainage, networks, centers,* or *cell assemblies.* Little use is made of maps or schemata, such as Tolman's sow-bug, Lewin's fields and vectors, or block diagrams representing organisms as adaptive machines. The advantage in representing processes without the use of metaphor, map, or hypothetical structure is that one is not misled by a spurious sense of order or rigor. Early in his career Freud wrote to Fliess that he had put psychology on a firm neurological basis. The theory permitted him "to see the details of neurosis all the way to the very conditioning of consciousness" (49). His letter emphasized number, structure, and terms borrowed from neurology, biology, and physics. He spoke of "the three systems of neurones, the 'free' and 'bound' states of quantity, the primary and secondary processes, the main trend and the compromise trend of the nervous system, the two biological rules of attention and defense." Terms of this sort encourage euphoria, and Freud was vulnerable; in his first report he was "wildly enthusiastic." Within a month or so he had abandoned the theory. He had the insight to tell Fliess that it seemed to him in retrospect "a kind of aberration."

Attitudes toward research

The experimental analysis of behavior is also generally characterized by an unhurried attitude toward the as-yet-unanalyzed or the as-yet-unexplained. Criticism often takes the line that the analysis is oversimplified, that it ignores important facts, that a few obvious exceptions demonstrate that its formulations cannot possibly be adequate, and so on. An understandable reaction might be to stretch the available facts and principles in an effort to cover more ground, but the general plan of the research suggests another strategy. Unlike hypotheses, theories, and models, together with the statistical manipulations of data which support them, a smooth curve showing a change in probability of a response as a function of a controlled variable is a fact in the bag, and there is no need to worry about it as one goes in search of others. The shortcomings and exceptions will be accounted for in time. The strategy is supported by the history of early criticisms of the *Behavior of Organisms*. It was said that the book was not about organisms but about the rat, and very small groups of rats at that. How could one be sure that other rats, let alone animals of other species, would behave in the same way? Only food and water were used as reinforcers, social reinforcers being conspicuously lacking. The stimuli— lights and buzzers—were crude and poorly controlled. Two levers should have been used so that the data would throw light on behavior at a choice point. And, after all, could we be sure that the rat was not pressing the lever simply because it had nothing else to do? These criticisms have all been answered without effort in the course of time simply as part of the normal development of the analysis.

Patience with respect to unexplored parts of a field is particularly important in a science of behavior because, as part of our own subject matter, we may be overwhelmed by the facts which remain to be explained. Subtle illusions, tricks of memory, the flashes which solve problems—these are fascinating phenomena, but it may be that genuine explanations within the framework of a science of behavior, as distinguished from verbal principles or "laws" or neurological hypotheses, are out of reach at the present time. To insist that a science of behavior give a rigorous account of such phenomena in its present state of knowledge is like asking the Gilbert of 1600 to explain a magnetic amplifier or the Faraday of 1840 to explain superconductivity. Early physical scientists enjoyed a natural simplification of their subject matters. Many of the most subtle phenomena were to come into existence only through technical advances in the sciences themselves. Others, though occurring in nature, were not recognized as parts of their fields. The behavioral scientist enjoys no such natural protection. He is faced with the full range of the phenomena he studies. He must therefore more explicitly resolve to put first things first, moving on to more difficult things only when the power of his analysis permits.

A final distinction. Those who engage in the experimental analysis of behavior are usually conspicuous for their enthusiasm. Bixenstine (16) has attributed an unwarranted optimism in all behavioral science to the methodological position taken by experimental analysts. This is perhaps to overestimate their influence, but in any case, he points to the wrong cause. He suggests that the optimism springs from release from the anxiety of theory construction. There is a more obvious explanation: the analysis works.

Note 4.1   Independent variables

The stimulus.   To the psychophysicist psychology is "the analysis of the stimulus." Students of perception, particularly under the influence of Gestalt psychology, emphasize the ways in which stimuli force us to respond to them. Students of feelings and emotion search for the things felt: hunger is stimulation arising from stomach contractions and thirst from a dry throat. Obese people eat more than normal because they are affected differently by "cues," and people are neurotic and psychotic because they see the world in a different way.

This predilection for stimuli owes much to the secure dimensions of physical things. Stimuli have duration and extent; they occupy an unquestioned position in time and space; they exist before anyone does anything about them and they survive afterwards. In contrast, behavior is evanescent. What men do and say are things of the moment. There is nothing left when a response has been completed except the responding organism. The behavior itself has gone off into history.

In spite of the fact that stimuli are thus reassuringly substantial, the psychologist is nevertheless seldom willing to deal with them as a physicist does. He shines a light into the eye of his subject as an engineer might shine a light into a photocell, but he wants to talk about what his cell—the organism—sees. Or he may inject a reference to the organism's history—for example, by calling a stimulus "novel." ("Familiar" more clearly refers to past history and there have been those, among them Gestalt psychologists, who have argued that familiarity is "in the stimulus." Some of the kinds of organization which are said to make stimuli particularly effective, by forcing a corresponding organization in the behavior of perceiving them, are also not physical properties. Past, present, or future responses may be used to impute "meaning" to a stimulus. (And nonmeaning as well; the nonsensical character of a list of syllables is not a physical property.) Psycholinguists are particularly likely to specify stimuli in terms of earlier contingencies in which they have appeared. "Sequential probabilities," "ambiguities," and "redundancies" are not "in the stimulus." A more obvious appeal to behavior is made in describing stimuli as anxiety provoking, frustrating, confusing, and so on.

On the other hand, physical properties of stimuli are sometimes invoked for the sake of objectivity or quantification when they are irrelevant. We accept the fact that not all properties of the environment are worth specifying. Visual stimuli are not important when our subject is blind, nor is electromagnetic radiation outside the visible range when our subject has normal vision. But other dimensions cannot be dismissed for such obvious reasons. Suppose we are interested in how accurately a person can estimate the number of spots on a page. The number ranges, say, from one to one hundred. This is an objective fact, but the numbers 1 to 100 do not therefore compose a single dimension of the stimulus to which speed or accuracy of estimation can be related. (For one thing the behavior of looking at a small number of spots differs from the behavior of looking at a large number.) The pattern of a maze and its length, like the pattern and length of a list of nonsense syllables, is a physical fact, but not therefore necessarily a useful property of a "stimulus." (Overemphasis on quantifiability causes trouble with other kinds of independent variables. A "twenty-four-hour hunger" describes an objective condition, which can be reproduced by other experimenters, but twenty-four does not describe a quantity of hunger. "Number of reinforced trials" is an objective but possibly useless measure of a history of reinforcement.)

Uncontrollable independent variables. The ethologists study behavior as a function of *species status.* A graylag goose behaves in a given way because it is a graylag goose. To change the behavior we should have to change the species. No matter how important genetic variables may be, we do not manipulate them as such in predicting and controlling the behavior of a given organism.

Age is not unrelated to genetic variables since most of the behavior attributed to species status is not present at birth but must mature, possibly during critical periods of development. Age is taken as the principal independent variable in studying the development of various sensory and motor skills and so-called traits, concepts, and mental processes. The development of speech, for example, is sometimes followed simply as an increase with age in the number of words or grammatical forms a child uses. Delinquent behavior in a given culture is said to show "a peak in theft at fourteen and in rowdyism at seventeen."

Cycles are another kind of temporal patterning. A squirrel runs and rests in its squirrel cage, the stock market rises and falls, a nation swings from a warlike to a peaceful mood and back, and romantic periods of history alternate with classical. A progressive change establishes a *trend.* Autocorrelational techniques can be used to clarify cycles and trends, but unless we know that a cycle will maintain its period or a trend continue, we cannot use the results for purposes of prediction. Nor, of course, can time be manipulated as an independent variable.

Controllable variables are also lacking when behavior is predicted from other behavior. The tests used in mental measurement evoke samples of behavior from which characteristics of similar behavior, usually on a larger scale, can be predicted—but only because the sample and the predicted behavior are functions of common variables, usually not identified. The traits or factors extracted from test scores seem to have the status of independent variables, but they cannot be manipulated as such.

Note 4.2   The dependent variable

Topography of behavior can be recorded in many ways. The graphic arts first made it possible to represent an organism in action, and films and videoscopes are modern equivalents. The alphabet was invented as a means of recording verbal behavior, and the tape recorder now permits greater accuracy. A mere record of topography, however, will not suffice for a functional analysis. We cannot break behavior into parts of convenient size on the basis of topography alone. Thus, we cannot simply describe a bit of behavior and call it an operant, even if everyone agrees to abide by our specifications. Even in reflexes which have been surgically isolated, the response must be defined in terms of a correlated stimulus (126). An operant must behave like one; it must undergo orderly changes in probability when independent variables are manipulated. The effect on the environment is such a variable, and we can construct an operant by making reinforcement contingent upon a given topography. But false starts are common; what is taken as an operant may not behave like one and something else may. In an apparatus containing two operanda, for example, it may be necessary to consider not only the response to each, but the behavior of changing from one to the other (134).

An explicit description of topography is sometimes avoided by characterizing the dependent variable in more general terms. For example, behavior is classified as procreative, maternal, or combative. Classifications of this sort always involve independent variables. The topography of fighting, copulating, and caring for young is usually related to phylogenic and ontogenic variables which define useful classes, but this is not always true, and even so the consequences of behavior—together with their phylogenic or ontogenic significance—are involved.

Emphasis naturally falls on topography when behavior is studied as a function of the inaccessible or uncontrollable variables already mentioned. There are established fields in which the description of behavior is mainly narration. Ethology tells us how a bird of a given species builds its nest, courts its mate, and defends its territory. Developmental psychology tells us how a baby of a given age raises its head, turns over, and grasps objects. If the important independent variables are indeed only to be found in the phylogeny of the species or in age, this is perhaps all that can be done. But it is a mistake to confine an analysis to the structure of behavior when other variables are available.

An emphasis on topography of behavior at the expense of controlling relations is an example of the Formalistic Fallacy. It is common in linguistics and psycholinguistics. By rearranging fragments of recorded verbal behavior (e.g. "words") new records (e.g. "sentences") are generated, which are then treated as though they were verbal responses. By adding *not* to *It is raining*, for example, we generate *It is not raining*, and we may proceed to test its truth or falsity. But no one has yet said *It is not raining*, except in reading the words thus arranged, and a textual response is not true or false but merely accurate or inaccurate. The generated "sentence" looks like a record of verbal behavior but the behavior it appears to record has never been emitted under the control of characteristic variables. There is a great difference between the response *It is raining* written in the presence of appropriate stimuli and the same pattern produced by rearranging words on slips of paper.

The Formalistic Fallacy is most damaging when verbal behavior is analyzed as if it were generated through the application of rules. This is most likely to happen when verbal behavior is studied as a function of uncontrollable variables, since contingencies of reinforcement are not then available as an alternative to the generation of behavior from rules (see Chapter 6). In a study of "the child's acquisition of syntax" Bellugi and Brown (14) recorded the appearance of new words and new grammatical structures in the speech of two children over a period of time. As an example of a "generative" rule, they give the following: "In order to form a noun phrase select first one word from the small class of modifiers and select, second, one word from the large class of nouns." Thus, to say *My hand* the child first selects *my* from a list of modifiers and then *hand* from a list of nouns. No reference is made to the relation of the "generated" phrase to the circumstances under which it is acquired or emitted. How often has the child echoed the verbal stimulus *my hand?* How often has he heard stories in which characters referred to their hands? How often has he heard *hand* when his own hand has been important as a stimulus—when, for example, it has been hurt, touched, washed, or shaken? What verbal history has sharpened the distinction between *my* and *your?* How many other responses containing *hand* and *my* has the child already learned? It seems safe to overlook all this material if the child selects words and puts them together to compose phrases or sentences by applying rules with the help of a mental mechanism. But selection and composition in that sense are rare forms of verbal behavior, characteristic mainly of logicians, linguists, and psycholinguists. Only the Formalistic Fallacy suggests that the products of selection and composition are equivalent to the behavior acquired under the contingencies arranged by a verbal community.

Probability of response. A further qualification of the dependent variable in a science of behavior is needed. We are not so much concerned with the topography of a response as with the probability that it will be emitted. Probability is a difficult concept. For many purposes we may be content with rate of responding, but this is awkward when a single instance of behavior is attributed to more than one variable. Similar problems arise, together with many others, when probability is inferred from the occurrence or nonoccurrence of a response in a given "trial." Behavior at a choice point does not provide independent measures of the probabilities associated with the choices. A rat may turn right rather than left in a T-maze, but we can infer only that a right turn was more probable than a left. The percentage of right or left turns in a series of trials will not complete the account because the organism presumably changes from trial to trial, and averages for groups of rats exposed to the same contingencies are still less useful.

A common practice is to evaluate probability of response in terms of the magnitude of an *independent* variable. A response evoked by a brief stimulus, for example, is felt to be stronger than one which requires a longer exposure. The probability seems to lie on a continuum between the time which guarantees a response and the time at which no appropriate response is ever made. Similar continua seem to be established by making stimuli incomplete—as by omitting letters in a text, filtering out some frequencies in recorded speech, or putting visual stimuli out of focus. The probability is inferred from the point at which the response fails to occur as the duration, clarity, or completeness of the stimulus is reduced. In psychoanalytic theory a response is inferred to have unusual strength if it occurs when it is not particularly appropriate to the occasion. Rorschach patterns and the vague auditory stimuli of the Verbal Summator (127) are presumed to evoke responses having special strength.

Probability of response is also sometimes inferred from how quickly the response is acquired or brought under stimulus control. If a response of complex topography is acquired only slowly, it is assumed that it began in very low strength. When an organism has been conditioned to respond to a given pattern, the probability that it will respond to a different pattern is sometimes argued from the speed with which it forms a discrimination. If it learns to distinguish patterns quickly, it is assumed that learning to respond to one pattern does not make a response to the other highly probable. Speed of learning is also sometimes used to measure probability attributed to deprivation or aversive stimulation.

Speed of forgetting is also, as we have noted, used to infer probability; a response which can be recalled a long time after acquisition is presumed to have been stronger when acquired. The principle is also basic to psychoanalysis; the responses we now recall were the strong responses of long ago. Further information can be extracted by varying the conditions under which recall occurs. A recollection which has little relevance to a current situation suggests unusual strength. A response recalled in the presence of distractions or conflicting variables is also held to be strong. (The number of psychological experiments which use "amount remembered" as a dependent variable is not to be taken as showing an extraordinary interest in the process of forgetting, for many of them are concerned with processes which could be more directly investigated with measures of probability.)

Behavior as a dependent variable is often neglected when the investigator turns his attention to internal processes, real or fancied. The study of verbal learning, for example, is more likely to be concerned with proactive and retroactive inhibition, reminiscence, or obliviscence than with the actual behavior of the subject, which is often not carefully analyzed. Behavior studied as a function of time—as growth, development, trends, or cycles—also often takes second place to supposed underlying processes. And no matter how elegant the mathematical procedures used in quantifying traits and abilities, they are almost always applied to relatively crude measures (for example, responses to a questionnaire) evoked under relatively uncontrolled conditions (the questionnaire). The emphasis is not upon the behavior but upon what seems to lie behind it.

Note 4.3 Significance

The psychological literature contains a prodigious number of charts, graphs, tables, and equations reporting quantitative relations among unimportant or useless variables. Much of this may be attributed to professional contingencies of reinforcement, under which what a psychologist says must be above all irrefutable. He can satisfy the contingencies by selecting a measurable aspect of behavior and a measurable condition and examining the relation between them. If he uses the right instruments and treats his data in the right ways, his result will be statistically "significant" even when no relation is found. The significance can be increased by devising a hypothesis which the result confirms or disproves or a general principle which it illustrates. The main thing is to avoid being wrong.

There are no contingencies in which positive results figure in a comparable way. Scientific progress is usually slow, and an important step is not necessarily recognized as such as soon as it is taken. Only a few discoveries are sudden enough to be contingent upon the scientist's investigatory behavior in such a way as to shape and maintain it. The dedication of the scientist is usually the product of a favorable program of weak reinforcements. Additional sources of reinforcement are therefore important. The experimental analysis of behavior has no doubt profited from the fact that its results have led rather quickly to a behavioral technology, but the laboratory scientist profits from any result which clarifies his central conception. It is reinforcing to find variables which change in an orderly fashion and which permit one to formulate behavior as a scientific system, in the sense in which that term was used, for example, by Willard Gibbs.

A concern for basic dimensions helps the young psychologist in another way. When Freud first turned from biology to psychoanalysis, he wrote to a friend (49): "What horrifies me more than anything else is all the psychology I shall have to read in the next few years." The literature faced by the young psychologist today is several thousand times as extensive. It cannot be read as a whole. A field of specialization helps, but most fields are still large. Some principle of selection is needed, and a useful guide is the significance of the variables studied. A glimpse of the coordinates of the graphs in an article will usually suffice. A good rule of thumb is as follows: do not spend much time on articles in which changes in behavior are followed from trial to trial or in which graphs show changes in the time or number of errors required to reach a criterion, or in amount remembered, or in percent of correct choices made, or which report scores, raw or standard. Sometimes a look at the apparatus will help. Dimensions are probably suspect if the work was done with mazes, T-mazes, jumping stands, or memory drums. The young psychologist will miss something in following these rules (he will find something of value almost everywhere), but he must run some risk. It is a matter of personal strategy, and an emphasis on basic dimensions makes it possible to plan a promising campaign.

Note 4.4 Progress

This is not the place for a survey of data, but some indication of the technical progress which has been made in the experimental analysis of behavior may be useful. Current practices contrast sharply with those reported thirty years ago in *The Behavior of Organisms* (129).

(1) The experimental space is more carefully controlled. Many versions have been standardized.

(2) Experiments last, not for an hour, but for many hours, days, weeks, or even months.

(3) The past history of the organism is more carefully controlled, possibly from birth.

(4) Many more species have been studied, including man (retardates, psychotics, normal children, and normal adults).

(5) Stimuli are more precisely controlled.

(6) Topography of response, including intensive and temporal properties, is more accurately reported and measured.

(7) An operant as a class or response is better defined and cumulative records are therefore smoother.

(8) Many more reinforcers have been studied—including, in addition to food and water, sexual stimulation, the opportunity to behave aggressively, and the production of novel stimuli.

(9) Rate of responding continues to be represented in a cumulative records, but details are clarified in analyses of interresponse times and with on-line computer processing—the latter, in particular, when contingencies are based on characteristics of rate or changes in rate.

(10) Many more schedules of intermittent reinforcement have been studied.

(11) Concurrent and sequential arrangements of contingencies permit the study of aspects of behavior which were once attributed to higher mental processes, among them many which bear upon decision-making.

(12) The experimental space often contains two or more organisms with interlocking contingencies which generate "synthetic social relations."

Note 4.5   A technology of behavior

Science and technology have always been closely interwoven. Practical problems are often solved first, and the solutions are then taken over by basic science; the craftsman's rules of thumb are the beginnings of scientific laws, as Ernst Mach pointed out long ago. On the other hand, as basic research flourishes, its methods and results come to be applied to practical affairs. Much of the technology which emerges may have no earlier rule-of-thumb counterpart. Psychology offers many examples. Techniques of mental measurement were invented to solve practical problems in education and only later came to be used in basic analyses of traits and abilities. Introspective psychology, on the other hand, emerged from philosophical inquiries into the nature of man's knowledge of the world around him, but it gave rise to instruments and methods which were later used to solve practical problems in adjusting to that world. Studies in learning (and in teaching and training) have almost always been a mixture of basic and applied research.

The technological successes of psychology have not, however, been remarkable. The psychologist often finds himself in a subordinate position; he supplies information but plays little or no part in its use. He determines the facts upon which decisions are made but takes no part in making them. Clinical psychologists often find themselves in this position with respect to psychiatrists. School psychologists report to the teacher or administrator who takes action. It is the statesman or politician who uses the results of opinion polls, and boards of directors who plan production in the light of market analyses. When a psychologist occasionally moves into a decision-making spot, he is usually no longer regarded as a psychologist. Possibly this only shows good judgment; the psychologist knows what he knows and is unwilling to take responsibility for acting upon it. Another explanation is to be found in the history of psychology. No other science has ever had to move against such a mass of folklore, superstition, and error; and it is not surprising that psychologists have put a high price on the factual and objective. They have struggled assiduously to escape from the limitations of personal experience. Measurement and quantification—in a word, objectivity—have been at a premium. If you want to know what a man actually hears or sees, control the stimulating environment. If you want to know what he actually does or says, record his behavior as precisely as possible. If you want to know what he is inclined to do or say, sample his opinions and beliefs. If you want to know what he is really like, quantify his behavior with inventories, questionnaires, and tests. Guarantee the significance of your answers by examining many cases, and draw your conclusions only with the help of logical and statistical methods.

The social sciences have also advanced beyond earlier treatments of their subject matters mainly by emphasizing objectivity. The social scientist has been called the man with a notebook—observing, sampling, recording what he sees, rather than trusting to casual impression and memory. Even historians have entered upon a phase of this kind, searching for materials which can be treated statistically in lieu of the personal reminiscences of eyewitnesses. The result tends to be a form of structuralism (see page 12) or behaviorism (see page 13) where the emphasis falls on topography to the virtual exclusion of independent variables. It is not surprising that the use of the results should remain in other hands.

There is another result. Psychology as a basic science has failed to supply a conception which recommends itself to specialists in other fields of human behavior. Sociology, anthropology, law and jurisprudence, economics, education, political science, religion, linguistics, literary criticism, philosophy, history—each has its own theory, model, or conception of man, drawn in part from common sense and in part from outmoded philosophical systems, with local improvisations as needed. A formula evolved in one field proves awkward in another. The student whose behavior is the concern of the educational specialist bears little resemblance to Economic Man. Man the Political Animal is not a promising patient in psychotherapy. Yet it is the same man who is being studied in all these fields, and it ought to be possible to talk about him in the same way. Psychoanalysis has come closest to supplying a common formulation, but it arose as a form of therapy and some touch of psychopathology survives when it is applied to everyday life. In spite of many claims to the contrary, it has not contributed a workable theory which is generally useful.

The experimental analysis of behavior may be on the point of doing so. The scientific method which has made it successful in the laboratory makes it almost immediately available for practical purposes. It is not concerned with testing theories but with directly modifying behavior. Its procedures are therefore relevant whenever a change in behavior is a consideration. It is less interested in the topography or structure of behavior than in the variables of which it is a function. It usually confines itself to the more convenient variables, but the interaction between organism and environment represented by the concept of contingencies of reinforcement has great generality. A particular field no doubt calls for special knowledge and will bring new discoveries, but a basic conception common to all fields is nevertheless a possibility.

Although a technology of behavior is thus in the making, we are not on the verge of solving all our problems. Human behavior is extraordinarily complex (it is no doubt the most complex subject matter ever submitted to scientific analysis), and a great deal remains to be learned. Technical knowledge is needed. We cannot deal effectively with human behavior by applying a few general principles (say, of reward and punishment) any more than we can build a bridge simply by applying the principles of stress and strain. The two fields in which an experimental analysis of behavior has already yielded the most extensive technology (education and psychotherapy) are those closest to psychology itself and hence those to which specialists in behavior are most likely to turn. Even there, however, a strong tradition favoring pure research keeps many of those who would be most successful away from technical applications. Elsewhere much of what is known has not yet been put to use because those who are in a position to use it either do not know that it is available or are put off by misunderstandings of its nature or its implications. A new kind of professional training, preferably with laboratory experience, is needed. In the long run, the effective management of human affairs will probably require a change in the way in which everyone thinks about himself and those with whom he comes into contact.

The need for an effective technology of behavior is obvious enough. Every generation seems to believe that the world is going to the dogs, but (to be ethological for a moment) we must also not forget the boy who cried Wolf! It is quite possible that we are in serious trouble. Man may be foolish enough to set off a nuclear holocaust—not by design but by one of those accidents which are so much admired by those who oppose design. We have not yet brought the powerful methodology of science to bear on many of our problems. Prescientific formulations of human behavior are still widely used, and supported by prescientific philosophies. A sweeping change is needed, and a successful science of behavior is perhaps the necessary first step.

Note 4.6 The critics

The experimental analysis of behavior is misunderstood in many ways and for many reasons, particularly in its implications for human affairs. With respect to its use in education, Paul Goodman writes (56): "To be candid, I think operant-conditioning is vastly overrated. It teaches us the not newsy proposition that if an animal is deprived of its natural environment and society, sensorily deprived, made mildly anxious, and restricted to the narrowest possible spontaneous motion, it will emotionally identify with its oppressor and respond—with low-grade grace, energy, and intelligence—in the only way allowed to it. The poor beast must do something, just to live on a little." Jules Henry, an anthropologist, has commented on "the uncritical extrapolation of experimental results from animals to man" in the following way: "Learning theory has two simple points to make and does so with talmudic ingenuity, variability, intricacy, and insistence. They are reinforcement and extinction. What has to be left out, because the subjects are mostly animals, is thought" (63). It would be interesting to try to apply these analyses to an issue of the *Journal of the Experimental Analysis of Behavior.*

Classroom demonstrations are often cited as if they epitomized the analysis. Pigeons have been taught to play a kind of ping-pong (146) and simple tunes on a toy piano, and these trivial achievements are offered as representing the nature and scope of operant conditioning. The analysis is often dismissed as "all a matter of conditioned reflexes" or of "habit formation in mazes." Reinforcement is sometimes said to be synonymous with reward or bribery or necessarily a matter of drive reduction. The range of the analysis is not recognized. Krutch (87) has argued that conditioned reflexes "shortcircuit" important processes in human behavior, which are presumably out of reach of a behavioral analysis. Ashby has written (6):

Children do behave like pigeons. And this is why the technique is so dangerous. Pigeons can be taught to play the piano but they cannot be taught to understand music; and except for very limited purposes (such as the memorizing of telephone numbers) rote learning without understanding is useless. Now the chief weakness of programmed instruction is that it rewards rote learning, and worse than that—it rewards only those responses which are in agreement with the programme. The doubter, the dissenter, the questioner—in short, anyone with an original mind—can get no stimulus or satisfaction out of the programme. Furthermore, it is the declared aim of those who compose programmes to make the steps so simple that the learner does not make mistakes, and so gets his reinforcement at every step. But making mistakes is an essential experience in learning.

But the behavior involved in understanding music can be analyzed experimentally, operant conditioning is not rote learning, programs can promote original behavior, and what is learned from making mistakes can be taught in other ways (155). Problem solving, creative thinking, intellectual and ethical self-management, and behavior governed by rules are also often said to be out of reach. Some of these will be discussed in Chapters 5 and 6. A very common complaint, to which we shall return in Chapter 8, is that consciousness is "ignored."

An experimental analysis of behavior is necessarily a science in progress. The assertion that it cannot explain some aspect of behavior must be qualified with the phrase "as of this date." The analysis has grown steadily more rigorous and powerful, and it is constantly reaching into new areas, but it no doubt has a long way to go. We do not dismiss the early stages of other sciences because they were not complete. Boyle's Law, as originally stated, was quite inadequate and had to be changed as other variables were considered and as more exact measures were taken. It was not discarded, however; it was simply qualified and extended.

The use of concepts and laws derived from an experimental analysis in the interpretation of daily life is also a source of misunderstanding. An analogy from another science may be helpful. Geophysics interprets the present condition of the accessible parts of the earth in terms of presumed conditions in the mantle and core. It appeals quite freely to physical laws derived from laboratory analyses of matter under various pressures and temperatures, even though it is merely an assumption that comparable states actually prevail in the interior of the earth. In the same way familiar facts about verbal behavior are interpreted with principles derived from the laboratory study of contingencies of reinforcement (141), even though the contingencies maintained by the verbal environment cannot be precisely ascertained. In both these examples, principles derived from research conducted under the favorable conditions of the laboratory are used to give a plausible account of facts which are not at the moment under experimental control. Neither account can at the present time be proved, but both are to be preferred to treatments which lack the same kind of experimental support.

Another common misunderstanding concerns extrapolation from animal to human behavior. Those who study living organisms—say, in genetics, embryology, or medicine—usually start below the human level, and students of behavior have quite naturally followed the same practice. The experimenter needs an organism which is readily available and cheaply maintained. He must submit it to daily regimens, often for long periods of time, confine it in easily controlled environments, and expose it to complex contingencies of reinforcement. Such organisms are almost necessarily simpler than men. Nevertheless, with very few exceptions, those who study them are primarily concerned with human behavior. Very few people are interested in the rat or pigeon for their own sakes.

The relevance of research on lower organisms to human behavior is sometimes flatly denied. Jules Henry, for example, has written, "When I extrapolate the laws of rat or pigeon learning to man, I break the law of homologous extrapolation because rats and pigeons are not homologous with man" (63). It turns out, however, that two species are homologous only if laws can be extrapolated from one to the other. Another writer has argued that although "theories . . . based on experimentation with pigeons [have] had considerable influence for good in education and clinical psychology . . . yet it seems likely that . . . pigeon results will be too simplistic for extensive use with humans" (6). This is almost certainly correct, since differences must always be taken into account, but useful similarities have been demonstrated over a fairly wide range of species. The fact is that methods first developed for the study of lower organisms, as well as the concepts and principles arising from that study, have been successfully applied to human behavior, both in a basic analysis and in many technological applications.

Although it is sometimes said that research on lower animals makes it impossible to discover what is distinctly human, it is only by studying the behavior of lower animals that we can tell what *is* distinctly human. The range of what has seemed to be human has been progressively reduced as lower organisms have come to be better understood. What survives is, of course, of the greatest importance. It must be investigated with human subjects. There is no evidence that research on lower organisms contaminates research on men or that those who study animals can have nothing important to say about men.

It is frequently implied that human dignity is threatened when principles derived from the study of lower animals are applied to man; but if we really believe that the proper study of mankind is man, we must not reject any relevant information. The use of animal vaccines in the treatment and prevention of human illness was once attacked on grounds of dignity, but medical science without the help of animal research is unthinkable. We not only study the endocrine systems of animals and apply the results to man, we use animal hormones.

A similar concern for human worth or dignity underlies a common misunderstanding of the practices of a scientific analysis. As Bannister has put it (10):

In order to behave like scientists we must construct situations in which our subjects are totally controlled, manipulated and measured. We must cut our subjects down to size. We construct situations in which they can behave as little like human beings as possible and we do this in order to allow ourselves to make statements about the nature of their humanity. I can think of no simple formula which can allow us to escape from this paradox but I think we might have the decency to acknowledge its presence. We ought not to use the curious notions of reductionism in order to try to convince ourselves that our chaining of our subjects is the ideal way to go about things. It may be that an imprisoned, miniscule man is all we are capable of studying but let us acknowledge that we do miserable experiments because we lack the imagination to do better ones, not claim that these are scientifically ideal because they are simple minded.

The experimental analysis of behavior is, of course, an *analysis*. The environment in which human behavior is observed is usually simplified so that one aspect (or at most a very few aspects) can be studied at one time. What we observe may not be very much like the behavior we see in the confusion of daily life, but it is still human behavior.

Simplification of the human environment is not an exclusively scientific practice. Artists, composers, writers, and scientists characteristically maximize the quality and quantity of their work by isolating themselves from unrelated features of the world about them. They build physical and social environments appropriate to a small part of their repertoires, and it is one of the objects of doing so that the behavior thus maximized should not closely resemble the behavior we meet with in daily life. We do not say that they have "cut themselves down to size" or "are behaving as little like human beings as possible" or that "they have imprisoned themselves as minuscule men," or that what they do is "all they are capable of doing." It is true that we often particularly admire those who think best in the heat of battle or who paint or compose or write in the wild abandon of a misspent life, for they must be unusual people to work under such circumstances and their work may be closer to real life; but though their achievements differ from those of the solitary worker, they will be no more human.

As the techniques of an experimental analysis of behavior become more powerful, more and more complex behavior is analyzed under more and more complex circumstances. We ignore some things for the sake of studying others, but we do not ignore them permanently. They will be studied in their turn. Nothing is lost in the process of analysis which can not be reconstituted. Every science has been subjected to similar criticisms at some time in its history; its methods have seemed to destroy the holistic aspects of its subject matter. But more and more of that subject matter is eventually accounted for.

The fact that it is hard to see what is happening in an experimental space (see page 9) should be carefully considered by those who object to the extrapolation of laboratory results to human affairs. Presumably they object because the extrapolations do not jibe with their observations of the world at large, but if we now ask them to look at the world in small, we shall find that their observations do not jibe with what *we know to be the case*. We know it because we have constructed the contingencies and can analyze their effects under especially advantageous conditions. It is quite possible that so many people have said so many different things about the world at large just because none of them has ever been able to confirm what he thinks he has seen. We extrapolate from relatively simple conditions to relatively complex, not to confirm what someone claims to have seen in the complex case, but to begin for the first time to see it in a new light.

Terminology is another common source of misunderstanding. When speaking or writing casually, the student of behavior is perhaps as likely as anyone else to mention sensations, feelings, ideas, thoughts, decisions, and so on. Critics sometimes cite instances of this to prove inconsistency, lack of logic, or bad faith. The astronomer is similarly inconsistent when he says that the sun rises or that the stars come out at night, but he would be a foolish astronomer indeed if he avoided such expressions in casual discourse. No one should be seriously misled by such expressions as "The idea occurred to me . . . ," "My memory of him is rather vague . . . ," or "I don't feel like going. . . ." When early astronomers were challenged, as they must have been when they continued to speak of the sunrise, their answer was presumably a quick translation into nongeocentric terms. The student of behavior must also be ready to translate if challenged, and in any serious enterprise he should be alert to the danger in unanalyzed, casual terms.

Another criticism of an experimental analysis of behavior is that it "apes" other sciences. This is not true. It adopts the basic scientific assumption of order and lawfulness in its subject matter, and it freely borrows any method which may be relevant to its subject matter, but it does not do this in order to resemble more prestigious sciences. Compared with information-theory or cybernetics, mathematical models, hypothetico-deductive systems, computer simulation, and general systems theory, it is unusually free of scientific role playing. It is in no hurry to be mathematical. Newton's brilliant success in putting order into a chaotic universe led men almost immediately to wonder whether the same thing might not be done for human behavior and society. Within a century Jean-Jacques Rousseau could exclaim, "Calculators, it is now up to you. Count, measure, compare." (It is tempting to suppose that he was clairvoyant, and that *calculateurs* meant "computers.") Another century and Gustav Fechner jumped out of bed with the exciting thought that the physical world and the world of the psyche might be *mathematically* related. Another century and mathematical psychology sustains the hope of avoiding the sheer labor of an empirical analysis—an analysis which is needed if we are to identify the entities and the relations among them which are to be treated mathematically.

5   Operant behavior

Purpose and behavior

We are interested in the behavior of an organism because of its effects on the environment. (One effect on the social environment is, of course, the arousal of our interest.) Some effects seem to throw light on the behavior which produces them, but their explanatory role has been clouded by the fact that they follow the behavior and therefore raise the specter of teleology.

An attempt has been made to solve the problem by creating a prior surrogate of a given effect. A quality or property of purpose is assigned to behavior to bring "what the organism is behaving for" into the effective present; or the organism is said to behave in a given way because it intends to achieve, or expects to have, a given effect; or its behavior is characterized as possessing utility to the extent that it maximizes or minimizes certain effects. The teleological problem is, of course, not solved until we have answered certain questions: what gives an action its purpose, what leads an organism to expect to have an effect, how is utility represented in behavior?

The answers to such questions are eventually to be found in past instances in which similar behavior has been effective. The original problem can be solved directly in the same way. Thorndike's Law of Effect was a step in that direction: the

105

approximately simultaneous occurrence of a response and certain environmental events (usually generated by it) changes the responding organism, increasing the probability that responses of the same sort will occur again. The response itself has passed into history and is not altered. By emphasizing a change in the organism, Thorndike's principle made it possible to include the effects of action among the causes of future action without using concepts like purpose, intention, expectancy, or utility. Up to that time, the only demonstrable causes of behavior had been antecedent stimuli. The range of the eliciting stimulus was later to be extended by Pavlovian conditioning, and the concept could be broadened to include the releasers of the ethologists, but only a small part of behavior can be predicted or controlled simply by identifying or manipulating stimuli. The Law of Effect added an important new class of variables of which behavior could be shown to be a function.

Thorndike's solution was probably suggested by Darwin's treatment of phylogenic purpose. Before Darwin, the purpose of a well-developed eye might have been said to be to permit the organism to see better. The principle of natural selection moved "seeing better" from the future into the past: organisms with well-developed eyes were descended from those which had been able to see better and had therefore produced more descendants. Thorndike was closer to the principle of natural selection than the above statement of his law suggests. He did not need to say that a response which had been followed by a certain kind of consequence was more likely to occur again but simply that it was not less likely. It eventually held the field because responses which failed to have such effects tended, like less favored species, to disappear.

Thorndike was concerned with how animals solved problems, rather than with the concept of purpose, and his Law of Effect did not end purposive formulations. The devices used for the study of behavior during the next quarter of a

century continued to emphasize an intentional relation between behavior and its consequences. The relation was represented spatially. In mazes, runways, and open fields, for
example, organisms ran *toward* their goals. In discrimination
apparatuses they chose the door which led *to* food. They
escaped *from* the dangerous side of shuttle-boxes or pulled
away from sources of dangerous stimulation. They drew objects *toward* them with rakes or strings. The experimenter
could see the purpose of an action in the spatial relation of
the organism and the objects toward which it was moving
or from which it was withdrawing. It was even asserted that
the organism itself should see a purposive relationship in
some such form in order to behave effectively. Köhler, for
example, criticized Thorndike on just this score (84).

The spatial representation of purpose, expectancy, or intention obscured one of the most important features of the
relation emphasized by Thorndike. The process he identified
remained unexplored for 30 years and during that time was
confused with rote habit formation and with various formulations of Pavlovian conditioning. In the late 1920's, however,
the consequences of behavior began to be studied with devices of another sort. Pavlov's technique for the study of
conditioned reflexes contributed to their development, even
though Pavlov himself was not primarily concerned with
consequences as such. In his basic studies, indeed, it might
be said that the organism did not receive food *for* doing anything; the salivation elicited by the conditioned stimulus did
not produce the food which followed. The experimental design, however, called for food to be introduced at a given
moment automatically. Once the procedure was familiar, it
was no great step to arrange devices in which a response
"produced" food in a similar fashion. In 1927 Ivanov-Smolensky (75), one of Pavlov's associates, reported an experimental arrangement, close to Thorndike's, in which a child
squeezed a rubber bulb to obtain chocolate. In the same year
D. K. Adams (1) reported a similar arrangement with cats.

In 1928, as we have seen, Miller and Konorski (101) presented food to a hungry dog when its leg was flexed, reflexly or passively, and eventually when flexion occurred alone. In 1932 Grindley (58) reported on similar work with guinea pigs. The essential features are seen when a rat operates a food dispenser by pressing a lever. None of these responses is a natural way of achieving its consequence. The behavior is nevertheless altered. The consequences of action change the organism regardless of how or why they follow. The connection need not be functional or organic—as, indeed, it was not in Thorndike's experiment.

Practical advantages

These early devices were not designed to eliminate spatial representations of purpose, but they all did so—and with far-reaching consequences. Some of these were practical. The experimenter could choose a response which was conveniently recorded; or one which the organism could execute rapidly and without fatigue for long periods of time; or one which minimized the peculiarities of a species and thus furthered a comparison between species with respect to properties not primarily related to the topography of behavior. In particular, it was possible to choose a response which was relatively free of extraneous variables and not likely to be confused with responses elicited or evoked by them. When a shuttle-box, for example, is used to study the effect of the postponement or termination of a shock, the behavior affected (running or jumping from one side to the other) is topographically similar to unconditioned responses to shock, such as startle or jumping into the air, and to more elaborate patterns of escape from a space in which shocks have been received. It may also resemble responses of both these sorts conditioned in the Pavlovian manner and elicited by the warning stimuli. The inevitable confusion can be avoided by making the postponement or termination of a shock contingent on an arbitrary response, such as pressing a lever in the Sidman arrangement, which is not otherwise related to the variables at issue. A response which is only temporally related to its consequences could also be conveniently studied with automatic equipment.

Another practical result was terminological. The term "operant" distinguishes between reflexes and responses which operate directly on the environment (128). The alternative term, *instrumental*, suggests the use of tools. To say that a rat "uses a lever to obtain food" has purposive overtones, and where nothing can be identified as an instrument, it is often said that the organism "uses a response" to gain an effect. For example, verbal behavior is interpreted as "the use of words," although the implication that words exist as things apart from behavior unnecessarily complicates an analysis (141). Another change was from *reward* to *reinforcement*. Reward suggests compensation *for* behaving in a given way, often in some sort of contractual arrangement. Reinforcement in its etymological sense designates simply the strengthening of a response. It refers to similar events in Pavlovian conditioning, where reward is inappropriate. These changes in terminology have not automatically eliminated purposive expressions (such as "The pigeon was reinforced *for* pecking the key"), but a given instance can usually be rephrased. Comparable teleological expressions are common in other sciences, as Bernatowicz (15) has pointed out.

Rate of responding as a datum

A more important result of studying an arbitrary connection between a response and its consequences, together with the simplified procedures which then become available, has been to emphasize rate of responding as a property of behavior. Rate is one of those aspects of a subject matter which do not attract attention for their own sake and which undergo intensive study only when their usefulness as a dependent variable has been discovered. Other sciences have passed through comparable stages. The elements and compounds studied by the chemist have fascinating characters—they exist in many colors, textures, and states of aggregation and undergo surprising transmutations when heated, dissolved, combined, and so on. These are the characteristics which naturally first attract attention. They were, for example, the principal concern of the alchemists. In contrast, the mere weight of a given quantity of a substance is of little interest in its own right. Yet it was only when the weights of substances entering into reactions were found to obey certain laws that chemistry moved into its modern phase. Combining weight became important because of what could be done with it. Rate of responding has emerged as a basic datum in a science of behavior for similar reasons. It is less dramatic than traits of character, but in the long run a more promising datum.

Changes in rate of responding are studied with methods which also may seem strange to the student of the learning processes said to take place in some inner system. The latter can usually be investigated only with "statistics." If learning is never accurately represented in one performance, performances must be averaged. If statements about the inner system cannot be directly confirmed, hypotheses must be set up and theorems deduced and tested. If some properties of the inner system are meaningful only with respect to larger sets of facts, a procedure such as factor analysis may be needed. It is not surprising that research on this pattern has come to be judged by the sophistication of its statistical and logical techniques. Confidence in an experiment is proportional to the number of subjects studied, an experiment is good only if properly "designed," and results are significant only at a level determined by special tests.

Much of this is lacking in the experimental analysis of behavior, where experiments are usually performed on a few subjects, curves representing behavioral processes are seldom averaged, the behavior attributed to complex mental activity is analyzed directly, and so on. The simpler procedure is possible because rate of responding and changes in rate can be directly observed, especially when represented in cumulative records. The effect is similar to increasing the resolving power of a microscope; a new subject matter is suddenly open to direct inspection. Statistical methods are unnecessary. When an organism is showing a stable or slowly changing performance, it is for most purposes idle to stop to evaluate the confidence with which the next stage can be predicted. When a variable is changed and the effect on performance observed, it is for most purposes idle to prove statistically that a change has indeed occurred. (It is sometimes said in such a case that the organism is "used as its own control," but the expression, borrowed from a basically different methodology, is potentially troublesome.) Much can be done in the study of behavior with methods of observation no more sophisticated than those available, say, to Faraday, with his magnets, wires, and cells. Eventually the investigator may move on to peripheral areas where indirect methods become necessary, but until then he must forego the prestige which attaches to traditional statistical methods.

Some traditional uses must also be questioned. Learning curves remain inadequate no matter how smooth they are made by averaging cases. Statistical techniques may eliminate noise, but the dimensions are still faulty. A curve which enables us to predict the performance of another organism does not therefore represent a basic process. Moreover, curves which report changes in variables having satisfactory dimensions can often not be averaged. The idiosyncrasies in a cumulative record do not necessarily show caprice on the part of the organism or faulty technique on the part of the experimenter. The complex system we call an organism has an elaborate and largely unknown history which endows it with a certain individuality. No two organisms embark upon an experiment in precisely the same condition nor are they affected in the same way by the contingencies in an experimental space. (It is characteristic of most contingencies that they are not precisely controlled, and in any case they are effective only in combination with the behavior which the organism brings to the experiment.) Statistical techniques cannot eliminate this kind of individuality; they can only obscure and falsify it. An averaged curve seldom correctly represents any of the cases contributing to it (123).

An analysis which recognizes the individuality of the organism is particularly valuable when contact is made with other disciplines such as neurology, psychopharmacology, and psychotherapy, where idiosyncratic sets of variables must also be considered. The rigor of the analysis is not necessarily threatened. Operant methods make their own use of Grand Numbers; instead of studying a thousand rats for one hour each, or a hundred rats for ten hours each, the investigator is likely to study one rat for a thousand hours. The procedure is not only appropriate to an enterprise which recognizes individuality, it is at least equally efficient in its use of equipment and of the investigator's time and energy. The ultimate test of uniformity or reproducibility is not to be found in the methods used but in the degree of control achieved, a test which the experimental analysis of behavior usually passes easily.

When effects on behavior can be immediately observed, it is most efficient to explore relevant variables by manipulating them in an improvised and rapidly changing design. Similar practices have been responsible for the greater part of modern science. This is not, however, the tenor of R. A. Fisher's *Design of Experiments*, which, as Lancelot Hogben (69) has said, gives the reader

... the impression that recourse to statistical methods is prerequisite to the design of experiments of any sort whatever. In that event, the whole creation of experimental scientists from Gilbert and Hooke to J. J. Thomson and Morgan has been groaning and travailing in fruitless pain together; and the biologist of today has nothing to learn from well-tried methods which have led to the spectacular advances of the several branches of experimental science during the last three centuries.

Statistics, like logic and scientific methodology in general, emphasizes the verbal behavior of the scientist: how reliable are his measures, how significant are the differences he reports, how confident can we be that what he says is true? His nonverbal behavior is much less easily codified and analyzed. In such considerations what the scientist *does* takes second place to what he *says*. Yet the *a priori* manipulation of variables, guided by directly observed effects, is superior to the *a posteriori* analysis of co-variation in many ways. It leads more rapidly to prediction and control and to practical recombinations of variables in the study of complex cases. Eventually, of course, the experimenter must behave verbally. He must describe what he has done and what he has seen, and he must conduct his research with this obligation in mind. But a compulsive preoccupation with validity or significance may be inimical to other, equally important obligations.

A nonstatistical strategy may also be recommended for its effect on the behavior of the investigator, who is perhaps as strongly reinforced during a successful experiment as the organism he studies. The contingencies to which he is submitted largely determine whether he will continue in similar work. Statistical techniques often inject a destructive delay between the conduct of an experiment and the discovery of the significance of the data—a fatal violation of a fundamental principle of reinforcement. The exceptional zeal which has often been noted in students of operant behavior is possibly attributable to the immediacy of their results.

The circumvention of an operant analysis

By accepting changes in rate of responding as basic behavioral processes and by emphasizing environmental variables which can be manipulated with the help of automatic equipment, research on operant behavior has been greatly simplified. But it has not been made easy. Technical advances have been offset by the demand for increasing rigor, by the problems which arise in studying one organism at a time, and by the attack on more and more complex arrangements of interrelated operants. Behavior—human or otherwise—remains an extremely difficult subject matter. It is not surprising that practices which seem to circumvent or simplify an operant analysis are common. In particular, verbal communication between subject and experimenter is widely used in lieu of the explicit arrangement of contingencies of reinforcement and the objective recording of behavior. The practice goes back to the study of mental life and is still favored by psychologists who formulate their subject matter in mental terms, but it survives as if it were a labor-saving device in many essentially behavioristic formulations.

The manipulation of independent variables appears to be circumvented when, instead of exposing an organism to a set of contingencies, the contingencies are simply described in "instructions." Instead of shaping a response, the subject is told to respond in a given way. A history of reinforcement or punishment is replaced by a promise or threat: "Movement of the lever will sometimes operate a coin dispenser" or ". . . deliver a shock to your leg." A schedule of positive or negative reinforcement is described rather than imposed: "Every response to the right lever postpones the shock but increases the number of responses to the left lever required to operate the coin dispenser." Instead of bringing the behavior under the control of a stimulus, the subject is told to behave as if a discrimination had been established: "Start when the light goes on, stop when it goes off." Thus instructed, the subject is asked either to behave appropriately or to describe behavior he might emit under such circumstances. The scope of the verbal substitute can be estimated by considering how a nonverbal organism, human or otherwise, could be similarly "instructed."

Descriptions of contingencies are, of course, often effective. Hypothetical consequences are commonly used for practical purposes ("Will you do the job if I pay you $50?" or "How would you feel about going if I told you that X would be there?"), and the subject is worth studying. Verbal instructions may be defended when the resulting behavior is not the primary object of interest; for example, the experimenter may show a subject how to operate a piece of equipment rather than shape his behavior through reinforcement so long as he is not concerned with the acquisition of the response but with what happens to it later. Verbal communication is not, however, a substitute for the arrangement and manipulation of variables.

There is no reason why a description of contingencies of reinforcement should have the same effect as exposure to the contingencies. A subject can seldom accurately describe the way in which he has actually been reinforced. Even when he has been trained to identify a few simple contingencies, he cannot then describe a new contingency, particularly when it is complex. We can scarcely expect him, therefore, to react appropriately to descriptions by the experimenter. Moreover, the verbal contingencies between subject and experimenter must be taken into account. Instructions must in some way promise or threaten consequences not germane to the experiment if the subject is to follow them.

The other major task in an operant analysis may seem to be circumvented when, instead of recording behavior so that rate or probability of response can be observed or inferred, the experimenter simply asks the subject to evaluate his tendency to respond or to express his preference for responding in one way rather than another. The subject may do so by describing his "intentions" or "plans" or by reporting "expectations" regarding the consequences of an action. Such behavior may be worth investigating, but it is not a substitute for the behavior observed in an operant analysis. Only in the simplest cases can a person correctly describe his ongoing behavior. The difficulty is not linguistic; the subject could be given an operandum and permitted to "model" the behavior—for example, to generate a cumulative record. It is highly unlikely that he would construct a curve closely resembling the curve he would generate if actually exposed to a specific set of contingencies, or even a curve he had already generated when so exposed. Changes in rate of responding are never easy to describe. They necessarily take place in time, and even a second observer cannot "see" them until they have been reduced to graphic form. The subject's own behavior presents other difficulties. If we ask him to say simply whether he will be more or less likely to respond, or will respond more or less rapidly, we have increased his chances of being right only by asking him to say less. Any report, no matter how specific, is subject to the verbal contingencies which induce a person to describe his behavior and possibly to similar contingencies elsewhere which may classify his behavior, for example, as right or wrong.

Verbal substitutes for arranged or observed variables may be used at different points in an investigation: contingencies may be described to the subject and his behavior then actually observed; he may be exposed to a set of contingencies and then asked to evaluate the nature or probability of his responses; and so on. Similar practices are used to evaluate the reinforcing or aversive properties of a given event or procedure, to predict the outcome of several variables operating at once, and so on, and are subject to the same criticism.

To those interested primarily in mental processes, verbal communication may not be an attempted circumvention or shortcut. On the contrary, an operant analysis may seem to be the long way around. The position is sometimes defended by insisting that the student of behavior always begins with an interest in mental life—possibly his own—and designs his experiments essentially to test hypotheses about it. Whatever the case may once have been, operant research has long since passed the point at which the experimenter can be guided by considering possible effects of variables on himself. The introspective vocabulary used in circumventing an experimental analysis is hopelessly inadequate for the kinds of facts currently under investigation. If one field is to borrow from the other, the debt will henceforth almost certainly be in the other direction; from the study of the behavior of other organisms, the experimenter is most likely to come to understand himself. In some theories of knowledge, introspective observations may be regarded as primary data, but in an analysis of behavior they are a form of theorizing which is not required or necessarily helpful.

Analyses of contingencies of reinforcement

The consequences of action and their effects on behavior also enter into theories of probability, decision-making, conflict, and games. The classical urn containing a given proportion of black and white balls, like other sample spaces, may be analyzed without reference to behavior, but it would be of little interest if the consequences of drawing either a black or white ball were not in some way reinforcing. (There has always been a close connection between probability theory and gambling, where every play is punished to the extent of its cost and some plays are also reinforced.) Probability theory also often takes into account the fact that this reinforcement will occur on an intermittent schedule and that as a consequence the drawer will experience a given subjective or felt probability, or exhibit a given probability of drawing again.

The probability that the drawer will draw again is usually assumed to be related to the probability function of the sample space. A relation is implied when it is said that a subject who has sufficient knowledge about a given system, possibly inferred from his experience with it, can behave "rationally." A relation is also implied when it is argued that irrational behavior requires explanation. For example, the fact that intermittent reinforcement raises the probability of responding above the value generated when all responses are reinforced has recently occasioned surprise. Any such relation is, of course, an empirical fact, to be determined experimentally. Standard operant equipment can be used to set up contingencies of reinforcement which have the effect of classical sample spaces. A schedule could, if necessary, be programmed by actually drawing balls from an urn. An organism can then be exposed to the schedule and the effect on its behavior observed.

In such a procedure the status of the probability function of the sample space (the schedule of reinforcement arranged by the programming equipment) is clear. The probability that the organism will respond at a given time is inferred from its rate. The relation between these two probabilities is complicated by the fact that rate of responding under a given schedule depends, as we have seen, on previous exposure to the schedule. When introduced into an experimental space for the first time, an organism may be said to show a certain "prior probability" of responding—the so-called operant level. A first response is or is not reinforced, and the rate rises or falls accordingly. This brief history contributes to what is now a different situation. When the organism responds again and is again possibly reinforced, the situation changes still more substantially. A given set of contingencies yields a performance which combines with the programming equipment to generate other contingencies which in turn generate other performances, and so on.

Many of these interactions between behavior and programming equipment have been carefully studied. Under a variable interval schedule of reinforcement, for example, the organism often responds at a nearly constant rate for long periods of time. All reinforcements therefore occur when it is responding at that rate, *although this condition is not specified by the equipment.* The rate becomes a discriminative and, in turn, a reinforcing stimulus, which opposes any change to a different rate—such as would otherwise be induced by, say, a psychopharmacological agent. As another example, when only the first response after the passage of a fixed interval of time is reinforced, the organism comes to exhibit a fairly stable performance in which the number of responses emitted during an interval approaches constancy. The organism is then being reinforced not only after a constant interval of time but after emitting a constant number of responses. The latter condition, *which is not specified by the equipment,* is characteristic of a fixed ratio schedule, and it generates a much higher rate of responding. As rapid responding appears, the stability of the fixed interval performance is destroyed, the number of responses per reinforcement is no longer constant, and a stable interval performance is restored as another cycle begins (46).

A third example is closer to probability theory. A schedule in which a response is reinforced upon completion of an appreciable fixed or variable number of responses must often be reached through a program, as we have seen. The number must first be small, but the schedule favors reinforcement when the organism is responding at a high rate, and it is soon possible to "stretch" the requirement. When a hungry rat is reinforced with food for running in a wheel, the required distance can be increased until more energy is consumed than is available in the food received (129). The behavior of the gambler, which almost always shows a similar "negative utility," is the result of the same kind of stretching. The variable ratio schedules inherent in gambling systems maintain behavior only after a history of reinforcement in which behavior has combined with the programming equipment to generate certain powerful terminal contingencies.

In summary, a scheduling system has no effect until an organism is exposed to it, and then it no longer fully determines the contingencies. Still other interactions between equipment and performance arise when a second response is introduced in order to study choice or decision-making. Suppose, for example, that a subject may press either of two keys, A and B, on which reinforcements are independently scheduled. The performance on either key can be accounted for only by examining the combined action of equipment and earlier performances *on both keys.* For example, if reinforcements are programmed on interval schedules, responding to A after B is more likely to be reinforced than responding to B after B, since the equipment may have set up a reinforcement on A while a response was being made to B. The behavior of changing from A to B or from B to A may be favored to the point at which the performance becomes a simple alternation (134). This yields the same rate on both keys, even though the schedules may be substantially different. The interaction may be corrected with a *change-over delay* in which, for example, a response to B is not reinforced if a response to A has been made during the preceding second, or in which the first response to either key after changing over is never reinforced (65). The contingencies on the two levers are nevertheless still subject to the other interactions mentioned previously. (By manipulating the change-over delay and other characteristics of the schedules, it may be possible to generate rates of responding on the two keys which would be predicted from some hypothesis of rationality or utility, but it would be a mistake to regard these as optimal conditions and possibly to stop the search when they have been found.)

Interactions between performance and programming system are still more complex if the performance changes the system, as in the so-called *adjusting* and *interlocking* schedules (46). Many examples are to be found in the theory of games and conflict, where the behavior of one organism alters the contingencies affecting another, and vice versa. The rules of any game can be represented by programming

equipment which is subject to modification by the performances of the players, but the actual contingencies of reinforcement are still more complex, for they include conditions
not specified by the equipment but generated by the earlier
performances of all parties.

That there is a limitation inherent in such analyses is
suggested by the fact that mathematical inquiries into probability, decision-making, conflict, and games confine themselves almost exclusively to ratio schedules. The contingencies
defined in sample spaces and rules practically always specify
reinforcement as a function of a number of responses, a restraint traceable perhaps to practical issues involving winning, losing, and ultimate utility. Yet the interactions between
equipment and performance are the same when reinforcement is scheduled by clocks or speedometers rather than by
counters, and the same processes are involved, as an experimental analysis has abundantly shown.

The properties of sample spaces, like the various conditions
under which choices are made, games played, or conflicts resolved, may be analyzed without taking behavior into account or, at most, by assuming selected performances. Those
interested primarily in such an analysis are likely to approach
behavior, if at all, by setting up hypotheses. The research
which follows has the nature of hypothesis testing and is
wasteful if the data collected lose their value when a hypothesis has been disproved or abandoned for any reason.
An experimental analysis of the behavior generated by the
contingencies in sample spaces may be conducted without
guessing at the results.

"Rule-governed behavior"[1]

Analyses of contingencies of reinforcement are related to
behavior in another way when they are used as guides or
rules. The behavior of a person who has calculated his

---

[1] The point of this section is developed further in Chapter 6.

chances, compared alternatives, or considered the consequences of a move is different from, and usually more effective than, the behavior of one who has merely been exposed to the unanalyzed contingencies. The analysis functions as a discriminative stimulus. When such a stimulus is perfectly correlated with reinforcement, the behavior under its control is maximally reinforced. On an interval schedule and in the absence of related stimuli, an organism emits unreinforced or "wasted" responses, but if the apparatus presents a conspicuous stimulus whenever a reinforcement becomes available, the organism eventually responds only in the presence of that stimulus and no responses are wasted. Clocks provide stimuli of this sort in connection with events occurring on interval schedules and are built and used for just that reason. Stimuli less closely correlated with reinforcement yield lesser improvements in efficiency. If a given setting on a clock cannot be sharply discriminated, for example, some responses will be emitted prior to "the time to respond" and some potentially effective responses may be delayed, but performance is nevertheless improved. A speedometer serves a similar function when reinforcement depends on a given rate of responding.

Analyses of sample spaces serve the same function as imprecise clocks and speedometers. Not every response under their control is reinforced, but there is still a net gain. When a man learns to play poker under the contingencies arranged by the cards and rules, his sampling of the possible contingencies is necessarily limited, even in prolonged play. He will play a more successful game, and after a much shorter history, if he consults a table showing his chances of success in making given plays. The contingencies in poker also depend upon the behavior of other players, and prior stimuli correlated with that behavior are therefore also useful. They are particularly important in a game such as chess. Chess playing may be shaped by the unanalyzed contingencies generated by the rules of the game and by the performances of opponents, but a player will play a better game, after a shorter history, if he can consult standard gambits, defenses, end-games, and so on, which show some of the likely consequences of given moves.

A stimulus commonly correlated with reinforcement and hence useful in improving efficiency is the record left by previous behavior. When a man finds his way from one place to another, he may leave traces which prove useful when he goes that way again. He wears a path which supplements the change taking place in his behavior and may even be useful to others who have not gone that way before. A path need not be constructed because it serves this function, but the advantages gained may reinforce the explicit leaving of traces. A trail is blazed, for example, precisely because it is more easily followed. Comparable reinforcing advantages have led men to construct pictures (maps) and verbal descriptions of paths.

As we shall see (page 148), many proverbs and maxims are crude descriptions of contingencies of social or nonsocial reinforcement, and those who observe them come under a more effective control of their environment. Rules of grammar and spelling bring certain verbal contingencies of reinforcement more forcefully into play. Society codifies its ethical, legal, and religious practices so that by following a code the individual may emit behavior appropriate to social contingencies without having been directly exposed to them. Scientific laws serve a similar function in guiding the behavior of scientists.

A person could, of course, construct rules of grammar and spelling, maxims for effective personal conduct, tables of probabilities in the games he plays, and scientific laws for his own use; but society usually analyzes the predictable contingencies for him. He constructs comparable stimuli for himself when he makes resolutions, announces intentions, states expectations, and formulates plans. The stimuli thus generated control his behavior most effectively when they are external, conspicuous, and durable—when the resolution is posted or the plan actually drafted in visible form—but they are also useful when recreated upon occasion, as by recalling the resolution or reviewing the plan. The gain from any such discriminative stimulus depends upon the extent to which it correctly represents the contingencies which led to its construction.

Discriminative stimuli which improve the efficiency of behavior under given contingencies of reinforcement are important, but they must not be confused with the contingencies themselves, nor their effects with the effects of those contingencies. The behavior of the poker player who evaluates his chances before making a given play merely resembles that of the player whose behavior has been shaped by prolonged exposure to the game. The behavior of one who speaks correctly by applying the rules of a grammar merely resembles the behavior of one who speaks correctly from long experience in a verbal community. The results may be the same, but the controlling variables are different and the behaviors are therefore different. Nothing which could be called following a plan or applying a rule is observed when behavior is a product of the contingencies alone. To say that "the child who learns a language has in some sense constructed the grammar for himself" (36) is as misleading as to say that a dog which has learned to catch a ball has in some sense constructed the relevant part of the science of mechanics. Rules can be extracted from the reinforcing contingencies in both cases, and once in existence they may be used as guides. The direct effect of the contingencies is of a different nature.

The distinction bears on two points already made. In the first place, the instructions used in circumventing an operant analysis also have the status of prior stimuli associated with hypothetical or real contingencies of reinforcement, but behavior in response to them is not the behavior generated by exposure to the contingencies themselves even when, on rare occasions, the two are similar. Subjects may report that they "understand instructions" and hence "know what to expect," but it does not follow that comparable reportable states of understanding or knowledge are generated by the contingencies themselves. In the second place—to return at last to the point with which this chapter began—when a man explicitly states his purpose in acting in a given way he may, indeed, be constructing a "contemporary surrogate of future consequences" which will affect subsequent behavior, possibly in useful ways. It does not follow, however, that the behavior generated by the consequences in the absence of any statement of purpose is under the control of any comparable prior stimulus, such as a felt purpose or intention.

Note 5.1   Purpose

The contingencies of reinforcement which define operant behavior are widespread if not ubiquitous. Those who are sensitive to this fact are sometimes embarrassed by the frequency with which they see reinforcement everywhere, as Marxists see class struggle or Freudians the Oedipus relation. Yet the fact is that reinforcement is extraordinarily important. That is why it is reassuring to recall that its place was once taken by the concept of purpose; no one is likely to object to a search for purpose in every human act. The difference is that we are now in a position to search effectively.

The words *intend, propose* (as a synonym for *purpose* as a verb), *expect, believe, think*, and *know* often seem to be concerned with the future. They are all used idiomatically with an infinitive or dependent clause describing action, as in *I intend to go, I propose to go,* or *I think that I shall go.* Such expressions suggest that the speaker will go, but they do not identify the past consequences which account for the probability that he will do so. We do not use terms of this sort idiomatically when the person cannot describe the variables of which his behavior is a function. We may be satisfied that a man goes to a meeting primarily because refreshments have been served at similar meetings in the past, but we concede that he did so "unconsciously." He may not have been surprised when refreshments were served, but we do not say that he went because he *expected* or *believed* that this would happen. A person may state his purpose or intention, tell us what he expects to do or get, and describe his beliefs, thoughts, and knowledge. (He cannot do this, of course, when he has not been "conscious" of the causal connections.) The contingencies are nevertheless effective *when a person cannot describe them.* We may ask him to describe them after the fact ("Why did you do that?"), and he may then examine his own behavior and discover his purpose or belief for the first time. He was not aware of his purpose when he acted, but he can state it afterward. A more explicit statement may be made prior to the act: a man may announce his purpose, state his intention, or describe the thoughts, beliefs, or knowledge upon which an action will be based. These cannot be reports of action because the action has not yet occurred; they appear instead to describe precursors. Once such a statement has been made, it may well determine action as a sort of self-constructed rule. It is then a true precursor having an obvious effect on subsequent behavior. When it is covert, it may be hard to spot; but it is still a form of behavior or a product of behavior rather than a mental precursor.

An experimental analysis permits us to relate behavior to a history of reinforcement and to other variables such as deprivation. We identify the variables and the relations among them. We may do this with respect to our own behavior provided we have been taught to do so by a given verbal community. Verbal communities which encourage introspection and self-observation are particularly likely to have this effect. Once we have observed variables affecting our own behavior, we may respond to them in other ways. In an extreme case we may analyze a set of contingencies of reinforcement, possibly a set to which we ourselves have not yet been exposed, and from the analysis derive rules enjoining or directing behavior similar to that which would be shaped by the contingencies. Subsequently we may follow these rules, possibly remaining untouched by the contingencies as such. There are then two extremes: (1) behavior shaped only by contingencies of reinforcement, in which case we respond "unconsciously," and (2) rule-governed behavior in which the contingencies from which the rules are derived may not have affected us directly. Between these extremes lie a wide range of degrees of "awareness." We can describe the probability of action by reporting that we expect to go, think we shall go, and so on. We may describe relevant variables by saying that we are going with the intention of getting food or knowing that we shall get food. We need a great deal of information in order to give an accurate translation of a single instance of verbal behavior in which one of these crucial terms appears. This is unfortunate, particularly for those who put purposes, thoughts, and knowledge high on their lists. In no translation do we need to use the substantive forms to refer to things.

There is an emotional element in *expectancy* or *expectation* which does not seem to be present in *purpose* or *belief*. Expectancy usually suggests positively reinforcing consequences. It may be idiomatic to say that we expect disaster, but we are more likely to say that we fear it. Most of the less respectable forms of expectancy, however, are confined to aversive consequences. A *premonition* is a prior warning, and one has *forebodings* only with respect to coming ills. *Anxiety*, in the sense of fear of an impending event, is more than expectancy, and so is *anticipation*, which seems to be as close as the English language comes to an antonym of anxiety. Anxiety involves emotional responses to a conditioned aversive stimulus, anticipation to a conditioned positive reinforcer.

Note 5.2 The definition of an operant

It is not enough to say that an operant is defined by its consequences. The consequences must have had the effect of making a condition of deprivation or aversive stimulation a current variable. The problem of causation in human behavior is said to be exemplified as follows (167):

"Is my act of flipping on the light switch the same act as my act of alerting the prowler, if in fact by flipping on the switch and illuminating the room, I do alert the prowler?" Although the question sounds as relevant as the medieval puzzler about how many angels can dance on a pinhead . . . it has highly practical implications in fixing intention and responsibility, and theoretical ones in helping to solve the age-old puzzler of free will *v.* determinism.

The topography of the response is described accurately enough as "flipping the switch." If the appearance of light is reinforcing—perhaps because in a lighted room behavior which has been reinforced in other ways is more likely to occur and behavior which has had aversive consequences less likely—the topography and the consequences define an operant. Alerting a prowler is clearly a different consequence which is contingent on the same topography of response and which enters into the definition of a different operant. The probability of flipping a switch is affected by both consequences. The question is relevant to "fixing intention and responsibility" as well as to "free will v. determinism" just because it concerns the effectiveness of contingencies of reinforcement. Flipping a switch has no meaning, purpose, or intention; but flipping a switch "to light the room" or "to alert a prowler" has, because these expressions refer to independent variables of which the probability of flipping a switch may be a function.

An effort is sometimes made to describe behavior without specifying topography in detail. It has been suggested, for example, that "rather than . . . find the motor equivalent of . . . responses,—the phenomena [may be] dealt with in functional terms and consequently ordered under two general behavior tendencies, namely, proximity seeking and proximity avoidance" (120). It is true that much behavior has the effect of bringing one closer to a person or object (E. B. Holt called such behavior "adient") or farther away ("abient"), but in describing behavior in this way we are specifying some of its consequences rather than its topography. What is described is therefore different from a "motor equivalent" not only in being more general but in introducing other data. "Proximity seeking" is not an operant, or any useful subdivision of behavior, unless all instances vary together under the control of common variables, and this is quite unlikely. Peterson has shown that imprinting in the young duckling is largely a matter of being reinforced by increasing proximity to the mother or imprinted object; increased proximity is reinforcing even when, thanks to a mechanical contrivance, the duckling achieves it by walking *away* from its mother. Adience and abience are spatial representations of purpose—of relations to positive and negative reinforcers; they are not topographical properties of behavior.

Several related issues have been raised by Charles Taylor (156) in criticizing the proposal that terms like "aggression," "guilt," and so on, should be done away with and that we should speak instead of the "explicit shaping of behavioral repertoires."

At one level the proposal seems totally confused. For the point of Freudian theory is that we can identify the "patterns of behavior" (that is, actions) in terms of "aggression" and "guilt": Some act is an act of aggression, the point of some other act is to alleviate guilt for aggression, and so on. It is only *qua* characterized in this way that these actions can be linked to their antecedents in the person's development, or perhaps predicted from this early development. To discover the "latent meaning" of, say, a neurotic ritual is not to indulge in a flight of fancy which could be inhibited without damage to the theory; it is to identify the action by the description under which it is linked to its antecedent conditions, by the part it plays in the psychic economy. Thus it seems nonsense to speak of the "patterns of behavior" *as against* guilt, aggression, etc. But on another level, [the] proposal is not only confused but totally destructive of the theory. For we might interpret "patterns of behavior" as "patterns of movement" (as against action). . . . But then nothing remains. For it is only as actions, and as actions with a certain meaning that these patterns can be linked in the theory with their antecedents. What is important is not that water is passing over my hands, but that I am washing my hands, that I am trying to cleanse them. The notions of action, desire, and so on are essential to Freud's theory: They form part of his "data language." To try to "translate" the theory into the data language considered adequate by those who do not share the same fundamental assumptions is to make nonsense of it. There is no such thing as Freud without psychology.

Such a purge "utterly destroys the theory" (it is designed to do so), but it does not destroy any of the valid relationships Freud discovered. Patterns of behavior are not simply patterns of movement. As we shall see again in Chapter 8, no behavior is aggressive because of its topography. A person who is at the moment aggressive is one who, among other characteristics, (1) shows a heightened probability of behaving verbally or nonverbally in such a way that someone is damaged (together with a lowered probability of acting in such a way that he is positively reinforced) and (2) is reinforced by such consequences. We may regard this as a state (or, better, pattern) of behavior or as an emotional state, comparable to a state of deprivation. Freud argued, for example, that events in a person's early life may be responsible for the fact that he now tends to act in ways which damage others and is reinforced by such damage. The fact that the current object of aggression only roughly resembles the original is in accord with established principles of generalization. If Freud's theory is simply the assertion that such relations may or do exist, then it had better be called a hypothesis or a statement of fact. The objectionable part of the theory is the mental apparatus which Freud invented to account for the relations and the causal status he ascribed to its parts.

A person who is likely to damage someone and to be reinforced by damaging him will probably "feel" something—the condition described as "being likely to act aggressively" and quite possibly autonomic responses generated by the same contingencies. He may respond to such stimulation and say "I feel aggressive," even though he has not acted in a conspicuous way; but what he feels in any case are collateral effects, not, as Freud asserted, causes. The pattern or state generated by an independent variable may be effective although "unconscious"; only when "conscious" is it felt as aggression.

Allowing water to pass over one's hands can perhaps be adequately described as topography, but "washing one's hands" is an "operant" defined by the fact that, when one has behaved this way in the past, one's hands have become clean—a condition which has become reinforcing because, say, it has minimized a threat of criticism or contagion. Behavior of precisely the same topography would be part of another operant if the reinforcement had consisted of simple stimulation (e.g., "tickling") of the hands or the evocation of imitative behavior in a child whom one is teaching to wash his hands.

To be observed, a response must affect the environment—it must have an effect upon an observer or upon an instrument which in turn can affect an observer. This is as true of the contraction of a small group of muscle fibers as of pressing a lever or pacing a figure 8. If we can see a response, we can make reinforcement contingent upon it; if we are to make a reinforcer contingent upon a response, we must be able to see it or at least its effects.

Most of the facts about operant conditioning—extinction, discrimination, stimulus generalization, and the effects of schedules of reinforcement—could have been discovered with a "preparation" similar to those used in reflex physiology in which the contraction of a limb or a single muscle operated a switch. Important facts would, however, then have been missed. Reinforcement strengthens responses which differ in topography from the response reinforced. When we reinforce pressing a lever, for example, or saying *Hello*, responses differing quite widely in topography grow more probable. This is a characteristic of behavior which has strong survival value (see Chapter 7), since it would be very hard for an organism to acquire an effective repertoire if reinforcement strengthened only identical responses.

We must not, however, assume the complete interchangeability of members of a response class (an operant) defined with respect to a change produced in the environment.

Note 5.3   Class versus instance

An operant is a class, of which a response is an instance or member. The usage is seldom respected. Strictly speaking, it is always instances which are counted in determining frequency, and from that frequency the probability of a *response* inferred. The probability is frequently taken, however, as the measure of the strength of an *operant*. Strength of response has no meaning except as a property of an instance, such as its force or speed. It is always a response upon which a given reinforcement is contingent, but it is contingent upon properties which define membership in an operant. Thus a set of contingencies defines an operant.

Contingencies cannot always be detected upon a given occasion. Although a response is reinforced, we cannot be sure what property satisfied the contingencies and hence defines the operant. The role of stimuli in defining contingencies is perhaps even more important. A response is reinforced in the presence of a given stimulus, but we cannot tell from a single instance what property of the stimulus is part of the contingencies. The "referent" of an abstract response is not identifiable upon any one occasion. Only by surveying many instances can we identify the properties of stimuli and responses which enter into the contingencies. This is not quite the traditional question of whether we can know particulars or universals, but it is interesting that the practice of imparting a universal meaning to the response itself as an alternative to surveying a large number of instances is close to the Platonic practice of letting ideas stand for universals.

A similar problem arose in the early history of evolution. As Mayr has shown (100), nineteenth century biologists were troubled by the distinction between species and individuals. Both Agassiz and Darwin, for quite different reasons, denied the existence of species as such. For Agassiz a species was an idea or thought. The relation between a species as a class and contingencies of survival (see Chapter 7) resembles the relation between an operant as a class and contingencies of reinforcement. The defining properties of both species and operants are practical; they are the characteristics (of individual organisms or responses) which are important in their respective contingencies.

Curiously enough, phylogenic responses are a sort of bridge between these two areas. An instinct is a class of which instinctive responses are instances. We observe only the instances, but we construct the instinct. Only instances have the effects upon which contingencies of survival operate.

6 An operant analysis of problem solving

The behavior observed when a man solves a problem is distinguished by the fact that it changes another part of his behavior and is reinforced and strengthened when it does so.[1] Two stages are easily identified in a typical problem. A hungry man faces a problem if he cannot emit any response previously reinforced with food; to solve it he must change either himself or the situation until a response occurs. The behavior which brings about the change is properly called problem solving and the response it promotes a solution. A question for which there is at the moment no answer is a problem. It may be solved, for example, by performing a calculation, by consulting a reference work, or by acting in any way which helps in recalling a previously learned answer.

Since there is probably no behavioral process which is not relevant to the solving of some problem, an exhaustive analysis of techniques would coincide with an analysis of behavior as a whole. This chapter is confined to the status and function of the terms appearing in an operant formulation.

Contingencies of reinforcement

When a response occurs and is reinforced, the probability that it will occur again in the presence of similar stimuli is

[1] For a more detailed analysis of problem solving, see (135, pp. 246–252) and (152, Chapter 6).

increased. The process no longer presents any great problem for either organism or investigator, but problems arise when contingencies are complex. For example, there may be no response available which satisfies a given set of contingencies; or competing responses may be evoked—among them emotional changes which weaken the very response upon which reinforcement is contingent or destroy the power of a reinforcer; or the contingencies may be satisfied only by a sequence or chain of responses, early members of which are too remote from the terminal reinforcer to be strongly affected by it until conditioned reinforcers have been set up.

In Thorndike's experiment the probability of turning the latch was at first quite low. The box evoked conditioned and unconditioned escape behavior, much of it incompatible with turning the latch and emotional responses which probably made the food less reinforcing when it was eventually reached. The terminal performance which satisfied the contingencies was a chain of responses: orienting toward and approaching the latch, touching the latch and turning it, orienting toward and passing through the opened door, and approaching and eating the food. Some links in this chain may have been reinforced by the food and others by escape from the box, but some could be reinforced only after other reinforcers had been conditioned. For these and other reasons the box presented a problem—for both the cat and Thorndike.

Thorndike thought he solved *his* problem by saying that the successful cat used a process of trial-and-error learning. The expression is unfortunate. "Try" implies that a response has already been affected by relevant consequences. A cat is "trying to escape" if it engages in behavior which either has been selected in the evolution of the species because it has brought escape from dangerous situations or has been reinforced by escape from aversive stimulation elsewhere during the life of the cat. The term "error" does not describe behavior, it passes judgment on it. The curves for trial-and-error learning plotted by Thorndike and many others do not represent any useful property of behavior—certainly not a single process called problem solving. The changes which contribute to such a curve include the adaptation and extinction of emotional responses, the conditioning of reinforcers, and the extinction of unreinforced responses. Any contribution made by an increase in the probability of the reinforced response is hopelessly obscured.

Even in Thorndike's rather crude apparatus it should be possible to isolate the change resulting from reinforcement. We could begin by adapting the cat to the box until emotional responses were no longer important. By opening the door repeatedly (while making sure that this event was not consistently contingent on any response), we could convert the stimuli generated by the door into conditioned reinforcers which we could then use to shape the behavior of moving into a position from which the latch would be likely to be turned. We could then reinforce a single instance of turning the latch and would almost certainly observe an immediate increase in the probability that the latch would be turned again.

This kind of simplification is common in the experimental analysis of behavior. It eliminates the process of trial and error and, as we have noted, disposes of the data which are plotted in learning curves. It leaves no problem and, of course, no opportunity to solve a problem. Clearly it is not the thing to do if we are interested in studying or in *teaching* problem solving. It is because programmed instruction eliminates much problem solving that some objections have been raised against it. The programmer solves the learner's problems for him. How does he do so? What must he not do if he is either to study or to teach problem solving?

Constructing discriminative stimuli

Consider a simple example not unlike Thorndike's puzzle box. You have been asked to pick up a friend's suitcase from an airport baggage claim. You have never seen the suitcase or heard it described; you have only a ticket with a number for which a match is to be found among the numbers on a collection of suitcases. To simplify the problem let us say that you find yourself alone before a large rotary display. A hundred suitcases move past you in a great ring. They are moving too fast to be inspected in order. You are committed to selecting suitcases essentially at random, checking one number at a time. How are you to find the suitcase?

You may, of course, simply keep sampling. You will almost certainly check the same suitcase more than once, but eventually the matching ticket will turn up. If the suitcases are not identical, however, some kind of learning will take place; you will begin to recognize and avoid cases which do not bear the matching number. A very unusual case may be tried only once; others may be checked two or three times, but responses to them will eventually be extinguished and the suitcase eliminated from the set.

A much more effective strategy is to mark each case as it is checked—say, with a piece of chalk. No bag is then inspected twice, and the number of bags remaining to be examined is reduced as rapidly as possible. Simple as it seems, this method of solving the problem has some remarkable features. Simply checking cases at random until the right one is found is of no interest as a behavioral process; the number of checks required to solve the problem is not a dimension of behavior. It is true that behavioral processes are involved in learning not to check cases which have already been marked because they bear nonmatching numbers, but the time required to find the right case throws no useful light on them. Mathematicians, showing perhaps too much confidence in psychologists, often take this kind of learning seriously and construct theoretical learning curves and design learning machines in which probabilities of responding change in terms of consequences, but the changes actually occurring in the processes of extinction and discrimination can be studied much more directly. (In a recent article H. D. Bloch (20) argues that a learning curve which is "fairly typical of those found for biological organisms in general" can be traced to an "embarrassingly simple" mechanism the explanation of which becomes "utterly transparent." The *euphoria mathematica* is scarcely justified. Bloch is not analyzing a behavioral process at all.)

It is the use of the chalk which introduces something new. Marking each suitcase as it is checked is a kind of precurrent behavior which furthers the reinforcement of subsequent behavior—by reducing the number of samplings needed to find the right suitcase. Technically speaking, it is constructing a discriminative stimulus—an S^Δ. The effect on the behavior which follows is the only reinforcement to which making such a mark can be attributed. And the effect must not be neglected, for it distinguishes the chalk marks from marks left by accident. One could "learn" the Hampton Court maze after a fresh fall of snow simply by learning not to enter any path showing footprints leaving it;[2] it is only when footprints have been found useful and, hence, when any behavior which makes them conspicuous is automatically reinforced that we reach the present case. A well-worn path over difficult terrain or through a forest is a series of discriminative stimuli and hence a series of reinforcers. It reinforces the act of blazing or otherwise marking the trail. Marking a *right* path is, technically speaking, constructing an S^D.

It is much easier to construct useful discriminative stimuli in verbal form. Easily recalled and capable of being executed

[2] More precisely, in a maze with no loops (i.e., where all wrong entrances are to culs-de-sac) the right path is marked after one successful passage through the maze by any odd number of sets of prints.

anywhere, a verbal response is an especially useful kind of chalk mark. Many simple "statements of fact" express relations between stimuli and the reinforcing consequences of responses made to them. In the expression *Red apples are sweet* for example, the word *red* identifies a property of a discriminative stimulus and *sweet* a property of a correlated reinforcer; red apples are "marked" as sweet. The verbal response makes it easier to learn to discriminate between sweet and sour apples, to retain the discrimination over a period of time, and, especially when recorded, to respond appropriately when the original discrimination may have been forgotten. (Whether one must describe or otherwise identify contingent properties in order to form a discrimination is not the issue. Lower organisms discriminate without responding verbally to essential properties, and it is unlikely that man gave up the ability to do so. He simply discovered the additional value of constructing descriptive stimuli which improve his chances of success.)

Transmission of constructed stimuli

A constructed external mark has another important advantage; it affects other people. A stranger can follow a well-worn path almost as well as the man who laid it down. Another person could take over the search for the suitcase using our marks—either after we had told him to ignore cases marked with chalk (that is, after the chalk mark had been made an effective discriminative stimulus through verbal instruction) or after he had learned to ignore marked cases—in a process which would still be quicker than learning to ignore some cases when all have remained unmarked. Two people could also search for the same case using each other's marks. Something of the sort happens when, for example, scientists are said to be "working on a problem."

The stimuli which a man constructs in solving problems can be helpful to other people precisely because the variables manipulated in self-management are those which control the behavior of men in general. In constructing *external* stimuli to supplement or replace *private* changes in his behavior, a man automatically prepares for the transmission of what he has learned. His verbal constructions become public property as his private discriminations could not. What he says in describing his own successful behavior (*I held the base firmly in my left hand and turned the top to the right*) can be changed into a useful instruction (*Hold the base firmly in your left hand and turn the top to the right*). The same variables are being manipulated and with some of the same effects on behavior.

The role of a public product of problem solving in the accumulation and transmission of folk wisdom is exemplified by a formula once used by blacksmiths' apprentices. Proper operation of the bellows of a forge was presumably first conditioned by the effects on the bed of coals. Best results followed full strokes, from wide open to tightly closed, the opening stroke being swift and the closing stroke slow and steady. Such behavior is described in the verse:

> Up high, down low,
> Up quick, down slow—
> > And that's the way to blow (119).

The first two lines describe behavior, the third is essentially a social reinforcer. A blacksmith may have composed the poem for his own use in facilitating effective behavior or in discussing effective behavior with other blacksmiths. By occasionally reciting the poem, possibly in phase with the action, he could strengthen important characteristics of his own behavior. By recalling it upon a remote occasion, he could reinstate an effective performance. The poem must also have proved useful in teaching an apprentice to operate the bellows. It could even generate appropriate behavior in an apprentice who does not see the effect on the fire.

Much of the folk wisdom of a culture serves a similar function. Maxims and proverbs describe or imply behavior and its reinforcing consequences. The reinforcement is positive in *A penny saved is a penny earned*, which may be paraphrased *Not-spending, like earning, is reinforced with pennies*. It is negative in *Procrastination is the thief of time*, where a connection is described between putting things off at the moment and being unpleasantly busy later. Many maxims describe social contingencies. The reinforcing practices of a community are often inconsistent or episodic, but contingencies which remain relatively unchanged for a period of time may be described in useful ways. *It is better to give than to receive* specifies two forms of behavior and states that the net reinforcement of one is greater than that of the other. (The Golden Rule is a curious instance. No specific response is mentioned, but a kind of consequence is described in terms of its effect on those who use the rule. In the negative form one is enjoined not to behave in a given way if the consequence would be aversive to oneself. In the positive form one is enjoined to behave in a given way if the consequences would be reinforcing to oneself. The rule may have been discovered by someone particularly sensitive to his effects on others, but once stated it should have proved generally useful.) Maxims usually describe rather subtle contingencies of reinforcement, which must have been discovered very slowly. The maxims should have been all the more valuable in making such contingencies effective on others.

The formal laws of governmental and religious institutions also specify contingencies of reinforcement involving the occasions upon which behavior occurs, the behavior itself, and the reinforcing consequences. The contingencies were almost certainly in effect long before they were formulated. Anyone who took another's property, for example, would often be treated aversively. Eventually men learned to behave more effectively under such contingencies by formulating them. A public formulation must have had additional advantages; with its help authorities could maintain the contingencies more consistently and members of the group could behave more effectively with respect to them—possibly without direct exposure. The codification of legal practices, justly recognized as a great advance in the history of civilization, is an extraordinary example of the construction of S^D's.

A well-known set of reinforcing contingencies is a language. For thousands of years men spoke without benefit of codified rules. Some sequences of words were effective, others were less so or not at all. The discovery of grammar was the discovery of the fairly stable properties of the contingencies maintained by a community. The discovery may have been made first in a kind of personal problem solving, but a description of the contingencies in the form of rules of grammar permitted men to speak correctly by applying rules rather than through long exposure to the contingencies. The same rules became helpful in instruction and in maintaining verbal behavior in conformity with the usages of the community.

Scientific laws also specify or imply responses and their consequences. They are not, of course, obeyed by nature but by men who deal effectively with nature. The formula $s = \frac{1}{2}gt^2$ does not govern the behavior of falling bodies, it governs those who correctly predict the position of falling bodies at given times.

As a culture produces maxims, laws, grammar, and science, its members find it easier to behave effectively without direct or prolonged contact with the contingencies of reinforcement thus formulated. (We are concerned here only with stable contingencies. When contingencies change and the rules do not, rules may be troublesome rather than helpful.) The culture solves problems for its members, and it does so by transmitting discriminative stimuli already constructed to evoke solutions. The importance of the process does not, of course, explain problem solving. How do men arrive at the formulas which thus prove helpful to themselves and others? How do they learn to behave appropriately under contingencies of reinforcement for which they have not been prepared, especially contingencies which are so specific and ephemeral that no general preparation is possible?

Problem-solving behavior

The question "Who is that just behind you?" poses a problem which, if the person is known by name, is solved simply by turning around and looking. Turning and looking are precurrent responses which generate a discriminative stimulus required in order to emit a particular name. One may also generate helpful stimuli by looking more closely at a stimulus which is not yet effectively evoking a response even though it is already in the visual field, and beyond "looking more closely" lie certain problem-solving activities in which a vague or complex stimulus is tentatively described or characterized. A stimulus is more likely to be seen in a given way when it has been described, and may then even be "seen in its absence" (see page 83). A crude description may contribute to a more exact one, and a final characterization which supports a quite unambiguous response brings problem solving to an end. The result is useful to others if, in public form, it leads them to see the same thing in the same way. The reactions of others which are reinforcing to those who describe vague situations may shape their descriptions, often exerting a control no less powerful than the situations themselves.

Behavior of this sort is often observed as a kind of running comment on contingencies of reinforcement to which one is being exposed. A child learns to describe both the world to which he is reacting and the consequences of his reactions. Situations in which he cannot do this become so aversive that he escapes from them by asking for words. Descriptions of his own behavior are especially important. The community asks him: *What did you do? What are you doing? What are you going to do? And why?* and his answers describe his behavior and relate it to effective variables. The answers eventually prove valuable to the child himself. The expression *I grabbed him because he was going to fall* refers to a response (grabbing) and a property of the occasion (he was going to fall) and implies a reinforcement (his falling would have been aversive to the speaker or others). It is particularly helpful to describe behavior which fails to satisfy contingencies, as in *I let go too soon* or *I struck too hard*. Even fragmentary descriptions of contingencies speed the acquisition of effective terminal behavior, help to maintain the behavior over a period of time, and reinstate it when forgotten. Moreover, they generate similar behavior in others not subjected to the contingencies they specify. As a culture evolves, it encourages running comment of this sort and thus prepares its members to solve problems most effectively. Cultures which divert attention from behavior to mental events said to be responsible for the behavior are notably less helpful.

It is possible to construct similar discriminative stimuli without engaging in the behavior. A piece of equipment used in the study of operant behavior is a convenient example of a reinforcing system. One may arrive at behavior appropriate to the contingencies it maintains through prolonged responding under them and in doing so may formulate maxims or rules. But the equipment itself may also be examined. One could look behind the interface between organism and apparatus and set down directions for behaving appropriately with respect to the system there discovered. The environment is such a reinforcing system, and parts of it are often examined for such purposes. By analyzing sample spaces and the rules of games, for example, we compose instructions which evoke behavior roughly resembling the behavior which would be generated by prolonged responding under the contingencies they maintain. Science is in large part a direct analysis of the reinforcing systems found in nature; it is concerned with facilitating the behavior which is reinforced by them.

(When prescriptions for action derived from an analysis of a reinforcing system differ from prescriptions derived from exposure to the contingencies maintained by the system, the former generally prevail. There are many reasons for this. A system is usually easier to observe than a history of reinforcement. The behavior summarized in a running comment may not be the terminal behavior which most adequately satisfies a given set of contingencies. A terminal performance may be marked by permanent though unnecessary features resulting from coincidental contingencies encountered *en route*. And so on.)

Contingencies are sometimes studied by constructing a model of a reinforcing environment. One may react to the model in simpler ways (for example, verbally) and acquire appropriate behavior more quickly. If rules derived from exposure to the model are to prove helpful in the environment, however, the contingencies must be the same, and a model is helpful therefore only if the reinforcing system has already been described. It is helpful simply in facilitating exposure to the contingencies and in studying the resulting changes in behavior.

Many instances of problem-solving behavior would be called *induction*. The term applies whether the stimuli which evoke behavior appropriate to a set of contingencies are derived from an exposure to the contingencies or from direct inspection of the reinforcing system. In this sense induction is not the deriving of a general rule from specific instances but the construction of a rule which generates behavior appropriate to a set of contingencies. Rule and contingency are different kinds of things; they are not general and specific statements of the same thing.

Deduction is still another way of constructing discriminative stimuli. Maxims, rules, and laws are physical objects, and they can be manipulated to produce other maxims, rules, and laws. Second-order rules for manipulating first-order rules are derived from empirical discoveries of the success of certain practices or from an examination of the contingency-maintaining systems which the first-order rules describe. In much of probability theory first-order rules are derived from a study of reinforcing systems. Second-order rules are discovered inductively when they are found to produce effective new first-order rules or deductively (possible tautologically) from an analysis of first-order rules or of the contingencies they describe.

Many rules which help in solving the problem of solving problems are familiar. "Ask yourself 'What is the unknown?'" is a useful bit of advice which leads not to a solution but to a modified statement to which a first-order rule may then be applied. Reducing the statement of a problem to symbols does not solve the problem but, by eliminating possibly irrelevant responses, it may make first-order problem solving more effective. Second-order, "heuristic" rules are often thought to specify more creative or less mechanical activities than the rules in first-order (possibly algorithmic) problem solving, but once a heuristic rule has been formulated, it can be followed as "mechanically" as any first-order rule (152).

Solving a problem is a behavioral event. The various kinds of activities which further the appearance of a solution are all forms of behavior. The course followed in moving toward a solution does not, however, necessarily reflect an important behavioral process. Just as there are almost as many "learning curves" as there are things to be learned, so there are almost as many "problem-solving curves" as there are problems. Logic, mathematics, and science are disciplines which are concerned with ways of solving problems, and the histories of these fields record ways in which particular problems have been solved. Fascinating as this may be, it is not a prime source of data about behavior. Strategies and instances in which strategies have actually been used have the same status whether a problem is solved by an individual, a group, or a machine. Just as we do not turn to the way in which a machine solves a problem to discover the electrical, mechanical, optical, or chemical principles on which it is constructed, so we should not turn to the way in which a man or a group solves a problem for useful data in studying individual behavior, communication, or coordinated action. This does not mean that we may not study individual, group, or machine behavior in order to discover better ways of solving problems or to reveal the limits of the kind of strategies which may be employed or the kinds of problems which may be solved.

Contingency-shaped versus rule-governed behavior

The response which satisfies a complex set of contingencies, and thus solves the problem, may come about as the result of direct shaping by the contingencies (possibly with the help of deliberate or accidental programming) or it may be evoked by contingency-related stimuli constructed either by the problem solver himself or by others. The difference between rule-following and contingency-shaped behavior is obvious when instances are pretty clearly only one or the other. The behavior of a baseball outfielder catching a fly ball bears certain resemblances to the behavior of the commander of a ship taking part in the recovery of a reentering satellite. Both move about on a surface in a direction and with a speed designed to bring them, if possible, under a falling object at the moment it reaches the surface. Both respond to recent stimulation from the position, direction, and speed of the object, and they both take into account effects of gravity and friction. The behavior of the baseball player, however, has been almost entirely shaped by contingencies of reinforcement, whereas the commander is simply obeying rules derived from the available information and from analogous situations. As more and more satellites are caught, it is conceivable that an experienced commander, under the influence of successful or unsuccessful catches, might dispense with or depart from some of the rules thus derived. At the moment, however, the necessary history of reinforcement is lacking, and the two cases are quite different.

Possibly because discriminative stimuli (as exemplified by maxims, rules, and laws) are usually more easily observed than the contingencies they specify, responses under their control tend to be overemphasized at the expense of responses shaped by contingencies. One resulting mistake is to suppose that behavior is always under the control of prior stimuli. Learning is defined as "finding, storing, and using again correct rules" (37), and the simple shaping of behavior by contingencies which have never been formulated is neglected. When the brain is described as an "organ for the manipulation of symbols," its role in mediating changes in behavior resulting from reinforcement is not taken into account.

Once the pattern has been established, it is easy to argue for other kinds of prior controlling entities such as expectancies, cognitive maps, intentions, and plans. We refer to contingency-shaped behavior alone when we say that an organism behaves in a given way with a given probability because the *behavior has been followed by a given kind of consequence in the past*. We refer to behavior under the control of prior contingency-specifying stimuli when we say that an organism behaves in a given way because *it expects a similar consequence to follow in the future*. The "expectancy" is a gratuitous and dangerous assumption if nothing more than a history of reinforcement has been observed (see page 106). Any actual formulation of the relation between a response and its consequences (perhaps simply the observation, "Whenever I respond in this way such and such an event follows") may, of course, function as a prior controlling stimulus.

The contingency-specifying stimuli constructed in the course of solving problems never have quite the same effects as the contingencies they specify. One difference is motivational. Contingencies not only shape behavior, they alter its probability; but contingency-specifying stimuli, as such, do not do so. Though the topography of a response is controlled by a maxim, rule, law, or statement of intention, the probability of its occurrence remains undetermined. After all, why should a man obey a law, follow a plan, or carry out an intention? It is not enough to say that men are so constituted that they automatically follow rules—as nature is said, mistakenly, to obey the laws of nature. A rule is simply an object in the environment. Why should it be important? This is the sort of question which always plagues the dualist. Descartes could not explain how a thought could move the pineal gland and thus affect the material body; Adrian acknowledged that he could not say how a nerve impulse caused a thought (2). How does a rule govern behavior?

As a discriminative stimulus, a rule is effective as part of a set of contingencies of reinforcement. A complete specification must include the reinforcement which has shaped the topography of a response and brought it under the control of the stimulus. The reinforcements contingent on prior stimulation from maxims, rules, or laws are sometimes the same as those which directly shape behavior. When this is the case, the maxim, rule, or law is a form of advice (141). *Go west, young man* is an example of advice when the behavior it specifies will be reinforced by certain consequences which do not result from action taken by the adviser. We tend to follow advice because previous behavior in response to similar verbal stimuli has been reinforced. *Go west, young man* is a command when some consequences of the specified action are arranged by the commander—say, the aversive consequences arranged by an official charged with relocating the inhabitants of a region. When maxims, rules, and laws are advice, the governed behavior is reinforced by consequences which might have shaped the same behavior directly in the absence of the maxims, rules, and laws. When they are commands, they are effective only because special reinforcements have been made contingent upon them. Governments, for example, do not trust to the natural advantages of obeying the law to ensure obedience. Grammatical rules are often followed not so much because the behavior is then particularly effective as because social punishments are contingent on ungrammatical behavior.

Rule-governed behavior is obviously unmotivated in this sense when rules are obeyed by machines. A machine can be constructed to move a bellows up high, down low, up quick, and down slow, remaining forever under the control of the specifying rules. Only the designer and builder are affected by the resulting condition of the fire. The same distinction holds when machines follow more complex rules. A computer, like a mechanical bellows, does only what it was constructed and instructed to do. Mortimer Taube (155) and Ulrich Neisser (105) are among those who have recently argued that the thinking of a computer is less than human, and it is significant that they have emphasized the lack of "purpose." But to speak of the purpose of an act is, as we saw in Chapter 5, simply to refer to its characteristic consequences. A statement of purpose may function as a contingency-specifying discriminative stimulus. Computers merely follow rules. So do men at times—for example, the blacksmith's apprentice who never sees the fire or the algorithmic problem solver who simply does what he has been taught or told to do. The motivating conditions (for machines and men alike) are irrelevant to the problem being solved.

Rules are particularly likely to be deficient in the sovereignty needed for successful government when they are derived from statistical analyses of contingencies. It is unlikely that anyone will ever stop smoking simply because of the aversive stimulation associated with lung cancer, at least not in time to make any difference, and it is therefore unlikely that giving up smoking will be shaped by these consequences. The actual contingencies have little effect on behavior under the control of contingency-specifying facts or rules. A formal statement of contingencies (*Cigarette smoking causes lung cancer*) needs the support of carefully engineered aversive stimuli involving sanctions quite possibly unrelated to the consequences of smoking. For example, smoking may be classified as shameful, illegal, or sinful and punished by appropriate agencies.

Some contingencies cannot be accurately described. The old family doctor was often a skillful diagnostician because of contingencies to which he had been exposed over many years, but he could not always describe these contingencies or construct rules which evoked comparable behavior in younger men. Some of the experiences of the mystic are ineffable in the sense that all three terms in the contingencies governing his behavior (the behavior itself, the conditions under which it occurs, and its consequences) escape adequate specification. Emotional behavior is particularly hard to bring under the control of rules. As Pascal put it, "the heart has its reasons which reason will never know." Nonverbal skills are usually much harder to describe than verbal. Verbal behavior can be reported in a unique way by modelling it in direct quotation (141). Nonverbal behavior is modelled so that it can be imitated but not as precisely or as exhaustively.

Rule-governed behavior is in any case never exactly like the behavior shaped by contingencies. The golf player whose swing has been shaped by its effect on the ball is easily distinguished from the player who is primarily imitating a coach, even though it is much more difficult to distinguish between a man who is making an original observation and one who is saying something because he has been told to say it; but when topographies of response are very similar, different controlling variables are necessarily involved, and the behavior will have different properties. When operant experiments with human subjects are simplified by instructing the subjects in the operation of the equipment (see page 114), the resulting behavior may resemble that which follows exposure to the contingencies and may be studied in its stead for certain purposes, but the controlling variables are different, and the behaviors will not necessarily change in the same way in response to other variables—for example, under the influence of a drug.

The difference between rule-following and contingency-shaped behavior may be observed as one passes from one to the other in "discovering the truth" of a rule. A man may have avoided postponing necessary work for years either because he has been taught that *Procrastination is the thief of time* and therefore avoids procrastination as he avoids thieves, or because he dutifully obeys the injunction *Do not put off until tomorrow what you can do today*. Eventually his behavior may come under the direct influence of the relevant contingencies—in doing something today he actually avoids the aversive consequences of having it to do tomorrow. Though his behavior may not be noticeably different (he continues to perform necessary work as soon as possible) he will now behave for different reasons, which must be taken into account. When at some future time he says *Procrastination is the thief of time,* his response has at least two sources of strength; he is reciting a memorized maxim and emitting a contingency-specifying statement of fact.

The eventual occurrence of a planned event works a similar change. Plans for a symposium are drawn up and followed. Eventually, almost incidentally it may seem, the symposium is held and certain natural consequences follow. The nature of the enterprise as an instance of human behavior has changed; in particular the probability that similar behavior will occur in the future has been altered. In the same way those half-formed expectancies called "premonitions" suddenly become important when the premonitored events occur. A similar change comes about when an actor, starting with memorized words and prescribed actions, comes under the influence of simulated or real reactions by other members of the cast, under the shaping effect of which he begins to "live" the role.

The classical distinction between rational and irrational

or intuitive behavior is of the same sort. The "reasons" which govern the behavior of the rational man describe relations between the occasions on which he behaves, his behavior, and its consequences. In general we admire the intuitive man, with his contingency-shaped behavior, rather than the mere follower of rules. For example, we admire the man who is "naturally" good rather than the merely law-abiding, the intuitive mathematician rather than the mere calculator. Plato discusses the difference in the *Charmides*, but he confuses matters by supposing that what we admire is speed. It is true that contingency-shaped behavior is instantly available, whereas it takes time to consult rules and examine reasons; but irrational behavior is more likely to be wrong and therefore we have reason to admire the deliberate and rational man. We ask the intuitive mathematician to behave like one who calculates—to construct a proof which will guide others to the same conclusion even though the intuitive mathematician himself did not need it. We insist, with Freud, that the reasons men give in explaining their actions should be accurate accounts of the contingencies of reinforcement which were responsible for their behavior.

Other kinds of problems

To define a problem, etymologically, as something explicitly put forth for solution (or, more technically, as a specific set of contingencies of reinforcement for which a response of appropriate topography is to be found) is to exclude instances in which the same precurrent activities serve a useful function although the topography of a response is already known. The distinction between contingency-shaped and rule-following behavior is still required. Sometimes the problem is not *what* to do but *whether* to do it. Problem-solving behavior is designed to strengthen or weaken an already identified response. Conflicting positive and negative consequences, of either an intellectual or ethical nature, are especially likely to raise problems of this sort—for example, when a strongly reinforced response has deferred aversive consequences or when immediate aversive consequences conflict with deferred reinforcers.

A relevant problem-solving practice is to emit the questionable response in tentative form—for example, as a *hypothesis*. Making a hypothesis differs from asserting a fact in that the evidence is scantier and punishment for being wrong more likely to follow. The emitted response is nevertheless useful, particularly if recorded, because it may enter into other problem-solving activities. For rather different purposes one acts verbally before acting in other ways by making a *resolution*. It is easier to resolve than to act; but the resolution makes the action more likely to take place. (A *promise* specifies a response and creates social contingencies which strengthen it, and contingencies of social origin are invoked when one "promises oneself" to do something in making a resolution.) A *statement of policy* is also a description of action to be taken. (Resolutions and statements of policy are often made because action itself is at the moment impossible, but they are relevant here only when the action they strengthen or weaken is not under physical constraint.) A joint secret statement of policy is a *conspiracy*; it describes cooperative action to be undertaken by a group.

Like the rules and plans appropriate to problems in which the topography of the solution is not known, hypotheses, statements of policy, and so on, are not to be inferred in every instance of behavior. People act without making resolutions or forming policies. Different people or groups of people (for example, "capitalists" in socialist theory) act in the same way under similar contingencies of reinforcement, even cooperatively, without entering into a conspiracy. The conclusion to which a scientist comes at the end of an experiment was not necessarily in existence as a hypothesis before or during the experiment.

Sometimes the problem is to arrive at a less than maximal

probability appropriate to intermittent reinforcement. A calculated probability, derived either by sampling a schedule of reinforcement or by directly inspecting the system maintaining such a schedule, controls an appropriate strength of response. But, again, a person is not always acting under the control of such a calculation or of any prior "felt" probability or sense of confidence, trust, or belief.

Sometimes the problem is to decide which of two or more responses to emit, the topographies of all alternatives being known. The concepts of choice and decision making have been overemphasized in psychological and economic theory. It is difficult to evaluate the probability that a single response will be made, but when two or more mutually exclusive responses are possible, the one actually emitted seems at least to be stronger than the others. For this reason early psychological research emphasized situations and devices in which only relative strength was observed (the rat turned right rather than left or jumped toward a circle rather than a square). Efforts to assess the separate probabilities of the competing responses were thus discouraged. Single responses were treated only as decisions between acting and not acting, within the time limits set by a "trial." The notion of relative strength is then practically meaningless, and "choose" simply means "respond." The problem of whether to act in one way or another differs from the problem of whether or not to act only because one of the aversive consequences of acting in one way is a loss of the opportunity to act in another. The same problem-solving activities are relevant. A decision announced before acting is essentially a resolution or statement of policy. The mere emission of one response rather than another, however, does not mean that a decision has been formulated.

The notion of a problem as something set for solution is even less appropriate when neither the topography of the behavior strengthened by precurrent activity nor its consequences are known until the behavior occurs. Artists, composers, and writers, for example, engage in various activities which further their production of art, music, and literature. (Sometimes they are required to produce works meeting quite narrow specifications, and their behaviors then exemplify explicit problem solving, but this is by no means always the case.) The artist or composer explores a medium or a theme and comes up with an unforeseen composition having unforeseen effects. A writer explores a subject matter or a style and comes up with a poem or a book which could not have been described or its effects predicted in advance. In this process of "discovering what one has to say," relevant precurrent behavior cannot be derived from any specification of the behavior to follow or of the contingencies which the behavior will satisfy. The precurrent behavior nevertheless functions by virtue of the processes involved in solving statable problems. For example, crude sketches and tentative statements supply stimuli leading to other sketches and statements, moving toward a final solution. Here again, it is a mistake to assume that the artist, composer, or writer is necessarily realizing some prior conception of the work he produces. The conditions under which Renoir was reinforced as he painted *The Boating Party* must have been as real as those under which a mathematician or scientist is reinforced for solving a set problem, but much less could have been said about them in advance.

Problem solving is often said to produce knowledge. An operant formulation permits us to distinguish between some of the things to which this term has been applied.

What is knowledge, where is it, and what is it about? Michael Polanyi (111, 112) and P. W. Bridgman (27, 28) have raised these questions with respect to the apparent discrepancy between scientific facts, laws, and theories (as published, for example, in papers, texts, tables of constants, and encyclopedias) and the personal knowledge of the scientist. Objective knowledge transcends the individual; it is more stable and durable than private experience, but it lacks color and personal involvement. The presence or absence of "consciousness" can scarcely be the important difference, for scientists are as "conscious" of laws as they are of the things laws describe. Sensory contact with the external world may be the beginning of knowledge, but contact is not enough. It is not even enough for "conscious experience," since stimuli are only part of the contingencies of reinforcement under which an organism distinguishes among the aspects and properties of the environment in which it lives. Responses must be made and reinforced before anything can be seen.

The world which establishes contingencies of reinforcement of the sort studied in an operant analysis is presumably "what knowledge is about." A person comes to know that world and how to behave in it in the sense that he acquires behavior which satisfies the contingencies it maintains. Behavior which is exclusively shaped by such contingencies is perhaps the closest one can come to the "personal knowledge" of Polanyi and Bridgman. It is the directed, "purposive" behavior of the blacksmith who operates his bellows because of its effect on the fire.

But there is another kind of behavior which could be called knowledge of the same things—the behavior controlled by contingency-specifying stimuli. These stimuli are as objective as the world they specify, and they are useful precisely because they become and remain part of the external world. Behavior under their control is the behavior of the apprentice who never sees the fire but acts as he instructs himself to act by reciting a poem. So far as topography goes, it may resemble behavior directly shaped by contingencies, but there remains an all important difference in controlling variables. (To say that the behaviors have different "meanings" is only another way of saying that they are controlled by different variables [141].)

The distinction which Polanyi (112) in particular seems to be trying to make is between contingency-shaped and rule-governed behavior rather than between behaviors marked by the presence or absence of "conscious experience." Contingency-shaped behavior depends for its strength upon "genuine" consequences. It is likely to be nonverbal and thus to "come to grips with reality." It is a personal possession which dies with the possessor. The rules which form the body of science are public. They survive the scientist who constructed them as well as those who are guided by them. The control they exert is primarily verbal, and the resulting behavior may not vary in strength with consequences having personal significance. These are basic distinctions, and they survive even when, as is usually the case, the scientist's behavior is due to both direct reinforcement and to the control exercised by the contingency-specifying stimuli which compose facts, laws, and theories.

Note 6.1   Why are rules formulated?

It is all very well to say that we extract rules from contingencies of reinforcement, either when we have been exposed to them or have had the chance to study the systems which arrange them, and that we gain by doing so because we and others can then follow the rules rather than submit to the possibly tedious process of having behavior shaped by the contingencies. But "extracting a rule" is complex behavior, and the natural reinforcement may be deferred. Why and how does the behavior arise?

Some fragmentary rules emerge as natural consequences of contingency-shaped behavior. Once a path has proved useful, it is not too difficult to explain any behavior which accentuates it. One blazes a trail because one thus intensifies discriminative stimuli which as such are also reinforcing. Retracing one's steps is perhaps the simplest use of a path, and marking a path so that it can be retraced is a common mythological theme. Footprints would evidently not have been conspicuous in the minotaur's labyrinth, and Theseus therefore unwound Ariadne's ball of thread as he entered. Hansel and Gretel found themselves in trouble when their trail of crumbs was eaten by birds.

A rather similar explanation holds for contingencies involving time. To complete a journey before dark it may be necessary to make an early start, and any stimulus correlated with time then becomes important. The position of the sun will do. It can be made more effective as a stimulus by measuring the altitude—say, in handwidths from the horizon. Shadows cast by the sun are easier to read, and a sundial is invented to cast them in standard ways. Sandglasses and water clocks produce visual stimuli which change with time at useful rates, but they are not modifications of natural clocks and the precurrent behavior of invention must have been more elaborate. The pendulum clock, of course, comes much later, when stimuli correlated with time are in common use and the mechanical arts well advanced. A clock is more useful when it can be read, and numbers are therefore added to sundials, sandglasses, and water clocks.

Paths and clocks, even when described verbally, are incomplete rules, for other parts of the contingencies in which they appear are not specified. Something closer to a complete rule may have emerged in the form of responses which are reinforced when they induce others to behave in given ways. A command or request specifies behavior and implies consequences, aversive in the command, positively reinforcing in the request. A warning or a piece of advice also specifies behavior and at least implies consequences. Contracts and bribes do the same. A student's assignment, a serf's corvée, a worker's quota, a soldier's task, and a citizen's duty specify something to be done and the aversive consequences which are avoided by doing it. Instructions and directions are usually forms of advice and warning.

The injunctive character of rules of this sort is eventually softened. The pure "mand" (141) may be replaced by a "tact" describing conditions under which specific behavior on the part of the listener will be reinforced. *Give me a drink!* yields to *I am thirsty.* The craftsman begins by ordering his apprentice to behave in a given way (or, as we have seen, by teaching him a poem to recite in order to give himself orders); but he may later achieve the same effect simply by describing the relation between what the apprentice does and the consequences. A scientific law does not enjoin anyone to behave in a given way; it simply describes the contingencies under which certain kinds of behavior will have certain kinds of consequences. Ethical, religious, and governmental laws presumably begin as injunctions but, like scientific laws, eventually merely describe contingencies, specifying behavior and its (usually punitive) consequences. The difference between a scientific and a governmental law is not that the one is discovered and the other made, for both are discovered. A government usually "makes a law" only when the culture is already maintaining or disposed to maintain the contingencies the law describes. The law is a description of prevailing ethical, religious, or governmental practices. In codifying the practices of a culture in praising and blaming, as well as in stating a scientific law, we are describing contingencies of reinforcement. We cannot give anyone credit for the consequences of his behavior until we have identified the behavior, the consequences, and the relation between them, nor can we blame anyone without a similar analysis. Both kinds of contingencies exist and shape behavior before they are analyzed or formulated in rules.

We might expect that a rule to guide one's own behavior would be formulated only rarely if at all. If one is already complying with a set of contingencies, why is a rule needed? Nevertheless, the scientist who examines a set of phenomena and formulates the law which "governs" it may do so mainly because he himself can then react more effevtively either now or later when the contingency-shaped behavior has weakened. Rules are stated more precisely because of social contingencies designed to induce a person to report what he is doing and why he is doing it. The verbal community generates "awareness" (135, Chapters 17 and 18) when it teaches an individual to describe his past and present behavior and behavior he is likely to exhibit in the future and to identify the variables of which all three are presumably functions. The description which is thus generated is not yet a rule, but the person may use the same terms to mand his own behavior (as a form of self-control), to make resolutions, to formulate plans, to state purposes, and thus to construct rules.

Note 6.2   The objectivity of rules

In contrasting contingency-shaped and rule-governed behavior we must take account of four things:

(1) A system which establishes certain contingencies of reinforcement, such as some part of the natural environment, a piece of equipment used in operant research, or a verbal community.

(2) The behavior which is shaped and maintained by these contingencies or which satisfies them in the sense of being reinforced under them.

(3) Rules derived from the contingencies, in the form of injunctions or descriptions which specify occasions, responses, and consequences.

(4) The behavior evoked by the rules.

The topography of (4) is probably never identical with that or (2) because the rules in (3) are probably never complete specifications of the contingencies in (1). The behaviors in (2) and (4) are also usually under the control of different states of deprivation or aversive stimulation.

Items (2) and (4) are instances of behavior and as such, ephemeral and insubstantial. We observe an organism in the act of behaving, but we study only the records which survive. Behavior is also subjective in the sense that it is characteristic of a particular person with a particular history. In contrast, (1) and (3) are objective and durable. The reinforcing system in (1) exists prior to any effect it may have upon an organism and it can be observed in the same way by two or more people. The rules of (3) are more or less permanent verbal stimuli. It is not surprising, therefore, that (2) and (4) often take second place to (1) and (3). (1) is said to be what a person acquires "knowledge about" and (3) is called "knowledge."

Maps.   In finding one's way in a complex terrain, the relation between the behavior and its reinforcing consequences can be represented spatially, as we have seen, and "purposive" comes to mean "goal directed." A special kind of rule is then available— a map. A city is an example of Item (1). It is a system of contingencies of reinforcement: when a person proceeds along certain streets and makes certain turns, he is reinforced by arriving at a certain point. He learns to get about in the city when his behavior (2) is shaped by these contingencies. This is one sense in which, as we say, he "acquires knowledge of the city." Whenever the reinforcement associated with arriving at a given point is relevant to a current state of deprivation, he behaves in ways which lead to his arrival at that point. A map on which a route is marked is an example of (3) and the behavior of following the map is an example of (4). Getting about the city by following a map (4) may resemble getting about the city as the effect of exposure to the contingencies (2), but the topographies will probably be different, quite apart from the collateral behavior of consulting the map in the former case. Since the map (3) appears to be a kind of objective "knowledge" of the city, it is easy to infer that (2) itself involves a map—Tolman's cognitive map, for example. It has been pointed out (151) that almost all the figures which describe apparatus in Tolman's *Purposive Behavior in Animals and Men* are maps. Terrain (1) is not only what is learned, it is what knowledge (3) is about. Learning then seems to be the discovery of maps.[1] But a map is plausible as a form of rule only when contingencies can be represented spatially. It is true that other kinds of psychological space have been hypothesized (for example, by Kurt Lewin) in order to account for behavior which is not an example of moving toward a goal or getting out of trouble, but the notion of a map and the concept of space are then strained.

The extent to which behavior is contingency-shaped or rule-governed is often a matter of convenience. When a trail is laid quickly (as at Hampton Court after a fresh fall of snow), there is no need to learn the maze at all; it is much more convenient simply to learn to follow the trail. If the surface leaves no mark, the maze must be learned as such. If the trail develops slowly, the maze may be learned first as if no path were available and the path which is eventually laid down may never be used. If the maze is difficult, however—for example, if various points in it are very much alike—or if it is easily forgotten, a slowly developing path may take over the ultimate control. In that case one eventually "discovers the truth" in a trail as one discovers the truth in a maxim.

It is the contingencies, not the rules, which exist before the rules

[1] The fact that it is much easier to learn to follow a marked than an unmarked route might suggest that the external path is being used in lieu of the internal pathways which figure so prominently in neurophysiology, but the two kinds of paths have very different functions.

are formulated. Behavior which is shaped by the contingencies does not show knowledge of the rules. One may speak grammatically under the contingencies maintained by a verbal community without "knowing the rules of grammar" in any other sense, but once these contingencies have been discovered and grammatical rules formulated, one may upon occasion speak grammatically by applying rules.

Some psychologists call operant conditioning "probability learning." Sometimes the reference is to the probability that an organism will respond in a given way (2) and sometimes to the probability that a response will be reinforced under the prevailing contingencies (1). "What is learned" is the latter; the organism is said to come to "know what behavior will have what effects under what circumstances."

Concepts. The items on our list which seem objective also tend to be emphasized when reinforcement is contingent upon the presence of a stimulus which is a member of a set defined by a property. Such a set, which may be found in nature or explicitly constructed, is an example of (1). Behavior is shaped by these contingencies in such a way that stimuli possessing the property evoke responses while other stimuli do not. The defining property is named in a rule (3) extracted from the contingencies. (The rule states that a response will be reinforced in the presence of a stimulus with that property). Behavior (4) is evoked by stimuli possessing the property, possibly without exposure to the contingencies. The "concept" is "in the stimulus" as a defining property in (1) and it is named or otherwise specified in the rule of (3). Since the topography of the response at issue is usually arbitrary, it is quite likely that the behaviors in (2) and (4) will be similar, and it is then particularly easy to suppose that one responds to (1) because one "knows the rule" in (3).

Note 6.3 Some kinds of rules

A scientific law or a maxim enjoining prudent behavior differs from a resolution, plan, or statement of purpose in the generality of the contingencies which it supplements or replaces. Laws and maxims describe long-lasting contingencies, and once discovered they can be transmitted to and used by others. A resolution, plan, or statement of purpose is constructed on the spot. It is much more likely to be an incomplete description of contingencies, but it has the same effect as a maxim or law to the extent that it identifies a response and the occasion upon which it may be reinforced. It may also invoke additional reinforcers, positive or negative. A person obeys a law and observes a maxim in part to avoid censure, possibly self-imposed, for failing to do so. He keeps a resolution, carries out a plan, and holds to a purpose in part for similar reasons.

A model to be imitated is a fragmentary rule specifying the topography of the imitative response. When we show someone how to do something, we compose an imitative model. This is a kind of instruction or direction. When we supply a copy or pattern to be drawn or otherwise reconstructed (say in needlework), we are also supplying a rule. There are many verbal examples (141). Echoic behavior, taking dictation, and copying handwriting all involve stimuli which can be interpreted as specifying topography of behavior. A text is a particularly interesting case. It is a fragmentary rule which directs the behavior of the reader, point for point.

We almost always restrict the word "study" to the acquisition of rule-governed behavior. Although we may study a piece of equipment if we are to do something with it, we do not usually say that we are studying when we learn to operate it. We do not say that a student is studying when he is actually driving a car or training device, but we say that he studies a manual on how to drive. The distinction seems to be that in the case of the manual, the verbal behavior he eventually acquires is specified in the text. There is no prior representation of the behavior of driving a car. It is contingency-shaped. It is easy to see how the prior representation is said to be learned, in the sense of stored within the learner. We recall a rule, fragmentary or otherwise. We recall parts of a manual on driving a car as we recite or paraphrase the text, but we do not say that we are recalling driving a car as we drive one.

In an early experiment on discrimination (129) a rat repeatedly pressed a lever and responses were reinforced provided a light was on. If the light had been made progressively dimmer until it could not be seen at all, the problem of "when to press the lever" would have become insoluble. The contingencies would have been indistinguishable from those of intermittent reinforcement. As long as the light was available, a human subject could have devised special ways of making it important as a discriminative stimulus. He could also have formulated a rule, for use by himself or others, either as an injunction ("Respond only when the light is on.") or as a description of the contingencies ("A response is followed by food only when the light is on.") The latter would be a scientific law in a limited universe.

When no light is visible, no rule can be formulated, but stimuli accidentally present when a response is reinforced may gain control. Pigeons show this kind of superstitious behavior and so do gamblers. A gambler who is conspicuously successful upon an occasion when he is wearing a particular tie will sometimes wear it again "for luck." (Luck as we shall see in Chapter 9, is an interesting explanatory fiction. Lady Luck stands in the same relation to a gambler as a Muse to a poet. A series of successes is attributed to a run of luck, and it is difficult to believe that there is not, indeed, some external cause.)

This does not mean that there are no useful rules regarding unpredictable schedules. "Don't gamble" is one. A gambling club advises its patrons, "When you hit a winning streak, stop while you're still ahead." If the club believes in winning streaks, it may offer this advice in order to get lucky players away from its tables, but there is a better reason. It is important that some players leave when they are winning, since the club would not be popular if all players stopped playing only when they had run out of money.

A betting system is a set of rules governing play. It is useful even when it does not, in fact, dictate successful play. Men are often punished for responding under the wrong circumstances and blamed for neglecting useful information. To respond with no indication of success is aversive, and one may escape by finding some apparent indicator. An overheard remark containing the name of a horse running in a race is the hunch upon which a bet is placed. One can then blame the hunch if the bet doesn't pay off.

A betting system has the effect of a water diviner (74). It costs money to dig a well, and the well may not bring in water. The mistake will be punishing, but one cannot avoid it by not digging. A dowser is therefore called in; and if the well fails to bring in water, he can be blamed. We flip a coin in making a difficult decision, and we can then blame a wrong choice on the coin. The Department of Defense, as well as large business organizations, uses decision-making systems, even when they are of questionable value, whenever there are no good reasons for deciding one way or the other. The system does not dictate good decisions, but it absolves everyone from blame for bad ones.

When a person is asked why he does something, or why he does it in a given way, his answer will usually refer to contingencies. He may correctly identify the variables controlling his behavior and in doing so he advances toward a rule which would govern similar behavior if the original contingencies were defective or lacking. He may be wrong, however; he may invent a set of variables. He is particularly likely to do so if the actual variables are grounds for punishment. This is rationalizing in the Freudian sense. When the set is defective, his explanation has the form of a belief. Thus he will not explain his superstitious behavior by confessing that he has been affected by adventitious contingencies. Instead, he will give "good reasons" for doing as he does. The superstitions transmitted by a culture are rules for which there are no corresponding contingencies. The paranoid is a specialist in extracting rules from defective contingencies. When a man is solving a problem, he may emit an effective solution before he can describe its place in the contingencies. For example, he may form a concept in the sense that he begins to respond consistently to a set of stimuli before he can name or describe the property defining the set. We usually say that he gets the idea only when he names the property, and we thus identify having an idea as being able to formulate a rule. We propose ideas to others in the form of rules, and the culture transmits what it has learned in that form.

A rule of thumb is no rule at all. Acting by rule of thumb is contingency-shaped behavior. The thumb may be a successful organ, but we do not need to explain its success by attributing rules to it. "Flying by the seat of one's pants" also seems to refer to contingency-shaped behavior as distinct from following instructions. It suggests that stimuli generated by the action of the plane on the body of the flyer are crucial, but flying can also be shaped by contingencies in which instrument readings are prominent.

Note 6.4 Differences between rule-governed and contingency-shaped behavior

A scientist may play billiards intuitively as a result of long experience, or he may determine masses, angles, distances, frictions, and so on, and calculate each shot. He is likely to do the former, of course, but there are analogous circumstances in which he cannot submit to the contingencies in a comparable way and must adopt the latter. Both kinds of behavior are plausible, natural, and effective; they both show "knowledge of the contingencies," and (apart from the precurrent calculations in the second case) they may have similar topographies. But they are under different kinds of stimulus control and hence are different operants. The difference appears when the scientist examines his behavior. In the first case he *feels* the rightness of the force and direction with which the ball is struck; in the second he feels the rightness of his calculations but not of the shot itself. (For an analysis of feelings, see Chapter 8.)

It is the control of nature in the first case with its attendant feelings which suggests to Polanyi and Bridgman a kind of personal involvement characteristic only of direct experience and knowledge (see page 155). The point of science, however, is to analyze the contingencies of reinforcement found in nature and to formulate rules or laws which make it unnecessary to be exposed to them in order to behave appropriately. What one sees in watching oneself following the rules of science is therefore different from what one sees in watching oneself behave as one has learned to do under the contingencies which the rules describe. The mistake is to suppose that only one of these kinds of behavior represents knowledge. Polanyi argues that "tacit knowing is . . . the dominant principle of all knowledge, and . . . its rejection would therefore automatically involve the rejection of any knowledge whatever" (111). It is true that an apprentice blacksmith may not know why he is operating the bellows as he does—

he may have no "feel" for the effect on the fire—but the rule, together with its effect on his behavior, is still a "form of knowledge."

Rogers (117) and Maslow (98) have tried to reverse the history of psychological science to return to a kind of knowledge generated by personal contingencies of reinforcement. They presumably do not question the effectiveness of the rules and prescriptions which may be drawn from a consideration of the circumstances under which people behave or can be induced to behave, but they give preference to personal knowledge which has the feeling of contingency-shaped behavior. It is not too difficult to make this feeling seem important—as important as it seemed to Polanyi and Bridgman in attempting to evaluate what we really know about the world as a whole.

Rogers and Maslow feel threatened by the objectivity of scientific knowledge and the possible absence of personal involvement in its use; but the personal and social behavior shaped by social contingencies has, except in rare instances, been as cold, scheming, or brutal as the calculated behavior of a Machiavelli. We have no guarantee that personal involvement will bring sympathy, compassion, or understanding, for it has usually done just the opposite. Social action based upon a scientific analysis of human behavior is much more likely to be humane. It can be transmitted from person to person and epoch to epoch, it can be *freed* of personal predilections and prejudices, it can be constantly tested against the facts, and it can steadily increase the competence with which we solve human problems. If need be, it can inspire in its devotées a feeling of rightness. Personal knowledge, whether contingency-shaped or rule-governed, is not to be judged by how it feels but by the help it offers in working toward a more effective culture.

The behavior evoked by a rule is often simpler than the behavior shaped by the contingencies from which the rule is derived. The rule covers only the essentials; it may omit features which give contingency-shape behavior its character. The sanctions which make a rule effective also often make the behavior "cold." Some rule-governed behavior, however, may be more complete and effective than contingency-shaped behavior. This is particularly the case when the contingencies are defective. Rules can be derived from a study of a reinforcing system (such as a sample space) or from large samples of behavior reinforced by such a system, and they will evoke behavior when reinforcing consequences are very rare and contingency-shaped behavior therefore unlikely. Maxims concerned with perseverance, for example, provide a necessary supplement to contingencies which are weak in this sense. Consequences which have a negligible effect in shaping behavior may yield important actuarial rules. Few people drive a car at a moderate speed and keep their seat belts fastened because they have actually avoided or escaped from serious accidents by doing so. Rules derived from contingencies affecting large numbers of people bring these consequences to bear upon the individual. Ethical and legal consequences work synergically with the natural consequences which by themselves are ineffective.

Long-deferred consequences, ineffective in shaping behavior, may also lead to useful rules. Ultimate utility is seldom important in the shaping of behavior but may be maximized if certain rules are followed. Rules of this sort are particularly valuable when they oppose powerful contingencies. It is easy to consume now and suffer shortages later, or to smoke now and die of lung cancer later; but rules derived from actuarial data or from economics and physiology may enable the long-term consequences to offset the immediate.

Rule-governed behavior is particularly effective when the contingencies would otherwise shape unwanted or wasteful behavior. A species which has developed the capacity to learn from one experience—to change its behavior as the result of a single reinforcement—is vulnerable to adventitious reinforcement. The reinforcer which follows a response need not be "produced by it." It may generate superstitious behavior. A study of many instances, or of the reinforcing system, may lead to a rule opposing the effects of coincidences. A general rule enjoining a person not to acquire a response when adventitiously reinforced is unlikely, but a large number of rules describing "genuine" connections between behavior and consequences may emphasize the uniqueness and hence the improbability of a given instance. Some general rules about spatial, temporal, and physical causality have this effect. If we shake a fist at a passing airplane and the plane suddenly veers, we are perhaps no more likely to shake our fist again to cause a plane to veer; but it is characteristic of superstitious behavior that we engage in it even though we "know by the rule" that it has no effect. The culture may ridicule superstitious responses to the point at which we engage in them only as a form of humor, but it is unlikely to eliminate them altogether.

Many classical distinctions can be reduced to the distinction between rule-governed and contingency-shaped behavior.

(1) *Deliberation* vs. *impulse.* Deliberate or reasoned behavior is marked either by an examination of possibly relevant rules and the selection of one or more to be obeyed or by an examination of current contingencies and the derivation of a rule on the spot. Acting on impulse is not preceded by behavior of this sort.

(2) *Ultimate* vs. *proximate gains.* Rules tend to bring remote consequences into play; without rules only immediate consequences affect behavior.

(3) *Culture-bound* vs. *"natural" behavior.* Rules evolve with the culture and differ among cultures; behavior shaped by nonsocial contingencies is as universal as the contingencies.

(4) *Surface* vs. *depths.* Rule-governed behavior is superimposed upon men. It is the veneer of civilization. Depth psychology is concerned with the "real" contingencies.

(5) *Contrived* vs. *natural.* Rules are often followed for reasons which are unrelated to the reinforcers in the contingencies from which they are derived. Contingency-shaped behavior varies with the deprivation or aversive stimulation related to those reinforcers.

(6) *Intellect* vs. *emotion.* Rule-governed behavior may be cold and Stoical; contingency-shaped behavior is likely to be hot and Epicurean. The protestant *vs.* the hedonist ethic.

(7) *Logical argument* vs. *intuition.* The behavior shaped by the contingencies which arise as one solves a problem may yield a solution "intuitively." The solution appears, the problem is disposed of, and no one knows why. The intuitive mathematician will, however, probably be asked for a proof. He will be asked to supply rules which will lead others from a statement of the problem to the solution.

(8) *Anxiety* vs. *joy.* The ethical, legal, and other sanctions which enforce rules are usually aversive and the emotional responses associated with rule-governed behavior ("anxiety") are then

evoked by preaversive stimuli. The strong positive reinforcers which shape behavior directly are more likely to be associated with "joy."

(9) *Monotony* vs. *variety*. Rule-governed behavior is usually designed to satisfy contingencies, not to duplicate other features of the behavior shaped by them. Contingency-shaped behavior is therefore likely to have a greater variety or richness.

(10) *Conscious* vs. *unconscious*. Since it is often the function of a rule to identify stimuli, responses, and their consequences, reasoned behavior is marked by reflection and awareness (see Chapter 8). Freud assigned contingency-shaped behavior to the unconscious. Presumably one must be conscious of one's own behavior, either to discover a rule or to follow one.

(11) *Knowing* vs. *knowing how*. The knowledge which appears to be objectified in rules is owned or held by those who know the rules. Contingency-shaped behavior, simply as knowing how to do things, is less likely to suggest a prior form of possession. In experimental science the distinction is carried by *rationalism* vs. *empiricism* and in theoretical science by *reason* vs. *intuition*.

(12) *Formula* vs. *art*. As Francis Bacon said, a painter or musician excels "by a kind of felicity and not by rule," where felicity seems to refer to the happy consequences which guide the artist in lieu of rules in the production of art.

(13) *Reason* vs. *faith*. Logical arguments for the existence of God may produce rules governing pious conduct, but the behavior of the mystic is shaped by events which testify to the immediate presence of God. (The mystic cannot share his experience in the sense of formulating rules which will generate similar behavior in those who are not subject to direct mystical contingencies.)

(14) *Rule* vs. *deed* (or *word* vs. *deed?*). Another theological issue: the good man may or may not know what is right, but he does what is right, and he does it because he is naturally good, not because he can follow good rules. He can therefore be credited with behaving well, not simply with following rules well. Compare the antinomianism of the hippy—in a condition often attributed to anomie.

(15) *Truth* vs. *belief*. The distinction between rule-governed and contingency-shaped behavior resolves an issue first raised in its modern form by C. S. Peirce, William James, and John Dewey:

the distinction between truth and belief. Truth is concerned with rules and rules for the transformation for rules. And it has the objectivity associated with analyses of contingencies of reinforcement. Belief is a matter of probability of action and the probability is a function of the contingencies—either the unanalyzed contingencies to be found in the environment or the contingencies contrived by a culture in teaching the truth.

(16) *Reason* vs. *passion* (or vs. *instinct* or vs. *nature*). "The greatest philosopher in the world," said Pascal, "standing on a plank broader than needed to support him but over a precipice, will be controlled by his imagination even though his reason convinces him that he is safe." It is not his imagination but earlier contingencies which evoke the behavior of being afraid (and some of these contingencies may be phylogenic). Reason, on the other hand, refers to an analysis of the actual contingencies, which might lead to a rule such as: "You may stand on the plank without falling." The conflict is between contingencies; each set controls its own response, and the responses are incompatible.

"The heart has its reasons which reason cannot know." Pascal may have been talking about reason and passion, but passion was not just emotion. Contingencies of reinforcement are "reasons" for acting, and when an analysis of these reasons gives rise to rules which govern effective action, it is not a pun to equate the result with reason in general. The physiological distinction between the head and the heart is, of course, now out of date, and so presumably is that between autonomic and skeletal nervous systems. We may appear to abandon reason when we "fly into a blind rage," but the head is involved in this as much as the heart, the skeletal as much as the autonomic nervous system. Nor will a distinction between instinctive and learned behavior suffice. Pascal seems to be saying simply that rule-governed and contingency-shaped behavior are different and that the former cannot simulate all the latter. Contingencies contain reasons which rules can never specify.

7   The phylogeny and ontogeny of behavior

Parts of the behavior of an organism concerned with the internal economy, as in respiration or digestion, have always been accepted as "inherited," and there is no reason why some responses to the external environment should not also come ready-made in the same sense. It is widely believed that many students of behavior disagree. The classical reference is to John B. Watson (164):

> I should like to go one step further now and say, "Give me a dozen healthy infants, well-formed, and my own specified world to bring them up in and I'll guarantee to take any one at random and train him to become any type of specialist I might select—doctor, lawyer, artist, merchant-chief and, yes, even beggerman and thief, regardless of his talents, penchants, tendencies, abilities, vocations, and race of his ancestors." I am going beyond my facts and I admit it, but so have the advocates of the contrary and they have been doing it for many thousands of years.

Watson was not denying that a substantial part of behavior is inherited. His challenge appears in the first of four chapters describing "how man is equipped to behave at birth." As an enthusiastic specialist in the psychology of learning he went beyond his facts to emphasize what could be done in spite of genetic limitations. He was actually, as Gray (57) has pointed out, "one of the earliest and one of the most careful workers in the area of animal ethology." Yet he is probably

172

responsible for the persistent myth of what has beeen called "behaviorism's counterfactual dogma" (67). And it is a myth. No reputable student of animal behavior has ever taken the position "that the animal comes to the laboratory as a virtual *tabula rasa,* that species differences are insignificant, and that all responses are about equally conditionable to all stimuli" (26).

But what does it mean to say that behavior is inherited? Lorenz (93) has noted that ethologists are not agreed on "the concept of 'what we formerly called innate.' " Insofar as the behavior of an organism is simply the physiology of an anatomy, the inheritance of behavior is the inheritance of certain bodily features, and there should be no problem concerning the meaning of "innate" that is not raised by any genetic trait. Perhaps we must qualify the statement that a man inherits a visual reflex, but we must also qualify the statement that he inherits his eye color.

If the anatomical features underlying behavior were as conspicuous as the wings of *Drosophila,* we should describe them directly and deal with their inheritance in the same way, but at the moment we must be content with so-called behavioral manifestations. We describe the behaving organism in terms of its gross anatomy, and we shall no doubt eventually describe the behavior of its finer structures in much the same way, but until then we analyze behavior without referring to fine structures and are constrained to do so even when we wish to make inferences about them.

What features of behavior will eventually yield a satisfactory genetic account? Some kind of inheritance is implied by such concepts as "racial memory" or "death instinct," but a sharper specification is obviously needed. The behavior observed in mazes and similar apparatuses may be "objective," but it is not described in dimensions which yield a meaningful genetic picture. Tropisms and taxes are somewhat more readily quantified, but not all behavior can be thus formulated, and organisms selected for breeding according to tropistic or taxic performances may still differ in other ways (43).

The probability that an organism will behave in a given way is a more promising datum, but very little has been done in studying its genetics. Modes of inheritance are not, however, the only issues.

The provenance of behavior

Upon a given occasion we observe that an animal displays a certain kind of behavior—learned or unlearned. We describe its topography and evaluate its probability. We discover variables, genetic or environmental, of which the probability is a function. We then undertake to predict or control the behavior. All this concerns a current state of the organism. We have still to ask where the behavior (or the structures which thus behave) came from. What we may call the ontogeny of behavior can be traced to contingencies of reinforcement, and in a famous passage Pascal suggested that ontogeny and phylogeny have something in common. "Habit," he said, "is a second nature which destroys the first. But what is this nature? Why is habit not natural? I am very much afraid that nature is itself only first habit as habit is second nature."

The provenance of "first habit" has an important place in theories of the evolution of behavior. A given response is in a sense strengthened by consequences which have to do with the survival of the individual and the species. A given form of behavior leads not to reinforcement but to procreation. (Sheer reproductive activity does not, of course, always contribute to the survival of a species, as the problems of overpopulation remind us. A few well-fed breeders presumably enjoy an advantage over a larger but impoverished population. The advantage may also be selective. It has recently been suggested (169) that some forms of behavior such as the defense of a territory have an important effect in restricting breeding.) Several practical problems raised by what may be called contingencies of selection are remarkably similar to problems which have already been approached experimentally with respect to contingencies of reinforcement.

An identifiable unit. A behavioral process, as a change in frequency of response, can be followed only if it is possible to count responses. The topography of an operant need not be completely fixed, but some defining property must be available to identify instances. An emphasis upon the occurrence of a repeatable unit distinguishes an experimental analysis of behavior from historical or anecdotal accounts. A similar requirement is recognized in ethology. As Julian Huxley has said, "This concept . . . of unit releasers which act as specific key stimuli unlocking genetically determined unit behavior patterns . . . is probably the most important single contribution of Lorenzian ethology to the science of behavior" (73).

The action of stimuli. Operant reinforcement not only strengthens a given response; it brings the response under the control of a stimulus. But the stimulus does not elicit the response as in a reflex; it merely sets the occasion upon which the response is more likely to occur. The ethologists' "releaser" also simply sets an occasion. Like the discriminative stimulus, it increases the probability of occurrence of a unit of behavior but does not force it. The principal difference between a reflex and an instinct is not in the complexity of the response but in, respectively, the eliciting and releasing actions of the stimulus.

Origins of variations. Ontogenic contingencies remain ineffective until a response has occurred. The rat must press the lever at least once "for other reasons" before it presses it "for food." There is a similar limitation in phylogenic contingencies. An animal must emit a cry at least once for other reasons before the cry can be selected as a warning because of the advantage to the species. It follows that the entire repertoire of an individual or species must exist prior to ontogenic or phylogenic selection, but only in the form of minimal units. Both phylogenic and ontogenic contingencies "shape" complex forms of behavior from relatively undifferentiated material. Both processes are favored if the organism shows an extensive, undifferentiated repertoire.

Programmed contingencies. It is usually not practical to condition a complex operant by waiting for an instance to occur and then reinforcing it. A terminal performance must be reached through intermediate contingencies (programmed instruction). In a demonstration experiment a rat pulled a chain to obtain a marble from a rack, picked up the marble with its forepaws, carried it to a tube projecting two inches above the floor of its cage, lifted it to the top of the tube, and dropped it inside. "Every step in the process had to be worked out through a series of approximations since the component responses were not in the original repertoire of the rat" (129). The "program" was as follows. The rat was reinforced for any movement which caused a marble to roll over any edge of the floor of its cage, then only over the edge on one side of the cage, then over only a small section of the edge, then over only that section slightly raised, and so on. The raised edge became a tube of gradually diminishing diameter and increasing height. The earlier member of the chain, release of the marble from the rack, was added later. Other kinds of programming have been used to establish subtle stimulus control to sustain behavior in spite of infrequent reinforcement, and so on (152).

A similar programming of complex phylogenic contingencies is familiar in evolutionary theory. The environment may change, demanding that behavior which contributes to survival for a given reason become more complex. Quite different advantages may be responsible for different stages. To take a familiar example, the electric organ of the eel could have become useful in stunning prey only after developing something like its present power. Must we attribute the completed organ to a single complex mutation, or were intermediate stages developed because of other advantages? Much weaker currents, for example, may have permitted the eel to detect the nature of objects with which it was in contact. The same question may be asked about behavior. Pascal's "first habit" must often have been the product of "programmed instruction." Many of the complex phylogenic contingencies which now seem to sustain behavior must have been reached through intermediate stages in which less complex forms had lesser but still effective consequences.

The need for programming is a special case of a more general principle. We do not explain any system of behavior simply by demonstrating that it works to the advantage of, or has "net utility" for, the individual or species. It is necessary to show that a given advantage is contingent upon behavior in such a way as to alter its probability.

Adventitious contingencies.   It is not true, as Lorenz (93) has asserted, that "adaptiveness is always the irrefutable proof that this process [of adaptation] has taken place." Behavior may have advantages which have played no role in its selection. The converse is also true. Events which follow behavior but are not necessarily produced by it may have a selective effect. A hungry pigeon placed in an apparatus in which a food dispenser operates every twenty seconds regardless of what the pigeon is doing acquires a stereotyped response which is shaped and sustained by wholly coincidental reinforcement. The behavior is often "ritualistic"; we call it superstitious (132). There is presumably a phylogenic parallel. All current characteristics of an organism do not necessarily contribute to its survival and procreation, yet they are all nevertheless "selected." Useless structures with associated useless functions are as inevitable as superstitious behavior. Both become more likely as organisms become more sensitive to contingencies. It should occasion no surprise that behavior has not perfectly adjusted to either ontogenic or phylogenic contingencies.

Unstable and intermittent contingencies. Both phylogenic and ontogenic contingencies are effective even though intermittent. Different schedules of reinforcement generate different patterns of changing probabilities. If there is a phylogenic parallel, it is obscure. A form of behavior generated by intermittent selective contingencies is presumably likely to survive a protracted period in which the contingencies are not in force, because it has already proved powerful enough to survive briefer periods, but this is only roughly parallel with the explanation of the greater resistance to extinction of intermittently reinforced operants.

Changing contingencies. Contingencies also change, and the behaviors for which they are responsible then change too. When ontogenic contingencies specifying topography of response are relaxed, the topography usually deteriorates; and when reinforcements are no longer forthcoming, the operant undergoes extinction. Darwin discussed phylogenic parallels in *The Expression of Emotions in Man and Animals.* His "serviceable associated habits" were apparently both learned and unlearned, and he seems to have assumed that ontogenic contingencies contribute to the inheritance of behavior, at least in generating responses which may then have phylogenic consequences. The behavior of the domestic dog in turning around before lying down on a smooth surface may have been selected by contingencies under which the behavior made a useful bed in grass or brush. If dogs now show this behavior less frequently, it is presumably because a sort of phylogenic extinction has set in. The domestic cat shows a complex response of covering feces which must once have had survival value with respect to predation or disease. The dog has been more responsive to the relaxed contingencies arising from domestication or some other change in predation or disease, and shows the behavior in vestigial form.

Multiple contingencies. An operant may be affected by more than one kind of reinforcement, and a given form of behavior may be traced to more than one advantage to the individual or the species. Two phylogenic or ontogenic consequences may work together or oppose each other in the development of a given response and presumably show "algebraic summation" when opposed.

Social contingencies. The contingencies responsible for social behavior raise special problems in both phylogeny and ontogeny. In the development of a language the behavior of a speaker can become more elaborate only as listeners become sensitive to elaborated speech. A similarly coordinated development must be assumed in the phylogeny of social behavior. The dance of the bee returning from a successful foray can have advantageous effects for the species only when other bees behave appropriately with respect to it, but they cannot develop the behavior until the dance appears. The terminal system must have required a kind of subtle programing in which the behaviors of both "speaker" and "listener" passed through increasingly complex stages. A bee returning from a successful foray may behave in a special way because it is excited or fatigued, and it may show phototropic responses related to recent visual stimulation. If the strength of the behavior varies with the quantity or quality of food the bee has discovered and with the distance and direction it has flown, then the behavior may serve as an important stimulus to other bees, even though its characteristics have not yet been affected by such consequences. If different bees behave in different ways, then more effective versions should be selected. If the behavior of a successful bee evokes behavior on the part of listeners which is reinforcing to the speaker, then the speaker's behavior should be ontogenically intensified. The phylogenic development of responsive behavior in the listener should contribute to the final system by providing for immediate reinforcement of conspicuous forms of the dance.

The speaker's behavior may become less elaborate if the listener continues to respond to less elaborate forms. We stop someone who is approaching us by pressing our palm against his chest, but he eventually learns to stop upon seeing our outstretched palm. The practical response becomes a gesture. A similar shift in phylogenic contingencies may account for the "intentional movements" of the ethologists.

Behavior may be intensified or elaborated under differential reinforcement involving the stimulation either of the behaving organism or of others. The more conspicuous a superstitious response, for example, the more effective the adventitious contingencies. Behavior is especially likely to become more conspicuous when reinforcement is contingent on the response of another organism. Some ontogenic instances, called "ritualization," are easily demonstrated. Many elaborate rituals of primarily phylogenic origin have been described by ethologists.

Some problems raised by phylogenic contingencies

Lorenz has recently argued that "our absolute ignorance of the physiological mechanisms underlying learning makes our knowledge of the causation of phyletic adaptation seem quite considerable by comparison" (93). But genetic and behavioral processes are studied and formulated in a rigorous way without reference to the underlying biochemistry. With respect to the provenance of behavior we know much more about ontogenic contingencies than phylogenic. Moreover, phylogenic contingencies raise some very difficult problems which have no ontogenic parallels.

The contingencies responsible for unlearned behavior

acted a very long time ago. The natural selection of a given form of behavior, no matter how plausibly argued, remains an inference. We can set up phylogenic contingencies under which a given property of behavior arbitrarily selects individuals for breeding, and thus demonstrate modes of behavioral inheritance, but the experimenter who makes the selection is performing a function of the natural environment which also needs to be studied. Just as the reinforcements arranged in an experimental analysis must be shown to have parallels in "real life" if the results of the analysis are to be significant or useful, so the contingencies which select a given behavioral trait in a genetic experiment must be shown to play a plausible role in natural selection.

Although ontogenic contingencies are easily subjected to an experimental analysis, phylogenic contingencies are not. When the experimenter has shaped a complex response, such as dropping a marble into a tube, the provenance of the behavior raises no problem. The performance may puzzle anyone seeing it for the first time, but it is easily traced to recent, possibly recorded, events. No comparable history can be invoked when a spider is observed to spin a web. We have not seen the phylogenic contingencies at work. All we know is that spiders of a given kind build more or less the same kind of web. Our ignorance often adds a touch of mystery. We are likely to view inherited behavior with a kind of awe not inspired by acquired behavior of similar complexity.

The remoteness of phylogenic contingencies affects our scientific methods, both experimental and conceptual. Until we have identified the variables of which an event is a function, we tend to invent causes. Learned behavior was once commonly attributed to "habit," but an analysis of contingencies of reinforcement has made the term unnecessary. "Instinct," as a hypothetical cause of phylogenic behavior, has had a longer life. We no longer say that our rat possesses a marble-dropping habit, but we are still likely to say that our spider has a web-spinning instinct. The concept of instinct has been severely criticized and is now used with caution or altogether avoided, but explanatory entities serving a similar function still survive in the writings of many ethologists.

A "mental apparatus," for example, no longer finds a useful place in the experimental analysis of behavior, but it survives in discussions of phylogenic contingencies. Here are a few sentences from the writings of prominent ethologists which refer to consciousness or awareness: "The young gosling . . . gets imprinted upon its mind the image of the first moving object it sees" (W. H. Thorpe, 158); "the infant expresses the inner state of contentment by smiling" (Julian Huxley, 73); "[herring gulls show a] lack of insight into the ends served by their activities" (Tinbergen, 159); "[chimpanzees were unable] to communicate to others the unseen things in their minds" (Frankenberger and Kortlandt, 85).

In some mental activities awareness may not be critical, but other cognitive activities are invoked. Thorpe (158) speaks of a disposition "which leads the animal to pay particular attention to objects of a certain kind." What we observe is simply that objects of a certain kind are especially effective stimuli. The ontogenic contingencies which generate the behavior called "paying attention" presumably have phylogenic parallels. Other mental activities frequently mentioned by ethologists include "organizing experience" and "discovering relations." Expressions of all these sorts show that we have not yet accounted for the behavior in terms of contingencies, phylogenic or ontogenic. Unable to show how the organism can behave effectively under complex circumstances, we endow it with a special cognitive ability which permits it to do so.

Other concepts replaced by a more effective analysis include "need" or "drive" and "emotion." In ontogenic behavior we no longer say that a given set of environmental conditions first gives rise to an inner state which the organism then expresses or resolves by behaving in a given way. We no longer represent relations among emotional and motivational variables as relations among such states, as in saying that hunger overcomes fear. We no longer use dynamic analogies or metaphors, as in explaining sudden action as the overflow or bursting out of dammed-up needs or drives. If these are common practices in ethology, it is evidently because the functional relations they attempt to formulate are not clearly understood.

Another kind of innate endowment, particularly likely to appear in explanations of human behavior, takes the form of "traits" or "abilities." Though often measured quantitatively, their dimensions are meaningful only in placing the individual with respect to a population. The behavior measured is almost always obviously learned. To say that intelligence is inherited is not to say that specific forms of behavior are inherited. Phylogenic contingencies conceivably responsible for "the selection of intelligence" do not specify responses. What has been selected appears to be a susceptibility to ontogenic contingencies, leading particularly to a greater speed of conditioning and the capacity to maintain a larger repertoire without confusion.

It is often said that an analysis of behavior in terms of ontogenic contingencies "leaves something out of account," and this is true. It leaves out of account habits, ideas, cognitive processes, needs, drives, traits, and so on. But it does not neglect the facts upon which these concepts are based. It seeks a more effective formulation of the very contingencies to which those who use such concepts must eventually turn to explain their explanations. The strategy has been highly successful at the ontogenic level, where the contingencies are relatively clear. As the nature and mode of operation of phylogenic contingencies come to be better understood, a similar strategy should yield comparable advantages.

Identifying phylogenic and ontogenic variables

The significance of ontogenic variables may be assessed by holding genetic conditions as constant as possible—for example, by studying "pure" strains or identical twins. The technique has a long history. According to Plutarch (*De Puerorum Educatione*) Licurgus, a Spartan, demonstrated the importance of environment by raising two puppies from the same litter so that one became a good hunter while the other preferred food from a plate. On the other hand, genetic variables may be assessed either by studying organisms upon which the environment has had little opportunity to act (because they are newborn or have been reared in a controlled environment) or by comparing groups subject to extensive, but on the average probably similar, environmental histories. Behavior exhibited by most of the members of a species is often accepted as inherited if it is unlikely that all the members could have been exposed to relevant ontogenic contingencies.

When contingencies are not obvious, it is perhaps unwise to call any behavior either inherited or acquired. Field observations, in particular, will often not permit a distinction. Friedmann (50) has described the behavior of the African honey guide as follows:

> When the bird is ready to begin guiding, it either comes to a person and starts a repetitive series of churring notes or it stays where it is and begins calling. . . .
> As the person comes to within 15 or 20 feet . . . the bird flies off with an initial conspicuous downward dip, and then goes off to another tree, not necessarily in sight of the follower, in fact more often out of sight than not. Then it waits there, churring loudly until the follower again nears it, when the action is repeated. This goes on until the vicinity of the bees' nest is reached. Here the bird suddenly ceases calling and perches quietly in a tree nearby. It waits there for the follower to open the hive, and it usually remains there until the person has departed with his loot of honey-comb, when it comes down to

the plundered bees' nest and begins to feed on the bits of comb left strewn about.

The author is quoted as saying that the behavior is "purely instinctive," but it is possible to explain almost all of it in other ways. If we assume that honey guides eat broken bees' nests and cannot eat unbroken nests, that men (not to mention baboons and ratels) break bees' nests, and that birds more easily discover unbroken nests, then only one other assumption is needed to explain the behavior in ontogenic terms. We must assume that the response which produces the churring note is elicited either (1) by any stimulus which frequently precedes the receipt of food (comparable behavior is shown by a hungry dog jumping about when food is being prepared for it) or (2) when food, ordinarily available, is missing (the dog jumps about when food is not being prepared for it on schedule). An unconditioned honey guide occasionally sees men breaking nests. It waits until they have gone, and then eats the remaining scraps. Later it sees men near but not breaking nests, either because they have not yet found the nests or have not yet reached them. The sight of a man near a nest, or the sight of man when the buzzing of bees around a nest can be heard, begins to function in either of the ways just noted to elicit the churring response. The first step in the construction of the final pattern is thus taken by the honey guide. The second step is taken by the man (or baboon or ratel, as the case may be). The churring sound becomes a conditioned stimulus in the presence of which a search for bees' nests is frequently successful. The buzzing of bees would have the same effect if the man could hear it.

The next change occurs in the honey guide. When a man approaches and breaks up a nest, his behavior begins to function as a conditioned reinforcer which, together with the fragments which he leaves behind, reinforces churring, which then becomes more probable under the circumstances and emerges primarily as an operant rather than as an emotional response. When this has happened, the geographical arrangements work themselves out naturally. Men learn to move toward the churring sound, and they break nests more often after walking toward nests than after walking in other directions. The honey guide is therefore differentially reinforced when it takes a position which induces men to walk toward a nest. The contingencies are subtle, but we should remember that the final topography is often far from perfect.

As we have seen, contingencies which involve two or more organisms raise special problems. The churring of the honey guide is useless until men respond to it, but men will not respond in an appropriate way until the churring is related to the location of bees' nests. The conditions just described compose a sort of program which could lead to the terminal performance. It may be that the conditions will not often arise, but another characteristic of social contingencies quickly takes over. When one honey guide and one man have entered into this symbiotic arrangement, conditions prevail under which other honey guides and other men will be much more rapidly conditioned. A second man will more quickly learn to go in the direction of the churring sound because the sound is already spatially related to bees' nests. A second honey guide will more readily learn to churr in the right places because men respond in a way which reinforces that behavior. When a large number of birds have learned to guide and a large number of men have learned to be guided, conditions are highly favorable for maintaining the system. (It is said that, where men no longer bother to break bees' nests, they no longer comprise an occasion for churring, and the honey guide turns to the ratel or baboon. The change in contingencies has occurred too rapidly to work through natural selection. Possibly an instinctive response has been unlearned, but the effect is more plausibly interpreted as the extinction of an operant.)

Imprinting is another phenomenon which shows how hard it is to detect the nature and effect of phylogenic contingencies. In Thomas More's *Utopia,* eggs were incubated. The chicks "are no sooner out of the shell, and able to stir about, but they seem to consider those that feed them as their mothers, and follow them as other chickens do the hen that hatched them." Later accounts of imprinting have been reviewed by Gray (57). Various facts suggest phylogenic origins: the response of following an imprinted object appears at a certain age; if it cannot appear then, it may not appear at all; and so on. Some experiments by Peterson (110), however, suggest that what is inherited is not the behavior of following but a susceptibility to reinforcement by proximity to the mother or mother surrogate. A distress call reduces the distance between mother and chick when the mother responds appropriately, and walking toward the mother has the same effect. Both behaviors may therefore be reinforced (68), but they appear before these ontogenic contingencies come into play and are, therefore, in part at least phylogenic. In the laboratory, however, other behaviors can be made effective which phylogenic contingencies are not likely to have strengthened. A chick can be conditioned to peck a key, for example, by moving an imprinted object toward it when it pecks or to walk away from the object if, through a mechanical arrangement, this behavior actually brings the object closer. To the extent that chicks follow an imprinted object simply because they thus bring the object closer or prevent it from becoming more distant, the behavior could be said to be "species-specific" in the unusual sense that it is the product of *ontogenic* contingencies which prevail for all members of the species.

Ontogenic and phylogenic behaviors are not distinguished by any essence or character. Form of response seldom if ever yields useful classifications. The verbal response *Fire!* may be a command to a firing squad, a call for help, or an answer to the question, *What do you see?* The topography tells us little, but the controlling variables permit us to distinguish three very different verbal operants (141). The sheer forms of instinctive and learned behaviors also tell us little. Animals court, mate, fight, hunt, and rear their young, and they use the same effectors in much the same way in all sorts of learned behavior. Behavior is behavior whether learned or unlearned; it is only the controlling variables which make a difference. The difference is not always important. We might show that a honey guide is controlled by the buzzing of bees rather than by the sight of a nest, for example, without prejudice to the question of whether the behavior is innate or acquired.

Nevertheless the distinction is important if we are to undertake to predict or control the behavior. Implications for human affairs have often affected the design of research and the conclusions drawn from it. A classical example concerns the practice of exogamy. Popper (114) writes:

> Mill and his psychologistic school of sociology . . . would try to explain [rules of exogamy] by an appeal to 'human nature,' for instance to some sort of instinctive aversion against incest (developed perhaps through natural selection . . .); and something like this would also be the naïve or popular explanation. [From Marx's] point of view . . . however, one could ask whether it is not the other way round, that is to say, whether the apparent instinct is not rather a product of education, the effect rather than the cause of the social rules and traditions demanding exogamy and forbidding incest. It is clear that these two approaches correspond exactly to the very ancient problem whether social laws are "natural" or "conventions." . . .

Much earlier, in his *Supplement to the Voyage of Bougainville,* Diderot (40) considered the question of whether there is a natural basis for sexual modesty or shame (*pudeur*). Though he was writing nearly a hundred years before Darwin, he pointed to a possible basis for natural selection. "The pleasures of love are followed by a weakness which puts one at the mercy of one's enemies. That is the only natural thing about modesty; the rest is convention." Those who are preoccupied with sex are exposed to attack (indeed, may be stimulating attack); hence, those who engage in sexual behavior under cover are more likely to breed successfully. Here are phylogenic contingencies which either make sexual behavior under cover stronger than sexual behavior in the open or reinforce the taking of cover when sexual behavior is strong. Ontogenic contingencies through which organisms seek cover to avoid disturbances during sexual activity are also plausible.

The issue has little to do with the character of incestuous or sexual behavior, or with the way people "feel" about it. The basic distinction is between provenances. And provenance is important because it tells us something about how behavior can be supported or changed. Most of the controversy concerning heredity and environment has arisen in connection with the practical control of behavior through the manipulation of relevant variables.

Interrelations among phylogenic and ontogenic variables

The ways in which animals behave compose a sort of taxonomy of behavior comparable to other taxonomic parts of biology. Only a very small percentage of existing species has as yet been investigated. (A taxonomy of behavior may indeed be losing ground as new species are discovered.) Moreover, only a small part of the repertoire of any species is ever studied (see Note 7.3). Nothing approaching a fair sampling of species-specific behavior is therefore ever likely to be made.

Specialists in phylogenic contingencies often complain that those who study learned behavior neglect the genetic limitations of their subjects, as the comparative anatomist might object to conclusions drawn from the intensive study of a single species. Beach, for example, has written (12): "Many ... appear to believe that in studying the rat they are studying all or nearly all that is important in behavior. . . . How else are we to interpret . . . [a] 457-page opus which is based exclusively upon the performance of rats in bar-pressing sit-

uations but is entitled simply *The Behavior of Organisms?*"
There are many precedents for concentrating on one species
(or at most a very few species) in biological investigations.
Mendel discovered the basic laws of genetics—in the garden
pea. Morgan worked out the theory of the gene—for the
fruitfly. Sherrington investigated the integrative action of
the nervous system—in the dog and cat. Pavlov studied the
physiological activity of the cerebral cortex—in the dog.

In the experimental analysis of behavior many species differences are minimized. Stimuli are chosen to which the
species under investigation can respond and which do not
elicit or release disrupting responses: visual stimuli are not
used if the organism is blind, or very bright lights if they
evoke evasive action. A response is chosen which may be
emitted at a high rate without fatigue and which will operate
recording and controlling equipment: we do not reinforce
a monkey when it pecks a disk with its nose or a pigeon when
it trips a toggle switch—though we might do so if we wished.
Reinforcers are chosen which are indeed reinforcing, either
positively or negatively. In this way species differences in
sensory equipment, in effector systems, in susceptibility to
reinforcement, and in possibly disruptive repertoires are
minimized. The data then show an extraordinary uniformity
over a wide range of species. For example, the processes of
extinction, discrimination, and generalization, and the performances generated by various schedules of reinforcement
are reassuringly similar. (Those who are interested in fine
structure may interpret these practices as minimizing the
importance of sensory and motor areas in the cortex and emotional and motivational areas in the brain stem, leaving for
study the processes associated with nerve tissue as such,
rather than with gross anatomy.) Although species differences exist and should be studied, an exhaustive analysis of
the behavior of a single species is as easily justified as the
study of the chemistry or microanatomy of nerve tissue in one
species.

A rather similar objection has been lodged against the extensive use of domesticated animals in laboratory research (78). Domesticated animals offer many advantages. They are more easily handled, they thrive and breed in captivity, they are resistant to the infections encountered in association with men, and so on. Moreover, we are primarily interested in the most domesticated of all animals—man. Wild animals are, of course, different—possibly as different from domesticated varieties as some species are from others, but both kinds of differences may be treated in the same way in the study of basic processes.

The behavioral taxonomist may also argue that the contrived environment of the laboratory is defective since it does not evoke characteristic phylogenic behavior. A pigeon in a small enclosed space pecking a disk which operates a mechanical food dispenser is behaving very differently from pigeons at large. But in what sense is this behavior not "natural"? If there is a natural phylogenic environment, it must be the environment in which a given kind of behavior evolved. But the phylogenic contingencies responsible for current behavior lie in the distant past. Within a few thousand years—a period much too short for genetic changes of any great magnitude—all current species have been subjected to drastic changes in climate, predation, food supply, shelter, and so on. Certainly no land mammal is now living in the environment which selected its principal genetic features, behavioral or otherwise. Current environments are almost as "unnatural" as a laboratory. In any case, behavior in a natural habitat would have no special claim to genuineness. What an organism does is a fact about that organism regardless of the conditions under which it does it. A behavioral process is none the less real for being exhibited in an arbitrary setting.

The relative importance of phylogenic and ontogenic contingencies cannot be argued from instances in which unlearned or learned behavior intrudes or dominates. Breland

and Breland (26) have used operant conditioning and programming to train performing animals. They conditioned a
pig to deposit large wooden coins in a "piggy bank." "The
coins were placed several feet from the bank and the pig required to carry them to the bank and deposit them. . . . At
first the pig would eagerly pick up one dollar, carry it to the
bank, run back, get another, carry it rapidly and neatly, and
so on. . . . Thereafter, over a period of weeks the behavior
would become slower and slower. He might run over eagerly
for each dollar, but on the way back, instead of carrying the
dollar and depositing it simply and cleanly, he would repeatedly drop it, root it, drop it again, root it along the way,
pick it up, toss it up in the air, drop it, root it some more,
and so on." They also conditioned a chicken to deliver plastic
capsules containing small toys by moving them toward the
purchaser with one or two sharp straight pecks. The chickens
began to grab at the capsules and "pound them up and down
on the floor of the cage," perhaps as if they were breaking
seed pods or pieces of food too large to be swallowed. Since
other reinforcers were not used, we cannot be sure that these
phylogenic forms of food-getting behavior appeared because
the objects were manipulated under food-reinforcement. The
conclusion is plausible, however, and not disturbing. A shift
in controlling variables is often observed. Under reinforcement on a so-called "fixed-interval schedule," competing behavior emerges at predictable points (103). The intruding
behavior may be learned or unlearned. It may disrupt a performance or, as Kelleher (80) has shown, it may not. The
facts do not show an inherently greater power of phylogenic
contingencies in general. Indeed, the intrusions may occur
in the other direction. A hungry pigeon which was being
trained to guide missiles (143) was reinforced with food on
a schedule which generated a high rate of pecking at a target
projected on a plastic disk. It began to peck at the food as
rapidly as at the target. The rate was too high to permit it
to take grains into its mouth, and it began to starve. A prod-

uct of ontogenic contingencies had suppressed one of the most powerful phylogenic activities. The behavior of civilized man shows the extent to which environmental variables may mask an inherited endowment.

Misleading similarities

Since phylogenic and ontogenic contingencies act at different times and shape and maintain behavior in different ways, it is dangerous to try to arrange their products on a single continuum or to describe them with a single set of terms.

An apparent resemblance concerns intention or purpose (see page 107). Behavior which is influenced by its consequences seems to be directed toward the future. We say that spiders spin webs in order to catch flies and that men set nets in order to catch fish. The "order" is temporal. No account of either form of behavior would be complete if it did not make some reference to its effects. But flies or fish which have not yet been caught cannot affect behavior. Only past effects are relevant. Spiders which have built effective webs have been more likely to leave offspring, and setting a net in a way that has caught fish has been reinforced. Both forms of behavior are therefore more likely to occur again, but for very different reasons.

The concept of purpose has had an important place in evolutionary theory. It is still sometimes said to be needed to explain the variations upon which natural selection operates. In human behavior a "felt intention" or "sense of purpose" which precedes action is sometimes proposed as a current surrogate for future events. Men who set nets "know why they are doing so," and something of the same sort may have produced the spider's web-spinning behavior which then became subject to natural selection. But men behave because of operant reinforcement even though they cannot "state their purpose"; and, when they can, they may simply be describing their behavior and the contingencies responsible for its strength. Self-knowledge is at best a by-product of contingencies; it is not a cause of the behavior generated by them. Even if we could discover a spider's felt intention or sense of purpose, we could not offer it as a cause of the behavior.

Both phylogenic and ontogenic contingencies may seem to "build purpose into" an organism. It has been said that one of the achievements of cybernetics has been to demonstrate that machines may show purpose. But we must look to the construction of the machine, as we look to the phylogeny and ontogeny of behavior, to account for the fact that an ongoing system acts as if it had a purpose.

Another apparent characteristic in common is "adaptation." Both kinds of contingencies change the organism so that it adjusts to its environment in the sense of behaving in it more effectively. With respect to phylogenic contingencies, this is what is meant by natural selection. With respect to ontogeny, it is what is meant by operant conditioning. Successful responses are selected in both cases, and the result is adaptation. But the processes of selection are very different, and we cannot tell from the mere fact that behavior is adaptive which kind of process has been responsible for it.

More specific characteristics of behavior seem to be common products of phylogenic and ontogenic contingencies. Imitation is an example. If we define imitation as behaving in a way which resembles the observed behavior of another organism, the term will describe both phylogenic and ontogenic behavior. But important distinctions need to be made. Phylogenic contingencies are presumably responsible for well-defined responses released by similar behavior (or its products) on the part of others. A warning cry is taken up and passed along by others; one bird in a flock flies off and the others fly off; one member of a herd starts to run and the others start to run. A stimulus acting upon only one member of a group thus quickly affects other members, with plausible phylogenic advantages.

The parrot displays a different kind of imitative behavior. Its vocal repertoire is not composed of inherited responses, each of which, like a warning cry, is released by the sound of a similar response in others. It acquires its imitative behavior ontogenically, but only through an apparently inherited capacity to be reinforced by hearing itself produce familiar sounds. Its responses need not be released by immediately preceding stimuli (the parrot speaks when not spoken to); but an echoic stimulus is often effective, and the response is then a sort of imitation.

A third type of imitative contingency does not presuppose an inherited tendency to be reinforced by behaving as others behave. When other organisms are behaving in a given way, similar behavior is likely to be reinforced, since they would probably not be behaving in that way if it were not. Quite apart from any instinct of imitation, we learn to do what others are doing because we are then likely to receive the reinforcement they are receiving. We must not overlook distinctions of this sort if we are to use or cope with imitation in a technology of behavior.

Aggression is another term which conceals differences in provenance. Inherited repertoires of aggressive responses are elicited or released by specific stimuli. Azrin, for example, has studied the stereotyped, mutually aggressive behavior evoked when two organisms receive brief electric shocks. But he and his associates have also demonstrated that the opportunity to engage in such behavior functions as a reinforcer and, as such, may be used to shape an indefinite number of "aggressive" operants of arbitrary topographies (8). Evidence of damage to others may be reinforcing for phylogenic reasons because it is associated with competitive survival. Competition in the current environment may make it reinforcing for ontogenic reasons. To deal successfully with any specific aggressive act we must respect its provenance. (Emotional responses, the bodily changes we feel when we are aggressive, like sexual modesty or aversion to incest, may

conceivably be the same whether of phylogenic or ontogenic origin; the importance of the distinction is not thereby
reduced.) Konrad Lorenz's recent book *On Aggression* (94)
could be seriously misleading if it diverts our attention from
relevant manipulable variables in the current environment
to phylogenic contingencies which, in their sheer remoteness,
encourage a nothing-can-be-done-about-it attitude.

   The concept of territoriality also often conceals basic differences. Relatively stereotyped behavior displayed in defend-
ing a territory, as a special case of phylogenic aggression,
has presumably been generated by contingencies involving
food supplies, breeding, population density, and so on. But
cleared territory, associated with these and other advantages,
becomes a conditioned reinforcer and as such generates behavior much more specifically adapted to clearing a given
territory. Territorial behavior may also be primarily ontogenic. Whether the territory defended is as small as a spot on
a crowded beach or as large as a sphere of influence in
international politics, we shall not get far in analyzing the
behavior if we recognize nothing more than "a primary passion for a place of one's own" (5) or insist that "animal
behavior provides prototypes of the lust for political power"
(41).

   Several other concepts involving social structure also
neglect important distinctions. A hierarchical pecking order
is inevitable if the members of a group differ with respect to
aggressive behavior in any of the forms just mentioned. There
are therefore several kinds of pecking orders, differing in
their provenances. Some dominant and submissive behaviors
are presumably phylogenic stereotypes; the underdog turns
on its back to escape further attack, but it does not follow
that the vassal prostrating himself before king or priest is
behaving for the same reasons. The ontogenic contingencies
which shape the organization of a large company or governmental administration show little in common with the
phylogenic contingencies responsible for the hierarchy in the

poultry yard. Some forms of human society may resemble the anthill or beehive, but not because they exemplify the same behavioral processes (3).

Basic differences between phylogenic and ontogenic contingencies are particularly neglected in theories of communication. In the inherited signal systems of animals the behavior of a "speaker" furthers the survival of the species when it affects a "listener." The distress call of a chick evokes appropriate behavior in the hen; mating calls and displays evoke appropriate responses in the opposite sex; and so on. De Laguna (39) has suggested that animal calls could be classified as declarations, commands, predictions, and so on, and Sebeok (121) has recently attempted a similar synthesis in modern linguistic terms, arguing for the importance of a science of zoosemiotics.

The phylogenic and ontogenic contingencies leading, respectively, to instinctive signal systems and to verbal behavior are quite different. One is not an early version of the other. Cries, displays, and other forms of communication arising from phylogenic contingencies are particularly insensitive to operant reinforcement. Like phylogenic repertories in general, they are restricted to situations which elicit or release them and hence lack the variety and flexibility which favor operant conditioning. Vocal responses which at least closely resemble instinctive cries have been conditioned, but much less easily than responses using other parts of the skeletal nervous system. The vocal responses in the human child which are so easily shaped by operant reinforcement are not controlled by specific releasers. It was the development of an undifferentiated vocal repertoire which brought a new and important system of behavior within range of operant reinforcement through the mediation of other organisms (141).

Many efforts have been made to represent the products of both sets of contingencies in a single formulation. An utterance, gesture, or display, whether phylogenic or ontogenic, is said to have a referent which is its meaning, the referent or meaning being inferred by a listener. Information theory offers a more elaborate version: the communicating organism selects a message from the environment, reads out relevant information from storage, encodes the message, and emits it; the receiving organism decodes the message, relates it to other stored information, and acts upon it effectively. All these activities, together with the storage of material, may be either phylogenic or ontogenic. The principal terms in such analyses (input, output, sign, referent, and so on) are objective enough, but they do not adequately describe the actual behavior of the speaker or the behavior of the listener as he responds to the speaker. The important differences between phylogenic and ontogenic contingencies must be taken into account in an adequate analysis. It is not true, as Sebeok contends, that "any viable hypothesis about the origin and nature of language will have to incorporate the findings of zoosemiotics." Just as we can analyze and teach imitative behavior without analyzing the phylogenic contingencies responsible for animal mimicry, or study and construct human social systems without analyzing the phylogenic contingencies which lead to the social life of insects, so we can analyze the verbal behavior of man without taking into account the signal systems of other species.

Purpose, adaptation, imitation, aggression, territoriality, social structure, and communication—concepts of this sort have, at first sight, an engaging generality. They appear to be useful in describing both ontogenic and phylogenic behavior and to identify important common properties. Their very generality limits their usefulness, however. A more specific analysis is needed if we are to deal effectively with the two kinds of contingencies and their products.

Note 7.1   Nature or nurture?

The basic issue is not whether behavior is instinctive or learned, as if these adjectives described essences, but whether we have correctly identified the variables responsible for the provenance of behavior as well as those currently in control. Early behaviorists, impressed by the importance of newly discovered environmental variables, found it particularly reinforcing to explain what appeared to be an instinct by showing that it could have been learned, just as ethologists have found it reinforcing to show that behavior attributed to the environment is still exhibited when environmental variables have been ruled out. The important issue is empirical: what *are* the relevant variables?

Whether we can plausibly extrapolate from one species to another is also a question about controlling variables. The ethologist is likely to emphasize differences among species and to object to arguing from pigeons to men, but the environmentalist may object in the same way to the cross-species generalizations of ethologists. If pigeons are not people, neither are graylag geese or apes. To take an important current problem as an example—the population of the world can presumably be kept within bounds without famine, pestilence, or war only if cultural practices associated with procreation can be changed with the aid of education, medicine, and law. It is also possible that man shows or will show when seriously overcrowded a population-limiting instinct, as certain other species appear to do. The question is not whether human procreative behavior is primarily instinctive or learned, or whether the behavior of other species is relevant, but whether the behavior can be controlled through accessible variables.

Extrapolation from one species to another is often felt to be more secure when the species are closely related, but contingencies of survival do not always respect taxonomic classifications. Recent work by Harlow and others on the behavior of infant monkeys is said to be particularly significant for human behavior because monkeys are primates; but so far as a behavioral repertoire is concerned, the human infant is much closer to a kitten or puppy than to an arboreal monkey. The kinship is not in the line of descent, but in the contingencies of survival. The monkey is more likely to survive if infants cling to their mothers, scream and run if left alone, and run to their mothers when frightened. The human baby cannot do much of this, and if it could, the behavior would have no great survival value in a species in which the mother leaves the young while foraging since highly excitable behavior in the infant would attract predators. Mild activity in hunger or physical distress and clinging and sucking when hungry are no doubt important for the human infant, but they lack the extremity of the responses of the infant monkey.

An emphasis on form or structure obscures the difference between inherited and acquired behavior because it means a neglect of the controlling variables in terms of which a distinction can be made. To define imitation simply as behaving as someone else is behaving is to mention stimuli and responses but to neglect the consequences, and it is the consequences which are either phylogenic or ontogenic. To define aggression as behavior which damages others is to fail to make the distinction for the same reasons.

Our increasing knowledge of controlling variables, both phylogenic and ontogenic, has already resolved some traditional issues. Not so long ago it might have been possible to debate whether a pigeon somehow or other learns to build its nest, but now that we have examined the behavior of pigeons under a fairly wide range of contingencies, we can be sure that it does not. A program which would shape the behavior of building a nest, with no contribution whatsoever from genetic endowment, can almost certainly not be arranged. If the pigeon had an inherited capacity to be reinforced by various stages in the construction of a nest, the assignment would be less difficult, but still staggering. It is quite out of the question to suppose that the necessary environmental contingencies arise by accident whenever a pigeon builds a nest. At the same time increasing information about how pigeons do build nests clarifies the phylogenic account.

Behavior which is not characteristic of all members of a species but recurs in more or less the same pattern in a few is likely to be said to show an *underlying* nature characteristic of the species. Thus, de Sade is said to have shown that man's "true instincts were to steal, rape, and murder," even though only a small percentage of men may do these things, at least in de Sade's culture. Without a culture or under extreme provocation, all men may be capable of doing so, but the extremity of the examples offered by de Sade suggests extreme *environmental* circumstances. As we have seen, a schedule of sexual reinforcement may be naturally "stretched" as the amount of behavior required for reinforcement increases with satiation and, on a different time scale, with age.

Note 7.2 Species-specific behavior

A complete inventory of the genetic behavioral endowment of a given species would cover all aspects of its behavior in all possible environments, including

(1) Skeletal and autonomic reflexes to all possible eliciting stimuli, including emotional responses under the most extreme provocation.

(2) All instinctive responses evoked by identifiable releasers in all possible settings, all necessary materials being available.

(3) All the behaviors which may be shaped and maintained by various contingencies of reinforcement, since a species is characterized in part by the positive and negative reinforcers to which it is sensitive and the kinds of topography which are within reach. For example, it is much harder to bring a pigeon under aversive control than a rat, monkey, or man. It is hard to teach a rat to let go of an object by reinforcing it when it does so. It is difficult to shape vocal behavior in most species below man, even when innate responses are common and imitative repertoires easily set up. The speed, order, and direction in which a repertoire can be modified under operant conditioning is also presumably a characteristic of a species.

(An interesting example of the availability of an unusual response in a porpoise arose when an effort was made to demonstrate operant conditioning to daily audiences (115). A female porpoise was reinforced for a new response each day, and all previously conditioned responses were allowed to go unreinforced. Standard responses such as "porpoising," "beaching," and "tail-slapping" made their appearance and were reinforced, one in each performance. The standard repertoire was soon exhausted, however, and the porpoise then began to execute responses which experienced trainers had never seen before and found hard to name or describe. Certain well-defined responses appeared which had previously been observed *only in other strains of porpoises*. These responses would not have been included in an inventory of the strain under observation had it not been for the unusual contingencies which made it highly probable that all available behavior would appear.)

(4) Behavior exhibited under unusual or conflicting sets of contingencies, particularly those involving punishment. (A disposition to neurotic or psychotic behavior and the forms taken by that behavior presumably vary among species.)

(5) Behavior characteristic of all levels of deprivation—extreme hunger or thirst as well as the most complete satiation.

The concept of a "natural environment" is appealing in part because it permits us to neglect behavior in other environments as if it were not characteristic of the species. Ethologists tend to show no interest, for example, in behavior under laboratory conditions or after domestication. Yet everything is the product of natural processes. We make a useful distinction between animals and men although we know that men are animals, we distinguish the natural from the social sciences although we know that society is natural, and we distinguish between natural and synthetic fibers although we know that the behavior of the chemist is as natural as that of a silkworm. There is nothing which is essentially human, social, or synthetic.

The "natural" environment in which the behavior of a species is studied by ethologists is usually only one of the environments in which the species is now living. It is significant that different natural environments often generate different behaviors. Kortlandt and his associates (86) are reported to have found that chimpanzees living in a rain forest differ greatly (are much less "advanced" or "humanized") than plains-dwelling chimpanzees. But which is the natural environment? Is a chimpanzee learning binary arithmetic in a laboratory (45) showing chimpanzee or human behavior? The chimpanzees who "manned" early satellites were conditioned under complex contingencies of reinforcement, and their behavior was promptly described as "almost human," but it was the contingencies which were almost human.

Note 7.3   Interrelations among phylogenic and ontogenic variables

Evolution is not appropriately described as a process of trial and error. A mutation is a trial only to those who insist that evolution has direction or purpose, and unsuccessful or lethal mutations do not disappear because they are errors. These terms are likely to turn up, however, in discussions of the evolution of behavior (rather than, say, of anatomical features) because of the currency of trial-and-error theories of learning. But operant conditioning is not, as we have seen, a matter of trial and error either.

A behavioral mutation is not simply a new form of response; the probability that it will be emitted is as important as its topography. A given topography of sexual behavior may be relevant to survival, but so is the probability that it will be displayed. Any susceptibility to reinforcement, positive or negative, has also presumably evolved by degrees rather than by saltatory changes. If the behavior reinforced by sexual contact has survival value, an increase in the power of the reinforcer should have survival value.

The process of operant conditioning has presumably emerged because of its phylogenic consequences, which must also have favored any increase in its speed. The extent to which a given kind of behavior is susceptible to operant reinforcement must also have been important. The human species took a great step forward when its vocal musculature, previously concerned with the production of responses of phylogenic significance, came under operant control, because the social contingencies responsible for verbal behavior could then begin to operate.

Behavior arising from ontogenic contingencies may make phylogenic contingencies more or less effective. Ontogenic behavior may permit a species to maintain itself in a given environment for a long time and thus make it possible for phylogenic contingencies to operate. There is, however, a more direct contribution. If, through evolutionary selection, a given response becomes easier and easier to condition as an operant, then some phylogenic behavior may have had an ontogenic origin. One of Darwin's "serviceable associated habits" will serve as an example. Let us assume that a dog possesses no instinctive tendency to turn around as it lies down but that lying down in this way is reinforced as an operant by the production of a more comfortable bed. If there are no phylogenic advantages, presumably the readiness with which the response is learned will not be changed by selection. But phylogenic advantages can be imagined: such a bed may be freer of vermin, offer improved visibility with respect to predators or prey, permit quick movement in an emergency, and so on. Dogs in which the response was most readily conditioned must have been most likely to survive and breed. (These and other advantages would increase the dog's susceptibility to operant reinforcement in general, but we are here considering the possibility that a particular response becomes more likely to be conditioned.) Turning around when lying down may have become so readily available as an operant that it eventually appeared without reinforcement. It was then "instinctive." Ontogenic contingencies were responsible for the topography of an inherited response. The argument is rather similar to Waddington's (162) suggestion that useful calluses on the breast of an ostrich, presumably of ontogenic origin, appear before the egg is hatched because a tendency to form calluses has evolved to the point at which the environmental variable (friction) is no longer needed.[1]

Temporal and intensive properties of behavior can also be traced to both ontogenic and phylogenic sources. For example, contingencies of survival and reinforcement both have effects on the speed with which an organism moves in overtaking prey or escaping from predators. A house cat, like its undomesticated relatives, creeps up on its prey slowly and then springs. Relevant contingencies are both phylogenic and ontogenic: by moving slowly the cat comes within jumping range and can then jump more successfully. The stalking pattern is effective because of the characteristic behavior of the prey. If a species comes fairly suddenly into contact with prey which is disturbed by quick movements, the stalking pattern should emerge first at the ontogenic

---

[1] I am indebted to Professor Leslie Reid for bringing Waddington's suggestion, and its behavioral implications, to my attention.

level; but under such conditions, those members of the species most susceptible to differential reinforcement of slow responding should survive and breed. The stalking pattern should then appear more and more quickly, and eventually in the absence of ontogenic contingencies.

Behavior which is not susceptible to operant reinforcement could not have evolved in this way. If the pilomotor response of an enraged cat frightens away its enemies, the disappearance of the enemy may be reinforcing (it could be used, for example, to shape the behavior of pressing a lever), but it is quite unlikely that the consequence has any reinforcing effect on the pilomotor response. It is therefore unlikely that the instinctive behavior had an ontogenic origin.

There are other kinds of interactions among the two kinds of contingencies. Phylogeny comes first and the priority is often emphasized by ethologists, sometimes with the implication that phylogenic problems must be solved before ontogenic contingencies can be studied. Ontogenic changes in behavior affect phylogenic contingencies. A given species does not, as is often said, choose between instinct and intelligence. As soon as a species becomes subject to ontogenic contingencies, phylogenic contingencies become less cogent, for the species can survive with a less adequate phylogenic repertoire. Man did not "choose intelligence over instinct"; he simply developed a sensitivity to ontogenic contingencies which made phylogenic contingencies and their products less important. The phylogenic contingencies still exist but exert less of an effect. The change may have serious consequences. It has often been pointed out, for example, that the ontogenic cultural practices of medicine and sanitation have overruled phylogenic contingencies which would normally maintain or improve the health of the species. The species may suffer when the culture no longer maintains medical and sanitary practices, or when new diseases arise against which only a natural resistance is a defense.

Some phylogenic contingencies must be effective before ontogenic contingencies can operate. The relatively undifferentiated behavior from which operants are selected is presumably a phylogenic product; a large undifferentiated repertoire may have been selected because it made ontogenic contingencies effective. The power of reinforcers must have arisen for similar reasons. It is tempting to say that food is reinforcing because it reduces hunger (Chapter 3), but food in the mouth is reinforcing when not swallowed or ingested, and man and other species eat when not hungry. The capacity to be reinforced by food must be traced to natural selection. Behavior reinforced with food has survival value mainly when an organism is hungry, and organisms which have developed the capacity to be active in getting food *only* when deprived of food have an advantage in being less often needlessly active. A similar variation in the strength of sexual behavior (in most mammals, though not in man) is more obviously of phylogenic origin. In a great many species the male is active sexually only when the behavior is likely to lead to procreation. The bitch in heat emits odors which greatly strengthen sexual behavior in the male dog, and she then cooperates in copulation. It might be argued that this shows a contemporary purpose, as implied in drive-reduction theories: sexual behavior is strong because it leads to fertilization. A plausible connection, however, is to be found in the phylogenic contingencies: under normal contingencies of survival a constantly active sexual behavior when ovulation is not frequent would displace behavior important for survival in other ways. Man appears to be one of a few species which can afford sexual behavior unrelated to ovulation.

The distinction between the inheritance of behavior of specified topography and the inheritance of the capacity to be reinforced by given consequences is relevant not only to imprinting but to the kind of fact offered in support of the concept of a racial unconscious. If archetypal patterns of behavior seem to recur without transmission *via* the environment, it may be because they are independently shaped by recurring contingencies to which racial sensitivities to reinforcement are relevant. The young boy discovering masturbation by himself may seem to be recalling a rhythmic topography exhibited by his ancestors (contributing perhaps to the topography of music and the dance); but the topography may be shaped simply by the reinforcing effects of certain contacts and movements, the capacity to be thus reinforced being possibly all that is inherited.

Common feelings. Inherited behavior may differ from learned in the way we feel about it. What we feel are events in, or states of, our body. When we behave primarily to avoid punishment, we may feel responses conditioned by punishing stimuli. We feel them as shame, guilt, or sin, depending upon the source of the punishment. If a culture punishes incestuous behavior, then any move made toward sexual contact with a close relative will presumably generate conditioned responses which are felt as anxiety. Phylogenic contingencies may induce a man to stay away from incestuous contacts either by providing an innate topography from which such contacts are missing, or by imparting a capacity to be automatically punished by them (when they give rise to an "instinctive abhorrence"). If incestuous contacts are automatically punishing for phylogenic reasons, we may look for a difference in the feelings associated with the avoidance of conditioned and unconditioned aversive stimuli. If the feelings differ, we should be able to decide whether incest is a taboo resulting from an instinctive abhorrence or an abhorrence resulting from a taboo.

Several classical issues which have to do with controlling variables are often stated in terms of feelings. When phylogenic contingencies have generated not only behavior having a specific topography but the capacity to be reinforced by the natural consequences of that behavior, the obvious redundancy may operate as a safety device. It may well be true that mothers "instinctively" nurse their young and are at the same time reinforced when they do so through an inherited sensitivity. The relevance of "pleasurable sensations" in accounting for instinctive behavior is an old theme. Cabanis (33) argued for the importance of the reinforcement. He also reported a curious practice in which a capon was plucked *le ventre*, rubbed with nettles and vinager, and set on eggs. The eggs were said to give relief from the irritation so that the capon continued to set on them and hatch them. By creating a strong aversive stimulus, from which the capon could escape by setting on eggs, the farmers who resorted to this practice created synthetic hens. Cabanis says that the capon continued to care for the hatched chicks, although the behavior could scarcely have been shaped or maintained through the aversive control. Perhaps all domestic chickens, male and female, possess the behavior in some strength (compare the example of the porpoise above).

The fact that an operant shaped by virtue of an inherited susceptibility to reinforcement may duplicate an instinct arising from the same phylogenic contingencies figured prominently in Darwinian discussions of purpose. There seemed to be an advantage in replacing remote and nearly inscrutable contingencies of survival with ontogenic contingencies where purpose referred to accessible and identifiable consequences (see page 106). Samuel Butler (31) argued that a hen felt relief after laying an egg and insisted that a poet felt the same kind of relief after writing a poem. We are still likely to say that a man eats to get relief from hunger pangs, and the English language has the idiom of "relieving oneself" to refer to defecation and urination. The argument is close to a theory of reinforcement as drive reduction. Confusion arises from the fact that food is both reinforcing and satiating. The connection is phylogenic: a nourishing substance becomes a reinforcer, so that any behavior leading to its ingestion is likely to be strengthened.

The sucking responses of a newborn infant are probably the best documented instinctive behavior in man. That the tactual and gustatory stimuli inevitably associated with sucking are also reinforcing is a supplementary fact rather than an explanation. The phylogenic contingencies have generated redundant mechanisms.

Note 7.4 Aggression

Aggression is sometimes defined as behavior which expresses feelings of hostility or hate, satisfies a need to hurt, is meant or intended to hurt, or can be traced to aggressive instincts or habits. These definitions remain incomplete until we have defined feelings, needs, meanings, intentions, instincts, and habits. Can aggressive behavior be defined in a better way?

Behavior is not aggressive simply because of its topography. Some forms of response, such as baring the teeth or biting, often turn out to be aggressive (as defined below), but this is not always true. Controlling variables must be specified, among them the variables toward which terms like meaning, need, and instinct point. One variable—the effect of the behavior—is important in traditional usage: behavior is aggressive if it harms others (or threatens to do so). A useful distinction may be drawn between phylogenic and ontogenic effects.

Phylogenic aggression. Tooth-and-claw competition was once the archetypal pattern of natural selection. What evolved was not only efficient teeth and claws but the reflexes and released behaviors in which they played a part. Classical examples with obvious survival value include the aggression of carnivores toward their prey, sexual competition between male and male (the aggression of male against female—in rape—is said to be confined to the human species), a mother's defense of her young, and the protection of a supply of food (the otherwise friendly dog snaps at anyone who tries to take away his bone). These specific contingencies of survival may have given rise to a more general controlling relation. Painful stimuli are associated with combat quite apart from the specific contingencies under which combat makes for survival, and they have come to release aggressive behavior on a great variety of occasions (8). Physical restraint and the absence of characteristic reinforcement ("frustration") are also effective, presumably for similar reasons.

Aggressive behavior of phylogenic origin is accompanied by autonomic responses which contribute to survival at least to the extent that they support vigorous activity. These responses are a major part of what is felt in aggression. Distinctions among jealousy, anger, rage, hatred, and so on, suggest specific phylogenic contingencies. Whether these are different autonomic patterns, or whether what is felt includes more than autonomic behavior, need not be decided here. (The relation of predator to prey is usually regarded as a special case. It may not give rise to "feelings of aggression" although other phylogenic variables may operate in the pursuit or killing of prey.) Many of the dynamic properties of phylogenic aggression remain to be analyzed: eliciting or releasing stimuli become more effective, either in evoking behavior or in arousing feelings, when repeated or when combined with other stimuli having the same effect; a period of active aggression may be followed by a period of quiescence in a kind of satiation which is not simply fatigue; and so on.

Ontogenic aggression. "Damage to others" may act as a reinforcer giving rise to a kind of aggressive behavior under the control of ontogenic variables. When we hurt someone by insulting him, cursing him, or telling him bad news, the topography of our behavior is determined by contingencies arranged by a verbal community. The contingencies have not prevailed long enough to permit any extensive natural selection of the behavior. When we hurt someone by using recently invented weapons, our behavior is also obviously acquired rather than inherited.

It is not enough to define ontogenic aggressive behavior simply by saying that it damages others. What are the dimensions of "damage"? Presumably the actual stimuli which reinforce aggressive action are to be found in the behavior of the recipient as he weeps, cries out, cringes, flees, or gives other signs that he has been hurt. (Counteraggression may be among these behaviors; an aggressive person is reinforced by "getting a rise" out of his opponent.) Aggressive behavior showing a wide range of topographies may be reinforced by these consequences.

Signs of damage also reinforce behavior which is not itself damaging. Thus, they reinforce the spectator at a wrestling or boxing match or professional football game, and he pays admission and watches the match or game because of them. (They are reinforcing even though he does not "identify himself" with the participants; but identification in such a case is also a form of aggressive behavior, largely imitative in nature [135].)

Damage to others may be reinforcing for several reasons. It may function as a conditioned reinforcer because signs of damage have preceded or coincided with reinforcers which do not otherwise have anything to do with aggression. Effective damage to a sexual competitor becomes reinforcing (if it has not been made so by phylogenic contingencies) when it is followed by unchallenged sexual reinforcement. Damage inflicted upon a thief becomes reinforcing when it is followed by the retention or return of possessions.

We have also to consider the possibility that a capacity to be reinforced by signs of damage may have evolved under the phylogenic contingencies which lead to phylogenic aggression. Individuals should have been selected when they behaved not only in such a way as to drive off predators or sexual competitors, but in such a way as to produce any stimuli commonly preceding these effects, such as the signs of damage associated with successful combat. Indeed the topography of combative behavior should be more quickly shaped and maintained by immediate signs of damage than by eventual success, as the details of a boxer's style are more effectively shaped by the immediate consequences of particular blows than by the final knockout.

Among the reinforcers which shape ontogenic aggression are any conditions which provide the opportunity to act aggressively, either phylogenically or ontogenically. If we are to define aggression in terms of its consequences, we should have to include the behavior of a pigeon pecking a key when the reinforcement is access to another pigeon which can be attacked. The reinforcing effect varies with the incitement, either phylogenic or ontogenic. The probability that the pigeon will peck the key varies with the probability that it will attack another pigeon when a pigeon is already present.

The feelings associated with ontogenic aggression will depend mainly upon the autonomic behavior elicited by the same contingencies. If damage to others is reinforcing simply because it has commonly been followed by such a reinforcer as food, the aggression to which it gives rise may be as "cold" as other forms of food-getting behavior. An innate capacity to be reinforced by damage to others traceable to phylogenic contingencies may give rise to the autonomic pattern associated with phylogenic aggression. To say that we are aggressive because we "take pleasure in hurting" adds no more to the analysis than to say that we eat because we take pleasure in eating. Both expressions simply indicate kinds of reinforcers.

Interactions and comparisons. A given instance of aggression can generally be traced to both phylogenic and ontogenic contingencies, since both kinds of variables are generally operative upon a given occasion. The fact that phylogenic contingencies have contributed to the capacity to be reinforced by ontogenic evidences of damage makes the interrelation particularly confusing. It is still worthwhile to look for the effective variables, particularly when an effort is made either to strengthen or weaken aggressive behavior.

The intensity of instinctive aggressive behavior presumably varies roughly with the incitement, at least according to the contingencies originally involved in its selection. If a mother's defense of her young in some modern environment seems exaggerated, we must turn to the original phylogenic contingencies for an explanation. The frequency and energy of ontogenic aggression may range more widely. An intermittent schedule of reinforcement may build a high probability of aggressive behavior even though the net damage is slight. There are natural programming systems having this effect. A man may spend much of his time in the mild aggression called complaining or nagging even though he only rarely evokes signs of damage, such as a burst of anger. He may be programmed into such a condition as the behavior of his listener slowly adapts or extinguishes. Other schedules of differential reinforcement build up violent forms of aggression. Personal systems of attack and counterattack escalate as readily as international if more and more violent behavior is needed to effect damage (to offset improved defenses or to achieve a net positive damage by exceeding the damage done by others). A set of social contingencies in which aggressive behavior escalates has been described elsewhere (135, p. 309); when two or more people are exchanging aggressive blows, the aversive stimulation of a blow received may evoke a harder blow in return.

Aggressive behavior which does not seem commensurate with its consequences is often puzzling. Killing is called "senseless" when relevant variables can not be identified. But aggression is never senseless in the sense of uncaused; we have simply overlooked either a current variable or a history of reinforcement.

Aggression might be defined as behavior which affects other organisms either phylogenically as a threat to their survival or ontogenically as a negative reinforcer. Both effects have opposites: behavior may promote the survival of others and positively reinforce them. There seems to be no antonym for aggression which covers behavior of both phylogenic and ontogenic origin. "Affection" is close; but it refers to feelings rather than to behavior or its consequences, as hatred refers to the emotional accompaniments of aggression. The phylogenic opposite of aggression has survival value with respect to a different object: survival is furthered by aggression toward competitors and by affection toward members of the same species. Maternal care, foraging for and protecting a mate or mates, and sexual behavior are examples of the latter. The consequences are reinforcing either because of an innate capacity to be reinforced by caring for others or because behavior which positively reinforces others is followed by other kinds of positive reinforcement. Both aggression and affection show a kind of reciprocity. We tend to act aggressively toward those who act aggressively toward us and to be affectionate toward those who show us affection.

A surprising number of the antonyms of aggression have aversive overtones. "Care," "solicitude," and "concern" all suggest anxiety lest the objects of affection be harmed, possibly coupled with a fear that they will no longer show affection. It has often been pointed out that love is close to hatred and that affection and aggression seem to be combined in certain forms of sadistic behavior. This has nothing to do with the essence of love or hatred or with anything in common in the accompanying feelings. It is the consequences which are close to one another and only then because both kinds of effects may be mediated by one person. Affectionate behavior, particularly when built up by intermittent reinforcement, may have strong aversive consequences which in turn evoke aggressive behavior toward the object of affection.

A tendency to kill members of the same species could promote the survival of the species. There may be advantages in limiting a population, in selecting or training especially good fighters who become valuable to the species when they turn on its enemies, and even in cannibalism, in an extreme emergency, as a way of preserving at least a few members. In general, however, intraspecies aggression is rare.

> The tyger preys not on the tyger brood;
> Man only is the common foe of man (54).

This is sometimes explained by saying that aggression toward members of one's own species is opposed by an instinctive inhibition, except in men. The concept of inhibition is not needed. We do not say that a carnivore refrains from eating vegetables because of an inhibition; its ingestive behavior is evoked only by certain kinds of stimuli. Even if it were true that tigers kill all animals except tigers, we should not need to hypothesize that tiger-killing is inhibited by a special mechanism. Contingencies of survival will explain a discrimination among kinds of prey.

Ontogenic intraspecies aggression also threatens the species. Cultural practices which minimize aggression against other members of a group, such as taboos against killing members of one's own family, tribe, or nation (note the definition of murder), obviously strengthen the group. The cultural sanctions are usually aversive: intragroup aggression is suppressed by punishment or the threat of punishment. This is inhibition in the original meaning of the word: the aggression is forbidden or interdicted. If we do not kill members of our own group, it is not because of some inner inhibition but because of identifiable variables in our culture.

Suicide.   It is difficult to see how aggressive action toward oneself could have survival value, particularly in the ultimate form of suicide. If suicidal behavior arose as a mutation, it should quickly have eliminated itself. Phylogenic contingencies in which the death of an individual benefits the species would probably favor the selection of behavior in which other members do the killing. (If intraspecies killing threatens the survival of the species, there is a remote chance that suicide would have survival value in making such behavior less probable.) Some forms of instinctive behavior may be damaging and possibly lead to the death of those who display them when the damage is associated with consequences having strong survival value. A difficult but necessary migration may provide the necessary conditions. So may a change of environment if behavior which once had survival value becomes damaging or lethal in a new setting.

Ontogenic contingencies are more likely to generate behavior which damages the behaver. Behavior which damages others is often damaging to the behaver in the sense that it exposes him to damage or leads him to accept damage without struggle. We may come to submit to damaging consequences because of ultimate positive reinforcement. We take a cold plunge because of the exhilarating glow which follows, submit to danger because we are reinforced by subsequent escape, and hurt ourselves so that others will feel sorry for us and give us attention. We submit to aversive stimuli in order to escape from stimuli which are even more aversive: we go to the dentist and submit to his drill to escape from a toothache. The religious flagellant whips himself to escape from conditioned aversive stimulation which he feels as guilt or a sense of sin. Animals can be induced to take a shock if, in doing so, they are then reinforced positively or negatively, and with careful programming they will continue to do so even when the shock becomes intense.

The ethical group arranges contingencies on this pattern if it gains when an individual inflicts damage on himself. Thus, the group may support a custom of suicide in the old or infirm. A culture which makes much of personal honor may support the practice of hara-kiri or induce heroes to expose themselves to necessarily fatal circumstances. Contingencies arranged by religious systems support mortification and maceration as well as martyrdom. A philosophy of "acceptance of life" recommends submission to aversive and potentially damaging conditions.

Accidental damaging consequences presumably do not define aggression. Although accidental killing was once punished by death, it is now recognized that such measures have no deterrent effect. Nor is the accidental killing of oneself counted as aggression. The man who runs his motor to keep his parked car warm or smokes a great many cigarettes or the citizens of a city who allow the air to be heavily polluted are not, strictly speaking, committing suicide. Nor is the culture whose practices prove fatal when the environment changes. Sanitation and medicine have emerged from ontogenic contingencies having to do with the avoidance of ill health and death, but it is conceivable that a group which maximize sanitation and medicine may be most vulnerable to a new virus, such as might arise from a mutation or come from some other part of the universe. Practices which up to now have had survival value, although of ontogenic origin, would then prove to have been lethal. Escalation of military power under ontogenic contingencies which seem to favor survival has frequently led to the destruction of civilizations and in the age of nuclear power may lead to the destruction of life on earth.

Death instinct. The fact that so much human behavior leads to death has suggested that man possesses a death instinct. There are many different kinds of phylogenic and ontogenic contingencies having this effect, however, and we are not likely to understand them or be able to do much about them if our attention is diverted from effective variables to a fictional cause. Men do behave in ways which are often damaging and even fatal to themselves and others, but a death instinct implies phylogenic contingencies in which this would have survival value. The ontogenic contingencies are much more plausible and conspicuous, and even there the contingencies involve more than damage or death.

The environmental solution.   The four solutions to the problem of aggression discussed in Chapter 3 deserve further comment. The sybaritic solution is to design relatively harmless ways in which people can be aggressive: a man beats another at tennis or chess rather than with a stick; he reads sadistic literature, sees sadistic movies, and watches sadistic sports. These practices probably reinforce aggression rather than "drain it off," unless the preoccupation with harmless forms leaves no time for harmful. To suppress aggression by punishment in the "puritan" solution is simply to shift the role of the aggressor. A chemical solution, as we have noted, may exist in the form of tranquilizers

The environmental solution becomes more plausible the more we know about the contingencies. Phylogenic aggression may be minimized by minimizing eliciting and releasing stimuli. Behavior acquired because of an inherited tendency to be reinforced by damage to others can be minimized by breaking up the contingencies—by creating a world in which very little behavior causes the kinds of damage which are reinforcing. We can avoid making damage-to-others a conditioned reinforcer by making sure that other reinforcements are not contingent upon behavior which damages. (To put it roughly, people who get what they want without hurting others are less likely to be reinforced by hurting others.) In short, we can solve the problem of aggression by building a world in which damage to others has no survival value and, for that or other reasons, never functions as a reinforcer. It will necessarily be a world in which non-aggressive behaviors are abundantly reinforced on effective schedules in other ways.

Note 7.5   A possible example of programmed phylogenic contingencies

The hypothesis of continental drift, which has recently received surprising confirmation, may explain certain cases of complex migratory behavior which are otherwise quite puzzling. Both European and American eels, for example, when ready to breed, leave their freshwater environments and journey to overlapping deep-sea breeding grounds in the middle Atlantic. The adults die there, but the young return to the appropriate continents. It is difficult to imagine that this extremely complex pattern in the behavior of both parents and offspring could have arisen in its present form through random mutations, selected by the survival of individuals possessing appropriate behavior. If we assume, however, that Europe and North America were once contiguous and that they moved only very slowly apart, the first journeys of the eels, or of those earlier forms which evolved as eels, could have been quite short. The present extreme behavior would have been gradually "shaped" through survival as the phylogenic contingencies changed. Each year only a slight extension of behavior would be demanded—possibly only a matter of inches—and the new contingencies could be met by most members of the species. Just as an animal with little or no innate tendency to home can be trained by releasing it at slowly increasing distances, so early forms of eels were "trained" by phylogenic contingencies as the distances to be traversed were extended by continental drift. This would help to explain the fact that the breeding grounds of European and American eels are close together or overlap.

The behavior of salmon in the North Atlantic may be the result of a similar program of phylogenic contingencies.[1]

---

[1] Dr. C. W. McCutchen has called my attention to the fact that Dr. Ronald Fraser in *The Habitable Earth,* published in 1964, points out that the green turtle that now migrates between Brazil and Ascension Island, an annual journey of 1,400 miles each way, may originally have gone at most 100 miles. Dr. Fraser does not discuss the importance of this fact for phylogenic programming.

III A CRITIQUE OF ALTERNATIVE EXPLANATIONS OF BEHAVIOR

8   Behaviorism at fifty

Behaviorism, with an accent on the last syllable, is not the scientific study of behavior but a philosophy of science concerned with the subject matter and methods of psychology. If psychology is a science of mental life—of the mind, of conscious experience—then it must develop and defend a special methodology, which it has not yet done successfully. If it is, on the other hand, a science of the behavior of organisms, human or otherwise, then it is part of biology, a natural science for which tested and highly successful methods are available. The basic issue is not the nature of the stuff of which the world is made or whether it is made of one stuff or two but rather the dimensions of the things studied by psychology and the methods relevant to them.

Mentalistic or psychic explanations of human behavior almost certainly originated in primitive animism. When a man dreamed of being at a distant place in spite of incontrovertible evidence that he had stayed in his bed, it was easy to conclude that some part of him had actually left his body. A particularly vivid memory or a hallucination could be explained in the same way. The theory of an invisible, detachable self eventually proved useful for other purposes. It seemed to explain unexpected or abnormal episodes, even to the person behaving in an exceptional way because he was thus "possessed." It also served to explain the inexplicable. An organism as complex as man often seems to behave capriciously. It is tempting to attribute the visible behavior to another organism inside—to a little man or homunculus. The wishes of the little man become the acts of the man observed by his fellows. The inner idea is put into outer words. Inner feelings find outward expression. The explanation is successful, of course, only so long as the behavior of the homunculus can be neglected (see Chapter 9).

Primitive origins are not necessarily to be held against an explanatory principle, but the little man is still with us in relatively primitive form. He was recently the hero of a television program called "Gateways to the Mind," one of a series of educational films sponsored by the Bell Telephone Laboratories and written with the help of a distinguished panel of scientists. The viewer learned, from animated cartoons, that when a man's finger is pricked, electrical impulses resembling flashes of lightning run up the afferent nerves and appear on a television screen in the brain. The little man wakes up, sees the flashing screen, reaches out, and pulls a lever. More flashes of lightning go down the nerves to the muscles, which then contract, as the finger is pulled away from the threatening stimulus. The behavior of the homunculus was, of course, not explained. An explanation would presumably require another film. And it, in turn, another.

The same pattern of explanation is invoked when we are told that the behavior of a delinquent is the result of a disordered personality or that the vagaries of a man under analysis are due to conflicts among his superego, ego, and id. Nor can we escape from the primitive features by breaking the little man into pieces and dealing with his wishes, cognitions, motives, and so on, bit by bit. The objection is not that these things are mental but that they offer no real explanation and stand in the way of a more effective analysis.

It has been about fifty years since the behavioristic objection to this practice was first clearly stated, and it has been about thirty years since it has been very much discussed. A whole generation of psychologists has grown up without really coming into contact with the issue. Almost all current textbooks compromise: rather than risk a loss of adoptions, they define psychology as the science of behavior *and* mental life. Meanwhile the older view has continued to receive strong support from areas in which there has been no comparable attempt at methodological reform. During this period, however, an effective experimental science of behavior has emerged. Much or what it has discovered bears on the basic issue. A restatement of radical behaviorism would therefore seem to be in order.

A rough history of the idea is not hard to trace. An occasional phrase in classic Greek writings which seemed to foreshadow the point of view need not be taken seriously. We may also pass over the early bravado of a La Mettrie who could shock the philosophical bourgeoisie by asserting that man was only a machine. Nor were those who simply preferred, for practical reasons, to deal with behavior rather than with less accessible, but nevertheless acknowledged, mental activities close to what is meant by behaviorism today.[1]

The entering wedge appears to have been Darwin's preoccupation with the continuity of species. In supporting the theory of evolution, it was important to show that man was not essentially different from the lower animals—that every human characteristic, including consciousness and reasoning powers, could be found in other species. Naturalists like Romanes began to collect stories which seemed to show that dogs, cats, elephants, and many other species were conscious and showed signs of reasoning. It was Lloyd Morgan, of course, who questioned this evidence with his Canon of Parsimony. Were there not other ways of accounting for what

---

[1] The doctrine of parallelism may have prepared the ground with its acknowledgment that the physical aspects of a man's behavior might be accounted for without referring to mental aspects.

looked like signs of consciousness or rational powers? Thorn-dike's experiments at the end of the nineteenth century were in this vein. He showed that the behavior of a cat in escaping from a puzzle-box might seem to show reasoning but could be explained instead as the result of simpler processes. Thorndike remained a mentalist, but he greatly advanced the objective study of behavior which had been attributed to mental processes.

The next step was inevitable: if evidence of consciousness and reasoning could be explained in other ways in animals, why not also in man? And if this was the case, what became of psychology as a science of mental life? It was John B. Watson who made the first clear, if rather noisy, proposal that psychology should be regarded simply as a science of behavior. He was not in a very good position to defend it. He had little scientific material to use in his reconstruction. He was forced to pad his textbook with discussions of the physiology of receptor systems and muscles and with physiological theories which were at the time no more susceptible to proof than the mentalistic theories they were intended to replace. A need for "mediators" of behavior which might serve as objective alternatives to thought processes led him to emphasize sub-audible speech. The notion was intriguing, because one can usually observe oneself thinking in this way, but it was by no means an adequate or comprehensive explanation. He tangled with introspective psychologists by denying the exist-ence of images. He may well have been acting in good faith, for it has been said that he himself did not have visual imagery; but his arguments caused unnecessary trouble. The relative importance of a genetic endowment in explaining behavior proved to be another disturbing digression.

All this made it easy to lose sight of the central argument—that behavior which seemed to be the product of mental activity could be explained in other ways. Moreover, the introspectionists were prepared to challenge it. As late as 1883 Francis Galton could write: "Many persons, especially women and intelligent children, take pleasure in introspection, and strive their very best to explain their mental processes" (51). But introspection was already being taken seriously. The concept of a science of mind in which mental events obeyed mental laws had led to the development of psychophysical methods and to the accumulation of facts which seemed to bar the extension of the principle of parsimony. What might hold for animals did not hold for men because men could see their mental processes.

Curiously enough, part of the answer was supplied by the psychoanalysts, who insisted that, although a man might be able to see some of his mental life, he could not see all of it. The kind of thoughts Freud called "unconscious" took place without the knowledge of the thinker. From an association, verbal slip, or dream it could be shown that a person must have responded to a passing stimulus, although he could not tell you that he had done so. More complex thought processes, including problem solving and verbal play, could also go on without the thinker's knowledge. Freud had devised, and never abandoned faith in, one of the most elaborate mental apparatuses of all time. He nevertheless contributed to the behavioristic argument by showing that mental activity did not, at least, *require* consciousness. His proofs that thinking had occurred without introspective recognition were, indeed, clearly in the spirit of Lloyd Morgan. They were operational analyses of mental life—even though, for Freud, only the unconscious part of it. Experimental evidence pointing in the same direction soon began to accumulate.

But that was not the whole answer. What about the part of mental life which a man can see? It is a difficult question, no matter what one's point of view, partly because it raises the question of what seeing means and partly because the events seen are private. The fact of privacy cannot, of course, be questioned. Each person is in special contact with a small part of the universe enclosed within his own skin. To take a noncontroversial example, he is uniquely subject to certain kinds of proprioceptive and interoceptive stimulation. Though two people may in some sense be said to see the same light or hear the same sound, they cannot feel the same distention of a bile duct or the same bruised muscle. (When privacy is invaded with scientific instruments, the form of stimulation is changed; the scales read by the scientist are not the private events themselves.)

Mentalistic psychologists insist that there are other kinds of events which are uniquely accessible to the owner of the skin within which they occur but which lack the physical dimensions of proprioceptive or interoceptive stimuli. They are as different from physical events as colors are from wave lengths of light. There are even better reasons, therefore, why two people cannot suffer each other's toothaches, recall each other's memories, or share each other's happinesses. The importance assigned to this kind of world varies. For some, it is the only world there is. For others, it is the only part of the world which can be directly known. For still others, it is a special part of what can be known. In any case, the problem of how one knows about the subjective world of another must be faced. Apart from the question of what "knowing" means, the problem is one of accessibility.

Public and private events

One solution, often regarded as behavioristic, is to grant the distinction between public and private events and rule the latter out of scientific consideration. This is a congenial solution for those to whom scientific truth is a matter of convention or agreement among observers. It is essentially the line taken by logical positivism and physical operationism. Hogben (69) has recently redefined "behaviorist" in this spirit. The subtitle of his *Statistical Theory* is "an examination of the contemporary crises in statistical theory from a behaviorist viewpoint," and this is amplified in the following way:

The behaviourist, as I here use the term, does not deny the convenience of classifying *processes* as mental or material. He recognizes the distinction between personality and corpse: but he has not yet had the privilege of attending an identity parade in which human minds without bodies are by common recognition distinguishable from living human bodies without minds. Till then, he is content to discuss probability in the vocabulary of *events*, including audible or visibly recorded assertions of human beings as such. . . .

The behavioristic position, so defined, is simply that of the publicist and "has no concern with structure and mechanism."

The point of view is often called operational, and it is significant that P. W. Bridgman's physical operationism could not save him from an extreme solipsism even within physical science itself. Though he insisted that he was not a solipsist, he was never able to reconcile seemingly public physical knowledge with the private world of the scientist (27, 28). Applied to psychological problems, operationism has been no more successful. We may recognize the restrictions imposed by the operations through which we can know of the existence of properties of subjective events, but the operations cannot be identified with the events themselves. S. S. Stevens has applied Bridgman's principle to psychology, not to decide whether subjective events exist, but to determine the extent to which we can deal with them scientifically (154).

Behaviorists have, from time to time, examined the problem of privacy, and some of them have excluded so-called sensations, images, thought processes, and so on, from their deliberations. When they have done so not because such things do not exist but because they are out of reach of their methods, the charge is justified that they have neglected the facts of consciousness. The strategy is, however, quite unwise. It is particularly important that a science of behavior face the problem of privacy. It may do so without abandoning the basic position of behaviorism. Science often talks about things it cannot see or measure. When a man tosses a penny into the air, it must be assumed that he tosses the earth beneath him downward. It is quite out of the question to see or measure the effect on the earth, but the effect must be assumed for the sake of a consistent account. An adequate science of behavior must consider events taking place within the skin of the organism, not as physiological mediators of behavior, but as part of behavior itself. It can deal with these events without assuming that they have any special nature or must be known in any special way. The skin is not that important as a boundary. Private and public events have the same kinds of physical dimensions.

In the fifty years since a behavioristic philosophy was first stated, facts and principles bearing on the basic issues have steadily accumulated. For one thing, a scientific analysis of behavior has yielded a sort of empirical epistemology. The subject matter of a science of behavior includes the behavior of scientists and other knowers. The techniques available to such a science give an empirical theory of knowledge certain advantages over theories derived from philosophy and logic. The problem of privacy may be approached in a fresh direction by starting with behavior rather than with immediate experience. The strategy is certainly no more arbitrary or circular than the earlier practice, and it has a surprising result. Instead of concluding that man can know only his subjective experiences—that he is bound forever to his private world and that the external world is only a construct—a behavioral theory of knowledge suggests that it is the private world which, if not entirely unknowable, is at least not likely to be known well. The relations between organism and environment involved in knowing are of such a sort that the privacy of the world within the skin imposes more serious limitations on personal knowledge than on the accessibility of that world to the scientist.

An organism learns to react discriminatively to the world around it under certain contingencies of reinforcement. Thus, a child learns to name a color correctly when a given response is reinforced in the presence of the color and extinguished in its absence. The verbal community may make the reinforcement of an extensive repertory of responses contingent on subtle properties of colored stimuli. We have reason to believe that the child will not discriminate among colors—that he will not see two colors as different—until exposed to such contingencies. So far as we know, the same process of differential reinforcement is required if a child is to distinguish among the events occurring within his own skin.

Many contingencies involving private stimuli need not be arranged by a verbal community, for they follow from simple mechanical relations among stimuli, responses, and reinforcing consequences. The various motions which comprise turning a handspring, for example, are under the control of external and internal stimuli and subject to external and internal reinforcing consequences. But the performer is not necessarily "aware" of the stimuli controlling his behavior, no matter how appropriate and skillful it may be. "Knowing" or "being aware of" what is happening in turning a handspring involves discriminative responses, such as naming or describing, which arise from contingencies necessarily arranged by a verbal environment. Such environments are common. The community is generally interested in what a man is doing, has done, or is planning to do and why, and it arranges contingencies which generate verbal responses which name and describe the external and internal stimuli associated with these events. It challenges his verbal behavior by asking, "How do you know?" and the speaker answers, if at all, by describing some of the variables of which his verbal behavior was a function. The "awareness" resulting from all this is a social product.

In attempting to set up such a repertoire, however, the verbal community works under a severe handicap. It cannot always arrange the contingencies required for subtle discriminations. It cannot teach a child to call one pattern of private stimuli "diffidence" and another "embarrassment" as effectively as it teaches him to call one stimulus "red" and another "orange" for it cannot be sure of the presence or absence of the private patterns of stimuli appropriate to reinforcement or lack of reinforcement. Privacy thus causes trouble, first of all, *for the verbal community*. The individual suffers in turn. Because the community cannot reinforce self-descriptive responses consistently, a person cannot describe or otherwise "know" events occurring within his own skin as subtly and precisely as he knows events in the world at large.[2]

There are, of course, differences between external and internal stimuli which are not mere differences in location. Proprioceptive and interoceptive stimuli have a certain intimacy. They are likely to be especially familiar. They are very much with us; we cannot escape from a toothache as easily as from a deafening noise. They may well be of a special kind; the stimuli we feel in pride or sorrow may not closely resemble those we feel in sandpaper or satin. But this does not mean that they differ in physical status. In particular, it does not mean that they can be more easily or more directly known. What is particularly clear and familiar to the potential knower may be strange and distant to the verbal community responsible for his knowing.

Conscious content

What *are* the private events to which, at least in a limited way, a man may come to respond in ways we call "perceiving" or "knowing"? Let us begin with the oldest, and in many ways the most difficult, kind represented by "the stubborn

[2] For an analysis of the ways in which the verbal community may partly solve its problem, see (130). Although the private world is defined anatomically as "within the skin," the boundaries are the limits beyond which the reinforcing community cannot maintain effective contingencies.

fact of consciousness." What is happening when a person observes the conscious content of his mind, when he "looks at his sensations or images"? Western philosophy and science have been handicapped in answering these questions by an unfortunate metaphor. The Greeks could not explain how a man could have knowledge of something with which he was not in immediate contact. How could he know an object on the other side of the room, for example? Did he reach out and touch it with some sort of invisible probe? Or did he never actually come in contact with the object at all but only with a copy of it inside his body? Plato supported the copy theory with his metaphor of the cave. Perhaps a man never sees the real world at all but only shadows of it on the wall of the cave in which he is imprisoned. Copies of the real world projected into the body could compose the experience which a man directly knows. A similar theory could also explain how one can see objects which are "not really there," as in hallucinations, after-images, and memories. Neither explanation is, of course, satisfactory. How a copy may arise at a distance is at least as puzzling as how a man may know an object at a distance. Seeing things which are not really there is no harder to explain than the occurrence of copies of things not there to be copied.

The search for copies of the world within the body, particularly in the nervous system, still goes on, but with discouraging results. If the retina could suddenly be developed, like a photographic plate, it would yield a poor picture. The nerve impulses in the optic tract must have an even more tenuous resemblance to "what is seen." The patterns of vibrations which strike our ear when we listen to music are quickly lost in transmission. The bodily reactions to substances tasted, smelled, and touched would scarcely qualify as faithful reproductions. These facts are discouraging for those who are looking for copies of the real world within the body, but they are fortunate for psychophysiology as a whole. At some point the organism must do more than create duplicates. It must see, hear, smell, and so on, as forms of *action* rather than of *reproduction*. *It must do some of the things it is differentially reinforced for doing when it learns to respond discriminatively.* The sooner the pattern of the external world disappears after impinging on the organism, the sooner the organism may get on with these other functions.

The need for something beyond, and quite different from, copying is not widely understood. Suppose someone were to coat the occipital lobes of the brain with a special photographic emulsion which, when developed, yielded a reasonable copy of a current visual stimulus. In many quarters this would be regarded as a triumph in the physiology of vision. Yet nothing could be more disastrous, for we should have to start all over again and ask how the organism sees a picture in its occipital cortex, and we should now have much less of the brain available in which to seek an answer. It adds nothing to an explanation of how an organism reacts to a stimulus to trace the pattern of the stimulus into the body. It is most convenient, for both organism and psychophysiologist, if the external world is never copied—if the world we know is simply the world around us. The same may be said of theories according to which the brain interprets signals sent to it and in some sense reconstructs external stimuli. If the real world is, indeed, scrambled in transmission but later reconstructed in the brain, we must then start all over again and explain how the organism sees the reconstruction.

An adequate treatment of this point would require a thorough analysis of the behavior of seeing and of the conditions under which we see (to continue with vision as a convenient modality). It would be unwise to exaggerate our success to date. Discriminative visual behavior arises from contingencies involving external stimuli and overt responses, but possible private accompaniments must not be overlooked. Some of the consequences of such contingencies seem well established. It is usually easiest for us to see a friend when we are looking at him, because visual stimuli similar to those present when the behavior was acquired exert maximal control over the response. But mere visual stimulation is not enough; even after having been exposed to the necessary reinforcement, we may not see a friend who is present unless we have reason to do so. On the other hand, if the reasons are strong enough, we may see him in someone bearing only a superficial resemblance or when no one like him is present at all. If conditions favor seeing something else, we may behave accordingly. If, on a hunting trip, it is important to see a deer, we may glance toward our friend at a distance, see him as a deer, and shoot.

It is not, however, seeing our friend which raises the question of conscious content but "seeing that we are seeing him." There are no natural contingencies for such behavior. We learn to see that we are seeing only because a verbal community arranges for us to do so. We usually acquire the behavior when we are under appropriate visual stimulation, but it does not follow that the thing seen must be present when we see that we are seeing it. The contingencies arranged by the verbal environment may set up self-descriptive responses describing the *behavior* of seeing even when the thing seen is not present.

If seeing does not require the presence of things seen, we need not be concerned about certain mental processes said to be involved in the construction of such things—images, memories, and dreams, for example. We may regard a dream, not as a display of things seen by the dreamer, but simply as the behavior of seeing. At no time during a daydream, for example, should we expect to find within the organism anything which corresponds to the external stimuli present when the dreamer first acquired the behavior in which he is now engaged. In simple recall we need not suppose that we wander through some storehouse of memory until we find an object which we then contemplate. Instead of assuming that we begin with a tendency to *recognize* such an object once it is found, it is simpler to assume that we begin with a tendency to *see* it. Techniques of self-management which facilitate recall—for example, the use of mnemonic devices—can be formulated as ways of strengthening behavior rather than of creating objects to be seen. Freud dramatized the issue with respect to dreaming when asleep in his concept of dreamwork —an activity in which some part of the dreamer played the role of a theatrical producer while another part sat in the audience. If a dream is, indeed, something seen, then we must suppose that it is wrought as such; but if it is simply the behavior of seeing, the dreamwork may be dropped from the analysis. It took man a long time to understand that when he dreamed of a wolf, no wolf was actually there. It has taken him much longer to understand that not even a representation of a wolf is there.

Eye movements which appear to be associated with dreaming are in accord with this interpretation, since it is not likely that the dreamer is actually watching a dream on the undersides of his eyelids. When memories are aroused by electrical stimulation of the brain, as in the work of Wilder Penfield, it is also simpler to assume that it is the behavior of seeing, hearing, and so on, which is aroused rather than some copy of early environmental events which the subject then looks at or listens to. Behavior similar to the responses to the original events must be assumed in both cases—the subject sees or hears—but the reproduction of the events seen or heard is a needless complication. The familiar process of response chaining is available to account for the serial character of the behavior of remembering, but the serial linkage of stored experiences (suggesting engrams in the form of sound films) demands a new mechanism.

The heart of the behavioristic position on conscious experience may be summed up in this way: seeing does not imply something seen. We acquire the behavior of seeing under stimulation from actual objects, but it may occur in the absence of these objects under the control of other variables. (So far as the world within the skin is concerned, it always occurs in the absence of such objects.) We also acquire the behavior of seeing-that-we-are-seeing when we are seeing actual objects, but it may also occur in their absence.

To question the reality or the nature of the things seen in conscious experience is not to question the value of introspective psychology or its methods. Current problems in sensation are mainly concerned with the physiological function of receptors and associated neural mechanisms. Problems in perception are, at the moment, less intimately related to specific mechanisms, but the trend appears to be in the same direction. So far as behavior is concerned, both sensation and perception may be analyzed as forms of stimulus control. The subject need not be regarded as observing or evaluating conscious experiences. Apparent anomalies of stimulus control, which are now explained by appealing to a psychophysical relation or to the laws of perception, may be studied in their own right. It is, after all, no real solution to attribute them to the slippage inherent in converting a physical stimulus into a subjective experience.

The experimental analysis of behavior has a little more to say on this subject. Its techniques have recently been extended to what might be called the psychophysics of lower organisms. Blough's adaptation of the Békésy technique—for example, in determining the spectral sensitivity of pigeons and monkeys—yields sensory data comparable with the reports of a trained observer (22, 23). Herrnstein and van Sommers have recently developed a procedure in which pigeons "bisect sensory intervals" (66). It is tempting to describe these procedures by saying that investigators have found ways to get nonverbal organisms to describe their sensations. The fact is that a form of stimulus control has been investigated without using a repertoire of self-observation or, rather, by constructing a special repertoire, the nature and origin of which are clearly understood. Rather than describe such experiments with the terminology of introspection, we may formulate them in their proper place in an experimental analysis. The behavior of the observer in the traditional psychophysical experiment may then be reinterpreted accordingly.

Mental way stations

So much for "conscious content," the classical problem in mentalistic philosophies. There are other mental states or processes to be taken into account. Moods, cognitions, and expectancies, for example, are also examined introspectively, and descriptions are used in psychological formulations. The conditions under which descriptive repertoires are set up are much less successfully controlled. Terms describing sensations and images are taught by manipulating discriminative stimuli—a relatively amenable class of variables. The remaining mental events are related to such operations as deprivation and satiation, emotional stimulation, and various schedules of reinforcement. The difficulties they present to the verbal community are suggested by the fact that there is no psychophysics of mental states of this sort. That fact has not inhibited the use of such states in explanatory systems.

In an experimental analysis, the relation between a property of behavior and an operation performed upon the organism is studied directly. Traditional mentalistic formulations, however, emphasize certain way stations. Where an experimental analysis might examine the effect of punishment on behavior, a mentalistic psychology will be concerned first with the effect of punishment in generating feelings of anxiety and then with the effect of anxiety on behavior. The mental state seems to bridge the gap between dependent and independent variables and is particularly attractive when these are separated by long periods of time—when, for example, the punishment occurs in childhood and the effect appears in the behavior of the adult.

The practice is widespread. In a demonstration experiment, a hungry pigeon was conditioned to turn around in a clockwise direction. A final, smoothly executed pattern of behavior was shaped by reinforcing successive approximations with food. Students who had watched the demonstration were asked to write an account of what they had seen. Their responses included the following: (1) the pigeon was conditioned to *expect* reinforcement for the right kind of behavior; (2) the pigeon walked around, *hoping* that something would bring the food back again; (3) the pigeon *observed* that a certain behavior seemed to produce a particular result; (4) the pigeon *felt* that food would be given it because of its action; and (5) the pigeon came to *associate* his action with the click of the food-dispenser. The observed facts could be stated respectively as follows: (1) the pigeon was reinforced *when* it emitted a given kind of behavior; (2) the pigeon walked around *until* the food container again appeared; (3) a certain behavior *produced* a particular result; (4) food was given to the pigeon *when* it acted in a given way; and (5) the click of the food-dispenser *was temporally related* to the pigeon's action. These statements describe the contingencies of reinforcement. The expressions "expect," "hope," "observe," "feel," and "associate" go beyond them to identify effects on the pigeon. The effect actually observed was clear enough: the pigeon turned more skillfully and more frequently; but that was not the effect reported by the students. (If pressed, they would doubtless have said that the pigeon turned more skillfully and more frequently *because* it expected, hoped, and felt that if it did so food would appear.)

The events reported by the students were observed, if at all, in their own behavior. They were describing what they would have expected, felt, and hoped for under similar circumstances. But they were able to do so only because a verbal community had brought relevant terms under the control of certain stimuli, and this was done *when the com-*

munity had access only to the kinds of public information available to the students in the demonstration. Whatever the students knew about themselves which permitted them to infer comparable events in the pigeon must have been learned from a verbal community which saw no more of their behavior than they had seen of the pigeon's. Private stimuli may have entered into the control of their self-descriptive repertoires, but the readiness with which they applied them to the pigeon indicates that external stimuli had remained important. The extraordinary strength of a mentalistic interpretation is really a sort of proof that in describing a private way station one is, to a considerable extent, making use of public information. (The speed and facility with which the mental life of a pigeon or person is reported are suspicious. Nothing is easier than to say that someone does something "because he likes to do it" or that he does one thing rather than another "because he has made a choice." But have we the knowledge about his private life which statements of that sort imply, or at least ought to imply? It is much more likely that we are employing a standard set of explanations which have no more validity—and in the long run are no more useful—than a standard set of metaphors.)

The mental way station is often accepted as a terminal datum, however. When a man must be trained to discriminate between different planes, ships, and so on, it is tempting to stop at the point at which he can be said to *identify* such objects. It is implied that if he can identify an object, he can name it, label it, describe it, or act appropriately in some other way. In the training process he always behaves in one of these ways; no way station called "identification" appears in practice or need appear in theory. (Any discussion of the discriminative behavior generated by the verbal environment to permit a person to examine his conscious content must be qualified accordingly.)

Cognitive theories stop at way stations where the mental action is usually somewhat more complex than identification.

For example, a subject is said to *know* who and where he is, what something is, or what has happened or is going to happen—regardless of the forms of behavior through which this knowledge was set up or which may now testify to its existence. Similarly, in accounting for verbal behavior, a listener or reader is said to understand the *meaning* of a passage, although the actual changes brought about by listening to, or reading, the passage are not specified. In the same way, schedules of reinforcement are sometimes studied simply for their effects on the *expectations* of the organism exposed to them, without discussing the implied relation between expectation and action. Recall, inference, and reasoning may be formulated only to the point at which *an experience is remembered or a conclusion reached*, behavioral manifestations being ignored. In practice, the investigator always carries through to some response, if only a response of self-description.

On the other hand, mental states are often studied as causes of action. A speaker thinks of something to say before saying it, and this explains what he says, although the sources of his thoughts are not examined. An unusual act is called "impulsive," without inquiring further into the origin of the unusual impulse. A behavioral maladjustment shows anxiety, the source of which is neglected. One salivates upon seeing a lemon because it reminds one of a sour taste, but why it does so is not specified. The formulation leads directly to a technology based on the manipulation of mental states. To change a man's voting behavior, we change his opinions; to induce him to act, we strengthen his beliefs; to make him eat, we make him feel hungry; to prevent wars, we reduce warlike tensions in the minds of men; to effect psychotherapy, we alter troublesome mental states. In practice, all these ways of changing a man's mind reduce to manipulating his environment, verbal or otherwise.

In many cases we can reconstruct a complete causal chain by identifying the mental state which is the effect of an environmental variable with the mental state which is the cause of action. But this is not always enough. In traditional mentalistic philosophies various things happen at the way station which alter the relation between the terminal events. The psychophysical functions and the perceptual laws which distort the physical stimulus before it reaches the way station have already been mentioned. Once the station is reached, other effects are said to occur. Mental states alter one another. A painful memory may never affect behavior, or may affect it in a different way, if another mental state succeeds in repressing it. Conflicting variables may be reconciled before reaching behavior if the subject engages in mental action called "making a decision." Dissonant cognitions generated by conflicting conditions of reinforcement will not be reflected in behavior if the subject can "persuade himself" that one condition was actually of a different magnitude or kind. These disturbances in simple causal linkages between environment and behavior can be formulated and studied experimentally as interactions among variables; but the possibility has not been fully exploited, and the effects still provide a formidable stronghold for mentalistic theories designed to bridge the gap between dependent and independent variables in the analysis of behavior.

Methodological objections

The behavioristic argument is nevertheless still valid. We may object, first, to the predilection for unfinished causal sequences. A disturbance in behavior is not explained by relating it to felt anxiety until the anxiety has in turn been explained. An action is not explained by attributing it to expectations until the expectations have in turn been accounted for. Complete causal sequences might, of course, include references to way stations, but the fact is that the way station generally interrupts the account in one direction or the other. For example, there must be thousands of instances in the psychoanalytic literature in which a thought or memory is said to have been relegated to the unconscious because it was painful or intolerable, but the percentage of those offering even the most casual suggestion as to why it was painful or intolerable must be very small. Perhaps explanations could have been offered, but the practice has discouraged the completion of the causal sequence.

A second objection is that a preoccupation with mental way stations burdens a science of behavior with all the problems raised by the limitations and inaccuracies of self-descriptive repertoires. We need not take the extreme position that mediating events or any data about them obtained through introspection must be ruled out of consideration, but we should certainly welcome other ways of treating the data more satisfactorily. Independent variables change the behaving organism, often in ways which survive for many years, and such changes affect subsequent behavior. The subject may be able to describe some of these intervening states in useful ways, either before or after they have affected behavior. On the other hand, behavior may be extensively modified by variables of which, and of the effect of which, the subject is never aware. So far as we know, self-descriptive responses do not alter controlling relationships. If a severe punishment is less effective than a mild one, it is not because it cannot be "kept in mind." (Certain behaviors involved in self-management, such as reviewing a history of punishment, may alter behavior; but they do so by introducing other variables rather than by changing a given relation.)

Perhaps the most serious objection concerns the order of events. Observation of one's own behavior necessarily follows the behavior. Responses which seem to be describing intervening states alone may embrace behavioral effects. "I am hungry" may describe, in part, the strength of the speaker's on-going ingestive behavior. "I was hungrier than I thought" seems particularly to describe behavior rather than an intervening, possibly causal, state. More serious examples of a possibly mistaken order are to be found in theories of psychotherapy. Before asserting that the release of a repressed wish has a therapeutic effect on behavior, or that when one knows why he is neurotically ill he will recover, we should consider the plausible alternative that a change in behavior resulting from therapy has made it possible for the subject to recall a repressed wish or to understand his illness.

Note 8.1 Private stimuli

To the mentalistic philosopher mental life is "the only thing he knows for certain—in himself, if not in others." From that point of view the behaviorist seems either to be saying that he doesn't see images, feel pains, and so on (thus opening himself to a charge of bad faith) or to be refusing to accept observed events as evidence. What he refuses to accept are the dimensions traditionally assigned to what he observes. Some of the objects of introspection are private (covert) responses. Watson was particularly intrigued with this possibility. So far as we know, the responses are executed with the same organs as observable responses but on a smaller scale. The stimuli they generate are weak but nevertheless of the same kind as those generated by overt responses. It would be a mistake to refuse to consider them as data just because a second observer cannot feel or see them, at least without the help of instruments.

Other common objects of introspection are proprioceptive and interoceptive stimuli and (particularly important in the case of feelings) responses of the autonomic nervous system. It would be absurd to deny the existence of events of this kind or the possibility that a person may respond to them and learn to describe them. It is equally absurd to argue that because they occur inside the skin they have nonphysical dimensions. The issue is particularly crucial when the behavior is discriminative. We may learn to see things with ease, but it is hard to learn to see that we are seeing them, in either their presence or absence. It is an interesting possibility that the concept of experience, as distinct from reality, would never have arisen had not certain exigencies in the social environment induced men to observe that they are responding to stimuli.

Pain is commonly offered as an example of immediate experience. Painful stimuli are inside the body and often very strong, and they do not need to be copied. Nevertheless it may be argued that they are not the same things as the "experience of pain." "The experience of pain . . . ," says Brand Blanshard (19), "is self-evidently not the same thing as a physical movement of any kind." Physical movement is not, for example, "dull" or "excruciating." It is nevertheless true that many adjectives used to describe pain were first applied to the things which caused pain. A dull pain is caused by a dull object and a sharp pain by a sharp object. "Excruciating" is taken from the practice of crucifixion. Even these intimate inner stimuli are thus described as things.

The experience of having an idea or an impulse or of engaging in cognitive processes is by no means self-evident. In our own culture the degree of preoccupation with experience is shown at one extreme in the thoroughgoing extrovert and at the other in the introspective psychologist. Whether we see these "mental events" at all depends upon our history of reinforcement. Descartes could not begin, as he thought he could, by saying, "Cogito ergo sum." He had to begin as a baby—a baby whose subsequent verbal environment eventually generated in him (though not in millions of his contemporaries) certain responses of which "cogito" was an example. The stimuli controlling that response (the events to which it refers) are almost inaccessible to the verbal community which builds descriptive repertoires, and they are therefore seldom described by, or observed by, two people in the same way. We react to these events because of contingencies of reinforcement which are perhaps as complex as many of those which generate the constructs of science.

Note 8.2 Awareness

When you observe that you are seeing something, so that you can say "Yes" when asked, "Do you see that?", are you simply seeing the thing again in a sort of "double take"? Why should seeing something twice have more awareness attached to it than seeing it once? Evidently, you are observing yourself in the act of seeing it, and that act is different from the thing seen. The act can occur when the thing seen is not present, and you can then say "Yes" to the question, "Can you see it in your imagination?" The double-take theory seems to require that you conjure up a copy of the thing (or retrieve it from the storehouse of memory), look at it, and then look at it again. But it is possible that to observe that you see something in memory is simply to observe the behavior once evoked when you saw the thing itself.

We are aware of what we are doing when we describe the topography of our behavior. We are aware of why we are doing it when we describe relevant variables, such as important aspects of the occasion or the reinforcement. The verbal community generates self-descriptive behavior by asking "What are you doing?" or "Why are you doing it?" and reinforcing our answers appropriately. The behavior with which we reply is not to be confused with the behavior generated by the original contingencies. It is not necessarily "linguistic," but it is verbal in the sense that we should have no reason to engage in it were it not for contingencies arranged by a verbal community. Such contingencies may respect separate features of our behavior—for example, they may be responsible for the fact that we know "what we have done" in the sense of being able to describe our response but not "why we did it" in the sense of being able to identify relevant variables.

Awareness may be needed in constructing rules which generate behavior appropriate to given contingencies (Chapter 6). When we construct rules without being subjected to the contingencies (for example, when we extract rules from an analysis of a reinforcing system such as a sample space), there is nothing in our behavior we need to be aware of; but when we construct a rule from observations of our behavior under exposure to the contingencies (without knowing about them in any other sense), we must be aware of the behavior and of the variables of which it is a function. An advanced verbal community generates a high level of such awareness. Its members not only behave appropriately with respect to the contingencies they encounter in their daily lives, they examine those contingencies and construct rules—on-the-spot rules for personal use or general rules which prove valuable to both themselves and the community as a whole.

A science of behavior does not, as is so often asserted, ignore awareness. On the contrary, it goes far beyond mentalistic psychologies in analyzing self-descriptive behavior. It has suggested better ways of teaching self-knowledge and the self-control which depends upon self-knowledge. It also emphasizes the importance of being aware at the right time. Sustained awareness can be a disadvantage; there is no reason why we should scrutinize every response we make or examine every occasion upon which we respond.

The discovery of rules and the awareness which the discovery demands are particularly important in learning and in solving problems. In fact, they are so important that many psychologists have, as we have seen, defined learning and problem solving as the extraction of rules. But nonverbal organisms solve problems without formulating rules and without being aware of what they are doing, and it would be surprising if man had lost this ability. Laboratory experiments often seem to show that a subject can describe a set of contingencies as soon as his behavior shows an effect, but the subjects come from a culture which has made the scrutiny of contingencies almost inevitable, particularly when participating in a laboratory experiment on learning or problem solving.

A subject can learn to respond without knowing that he has responded if the reinforced response is so subtle that he cannot perceive it (62). Whether his behavior can be controlled by stimuli which he cannot perceive under the contingencies which generate awareness is the issue raised by "subliminal stimuli." The term is not a contradiction. A man may be able to identify or describe a stimulus under contingencies arranged by a verbal community though he does not respond to it under nonverbal contingencies. For example, only when he is told the solution to a problem in concept formation, does he respond correctly. Stimuli are certainly effective in contingencies which the subject has had no reason to analyze. The question is not whether one necessarily sees contingencies as such when they take effect, but of what happens when a verbal community induces one to see them. Learning without awareness is simply a special case of behaving without awareness, and the latter is common. We are by no means always aware of what we are doing or why. We are perhaps more likely to be aware when we are learning something new, because it is at such times that self-descriptive behavior is of most use.

The behaviorist is often asked "What about the unconscious?" as if it presented an especially difficult problem, but the only problem is consciousness. All behavior is basically unconscious in the sense that it is shaped and maintained by contingencies which are effective even though they are not observed or otherwise analyzed. In some cultures, including our own, well-established practices of self-description generate consciousness in the present sense. We not only behave, we observe that we are behaving, and we observe the conditions under which we behave.

Freud's unconscious was not, however, simply behavior of which a person has not become aware. He emphasized special reasons why self-descriptive behavior may be lacking. Some of the most powerful contingencies arranged by the community to generate awareness involve punishment. To blame someone is to attribute aversive consequences to his behavior. The assertion "You did that!" asserts a connection between behavior (what the person *did*) and undesirable consequences (*that*). The accused is ordered to observe the causal connection. As a result, similar behavior or behavior having similar consequences may generate conditioned aversive stimuli, possibly felt as guilt or shame. Freud argued that it is the punishing consequences which repress self-description or consciousness. The contingencies remain effective but are not noted. To be told that we carry bad news with alacrity because we are reinforced when we hurt other people is to be told that our behavior in carrying news is punishable as an instance of hurting someone rather than admirable as a form of conveying information. It is easier for us to note that we carry bad news in order to supply a friend with important information than to note that we behave in precisely the same way in order to hurt him.

Note 8.3 Mind and matter

What is matter? — Never mind.
What is mind? — No matter.

—*Punch*, 1855

It is curious that *matter* and *mind* are synonyms rather than antonyms when referring to the importance of things. Evans and Evans (44) give "He mattered not whether he went" as one equivalent to "He did not mind whether he went." You should *mind* your *P*'s and *Q*'s because your *P*'s and *Q*'s *matter*.

Note 8.4 The copy theory

The dualistic argument runs something like this. We do not know the world as it is but only as it appears to be. We cannot know the real world because it is outside our bodies, most of it at a distance. We know only copies of it inside our bodies. We know them in the sense of being in contact with them, of being acquainted with them. (The word *acquainted* comes from the same root as *cognition*.) We grasp them or apprehend them, as we apprehend a criminal. We know them almost in the biblical sense of possessing them sexually. (Polanyi [113] has recently argued for a comparable intimacy *outside* the body. The knower invades the known rather than vice versa: "We may consider the act of comprehending a whole, as an interiorization of its parts, by virtue of which we come to dwell in these parts; this indwelling being logically similar to the way we live in our body." It is certainly "logical," for it has traditionally been argued that the homunculus can leave the body and invade other parts of the universe.)

The copy comes to us from the outside world. It can be intercepted by shutting our eyes, but by a special mental act it can be reinstated or recalled while our eyes are still closed or open on a different part of the world. Reinstatement is possible long after the copy is made, although the accuracy deteriorates. For that matter even on-the-spot copies are not true to life. When the world of experience is related to the real world in a fairly orderly way (Fechner thought the relation was logarithmic), it is said to be composed of sensations. When the discrepancy is greater (a straight line looks curved, a fixed point seems to move), it is said to be composed of perceptions or illusions. When there is no current relation at all, it is said to be composed of fantasies, dreams, delusions, and hallucinations.

The Ames demonstrations are particularly dramatic examples of the discrepancies between the world as it really is and as it seems to be. They make it clear that experience may triumph over reality. But how do we know about the world as it really is? In one of the Ames demonstrations the observer looks into a room through one window and sees it as a normal rectangular room and then through a window at the side and sees it as trapezoidal. But surely one window does not reveal the room as it appears to be and the other as it really is. Both windows show it only as it appears to be. The fact that the room is "really" trapezoidal is an inference, similar to the scientific inferences which lead to the proposition that the materials of which the room is composed are mostly empty space. Inferences never get us away from the experiential nature of original data, as Polanyi and Bridgman have recently insisted, taking their cue from Bishop Berkeley (see page 155). If we accept the Greek position that we can know only our sensations and perceptions, there is only one world, and it is the world of mind.

It is a little too simple to paraphrase the behavioristic alternative by saying that there is indeed only one world and that it is the world of matter, for the word "matter" is then no longer useful. Whatever the stuff may be of which the world is made, it contains organisms (of which we are examples) which respond to other parts of it and thus "know" it in a sense not far from "contact." Where the dualist must account for discrepancies between the real world and the world of experience, and the Berkeleyan idealist between different experiences, the behaviorist investigates discrepancies among different responses.

It is no part of such an investigation to try to trace the real world into the organism and to watch it become a copy. A recent article on "Vision and Touch" (116) begins as follows:

A visual perception is not simply a copy of the image on the retina. The image has two dimensions, the perceived object three. The image is upside down, but the object is seen right-side up. An image of a given size can be projected on the retina either from a small object that is nearby or from a large object that is distant, and yet one usually perceives the actual size of the object quite accurately. The image is received by millions of separate light-sensitive cells in the retina, but one sees a unified object with a definite shape.

The authors thus assume three things: (1) an object, (2) an optical image on the retina (and other transforms of that image in the nervous system), and (3) a "visual perception." The first two are physical, the third presumably something else. They are concerned with discrepancies: the image on the retina is not a good copy of the object. From the present point of view the object is *what is actually seen*. It is not inside the perceiver and hence cannot be intimately embraced, but it is what the perceiver perceives. We account for his behavior in terms of the object seen plus a possibly long history of exposure to similar objects. It is only the curious belief that there is a copy inside the body which leads psychologists to be concerned with supposed transformations.

The sequence of physical and physiological events which are involved when an organism perceives an object is, of course, a legitimate subject for study. The first stage, between the object and the surface of the perceiver, is part of physics. The second, the optics of the eye, is the physics of an anatomical structure. The third is physiological. It has been almost hopelessly misrepresented in dualistic theories, which have led physiologists to search for the inner structures which are seen. The nervous system is not engaged in making copies of stimuli; it plays, however, an important role in reacting to them in other ways (see Chapter 9).

A curious by-product of dualism is the belief that phenomena said to show extrasensory perception are parapsychological rather than paraphysical. Suppose we teach a pigeon to match the Rhine cards. The five cards appear in a row of transparent windows any one of which the pigeon can peck. Above the row is a sample card which may be any one of the five cards chosen at random. The pigeon is reinforced for pecking the card which matches the sample. Both the pigeon and the experimenter who arranges the contingencies have normal sensory access to all cards, and the pigeon fairly quickly begins to match the patterns successfully. Suppose, now, that the sample card is enclosed in a box where it can be seen by the experimenter but not by the pigeon, and let us suppose that the pigeon still matches the cards, at least better than it should do by chance. From the point of view of a science of behavior, the pigeon is still responding appropriately under specified physical contingencies of reinforcement. The experimenter has not actually followed the sequence of physical events leading from the exposed card to the eye of the pigeon, and as a psychologist he has no reason to investigate the sequence from the concealed card. Physicists, however, should be greatly disturbed. It is only because the psychologist has believed that the pigeon must conjure up a copy of the exposed card in its mind that he calls the phenomenon parapsychological.

The visual world has dominated the field of perception. It would be hard to "visualize" an auditory stimulus and we have no comparable term for auditory copy-making.

Tastes and smells would be particularly hard to copy, but they can be regarded as contact stimuli and hence susceptible to being known without copying. Touch is the obvious mode in which we know in the sense of making contact with. We are intimate with the things we touch and do not need to copy them. Looked at from without, the skin is part of the physical world; looked at from within, it is part of the world of experience. But alas, even here the copy is defective. The sense of touch ought to show a sharp isomorphic correspondence between things as they are and things as they appear to be, but the "retina" of the skin must form an even more unsatisfactory image than that of the eye. One "looks at" a touched point through overlapping networks of nerves. The two-point limen was an early sign of trouble.

The psychology of sensation, beginning in British Empiricism as the study of how we can know the real world, eventually became the physiology of end organs. But the operation of end organs could not explain all the facts of experience; hence a psychology of perception. When the nervous system was invoked, perception moved toward brain physiology. (Köhler, for example, explained the facts of visual perception with gestaltig brain-fields.) But the neurological problem is misunderstood, as we shall see in Chapter 9, as a search for inner copies.

The problems of perception have to do with the stimulus control of behavior. Different stimuli sometimes seem to have the same effect, and the same stimulus sometimes seems to have different effects. We can explain this, not by tracing the real world into the organism and seeing how it is altered, but by analyzing the contingencies of reinforcement. It is really not too hard to explain the fact that organisms react in different ways at different times. The views through the two windows in the trapezoidal room are not interesting because there are discrepancies in responses to "what must be the same physical object" but because a long history of reinforcement with respect to rectangular rooms —the kinds of things which happen in them and their appearances from different aspects—has generated surprisingly different responses. The curious effect of a rotating trapezoid is not some strange quirk of the inner copy of a stimulus in a brain-field, but the product of a long history of reinforcement with respect to rectangles seen from different aspects. The "constructs" of science differ from "immediate experience" in many ways (lacking, for example, the warmth, color, and intimacy of direct experience) because they are the products of particularly complex contingencies of reinforcement possibly involving long sequences of responses.

Note 8.5   The behavior of seeing

The editor of a handbook in psychology objected to a contributor's use of "discriminate" as a synonym for "see." He complained that *He discriminates a cat on the back fence* was not idiomatic. But Skeat's *Etymological Dictionary of the English Language* defines *discriminate* as *discern* or *distinguish*, both of which would have been acceptable. *He distinguishes or discerns a cat on the back fence is* idiomatic. There is a colloquial use of *make out* which is close: *Can you make that out? Can you make out what that is? Make* alone suffices in *What do you make of it?* These are all synonyms of *see* as a kind of behavior differentially reinforced with respect to a stimulus.

The behavior is not to be confused with precurrent responses which make it possible to see or to see better. *Looking at* a picture differs from *seeing* it, just as *listening to* music differs from *hearing* it. One may look without seeing and listen without hearing, or at least before seeing or hearing. The precurrent behavior is obvious when one looks toward a picture or listens by cupping a hand behind the ear, but there are presumably comparable behaviors of lesser magnitude. They are reinforced indirectly by what is then seen or heard. They are much more easily identified and described than seeing or hearing.

The verb "discriminate" has an advantage over see, discern, or make out, because it reminds us of the appropriate contingencies. The difficulty is that the contingencies emphasize the controlling stimulus but do not demand a specific form of response or a specific reinforcer. In studying discrimination, the stimulus is carefully manipulated, but the response and the reinforcement may be quite arbitrary. The question "Do you see that?" does not specify the topography of the behavior, although further details are specified in injunctions such as "Tell me what it is" or "Point to it." The expression "seeing something" refers to a wide range of behaviors generated by a wide range of contingencies having in common a particular stimulus. Perhaps that is all we report when we report that we see something. The report is roughly equivalent to the statement: "Specify the rest of the contingencies and if I do not then respond, it is not from any defect in the stimulus."

Between seeing a thing which is there now and recalling it when it is no longer there, lies an important middle ground in which the thing is not all there. The dog lover is automatically reinforced when he sees dogs (135, page 271). The behavior of seeing dogs is therefore strong. It is most easily evoked by actual dogs, but it is also within reach of a series of stimuli of decreasing verisimilitude: wax museum models, life-size paintings or photographs in full color, unpainted sculpture, black and white paintings or photographs, and pencil sketches. What is seen may be simply the stimulus, but it is likely to be more than is really there. Certainly that is true when such a person sees a dog in an ink blot or cloud pattern. The final step is seeing a dog when there is no relevant stimulus whatsoever—daydreaming of dogs rather than being reminded of them. The true lover is distinguished by the fact that he does not need stimuli in order to see his beloved. It is possible that religions have proscribed idolatry for that reason. The use of an idol in order to see a god is a sign of weakness. Secular pictures or statues may be proscribed for the same reason: "This looking at a thing in order to think of a person is the very basis of idolatry," said George Borrow (24), speaking about statues of Shakespeare as well as about Moses and graven images.

When we talk about seeing, we are talking about a common part of many responses. In any specific instance contingencies respect the topography of a response and the reinforcement contingent on both the stimulus and the response. If we are interested in stimulus control, we may adopt arbitrary responses and reinforcers (as is done in psychophysics, for example) or deal with characteristics of behavior common to many instances in which responses and reinforcers vary. The way station of sensation or perception seems to cut across a causal sequence at the point at which a stimulus has acted but a response has not yet been made. The dangers in such a formulation have been noted.

Even if there were private copies of the external world, we should still have to answer the question "what is seeing?" Put the copy seen wherever you like—at the surface of the organism, in the depths of the nervous system, or in the mind—and you still have to explain what happens when it is seen. The behaviorist does not need to support the notion of experience as a form of contact or possession and can therefore leave the environment where it is. The whole organism is then available in analyzing the behavior of seeing.

Note 8.6   Way stations

In tracing behavior back through a causal sequence, Freud stopped at the way stations in his mental apparatus which represented early experience. The evidence for the experience was seldom independently checked. It was argued that what the patient remembered was more important than what actually happened or whether anything happened at all. Mental precursors were thus inferred from some parts of the patient's behavior and used to explain other parts. Something similar is done when behavior exhibited in taking a mental test is said to explain behavior exhibited elsewhere.

The causal sequence is sometimes transected at the level of knowledge. Like perception, knowledge may function as the end product of stimulation or as the beginning of action. Verbal behavior which describes reality (which has the form of the "tact" defined in [141]) plays a similar role. A response of given topography is reinforced by the verbal community when it "corresponds" to a stimulus in conventional ways. The importance of the stimulus control brings the tact very close to the classical notion of passive perception or contemplative knowledge. It is one of the great accomplishments of the verbal community that it generates verbal behavior of this form. It does so because the close relation between the topography of behavior and the tacted stimulus is useful to it. A tact is, in a sense, a way station between the stimulus affecting the speaker and the action taken by the listener. It has the independent status claimed for a merely contemplative knowledge, and it may have suggested the possibility of private knowledge having a similar function. Nonverbal contingencies do not generate objective knowledge in the same sense.

It is often argued that science is concerned not only with prediction and control but with understanding or even with simple contemplation, but scientific knowledge is not an elaborated perception of the external world in the mind of the scientist but rather what scientists do about the world. When they construct rules (including laws, theories, models, maps), the rules are sometimes regarded as improved, stable, and manipulable forms of knowledge. The rules seem to replace images in the mind of the scientist and are therefore close to simple understanding or contemplation, but they are not to be found in anyone's mind.

Note 8.7 Feelings

We use "to feel" to denote the passive sensing of bodily stimuli, as we use "to see" and "to hear" to denote the sensing of stimuli which reach the body from a distance. We *feel* objects with which we are in contact as we *see* objects at a distance. Each mode of stimulation has its own sense organs. We use "to feel" in a more active sense to denote precurrent behavior which intensifies or clarifies stimuli. We feel a surface to discover how it feels, as we look at something to discover how it looks, or listen to something to discover how it sounds. We do not, however, feel states or events which are deep inside the body—like aches, pains, movement, or postures—in an active sense. There appears to be no behavior comparable to running the hand over a surface which clarifies such stimuli.

Things with which we are in contact do not raise the problem of knowing things at a distance. We know them without constructing copies. The passive feeling of wet glass is not the wet glass, nor is it a copy of wet glass in the sense in which a visual sensation or perception is said to be a copy of a thing seen. The felt pain of a toothache is not simply the inflamed nerve, but neither is it a copy of the inflammation. Possibly because we do not seem to construct copies of things felt, it is not argued that we recall feelings by conjuring up old copies. In a sense a feeling seems to be both the thing felt and the act of feeling it. The things with which a person is in contact at the surface of his body are public stimuli, accessible to the verbal community, and the community can therefore teach words like *smooth, rough, oily,* or *sticky* without difficulty. But things inside the body are not readily accessible, and verbal responses describing them are likely to be imprecise and unreliable.

Among the things inside the body which are felt are proprioceptive and interoceptive stimuli. We feel gas pains, lame muscles, dizziness, hunger pangs, a full bladder. We also feel behavior, including very weak behavior and conditions which precede or are associated with behaving. Autonomic reflex responses to conditioned stimuli are among the emotions which are felt—for example, "the anxiety" evoked by a preaversive stimulus. To "feel like vomiting" is either to feel stimuli which have preceded or accompanied vomiting, or to feel actual small-scale responses. We also feel operant behavior at a comparable level. When we say "I feel like going" we may be reporting incipient responses of going or conditions which have preceded or accompanied going. When we say "I don't feel like playing chess" in response to a suggestion, we may be reporting the absence of any behavior in response to the suggestion or of conditions which commonly accompany playing chess.

Many adjectives describing "states" of behavior presumably refer to combinations of such stimuli. "I feel hungry" is presumably a report of interoceptive stimulation such as hunger pangs, or small scale operant responses which have been reinforced by food, or possibly other conditions associated with a probability of getting food or eating. "I feel angry" may refer both to reflex and operant behavior characteristic of the emotion of anger. When a characteristic reinforcement has not been forthcoming, we may report "I feel discouraged" and thus describe a low probability of responding and some of the emotional effects of nonreinforcement.

The traditional argument is that when a man goes without food, he first grows hungry and that feelings of hunger then prompt him to eat. We observe simply that the probability that he will eat increases as a function of the length of time without food. He may feel certain bodily conditions associated either with the probability of eating or the shortage of food, and he may refer to these when he tells us that he feels hungry, provided the verbal community has taught him to do so. Internal states are the "referents" of his description of his feelings, and as such are among the independent variables controlling his verbal behavior. What is felt is certainly relevant to a causal sequence, but it does not follow that the act of feeling is an essential part of that sequence. According to Butterfield (32) Aristotle held that falling bodies accelerated because they were more jubilant as they found themselves nearer home, as a horse accelerates in approaching home as he returns from a journey. We no longer take the feelings of a falling body seriously. Why do we do so with a horse? It is true that a person who has gone without food for some time not only eats but feels hungry. A person who has been attacked not only responds aggressively but feels angry. A person who is no longer reinforced when responding in a given way not only responds less readily but feels discouraged or frustrated. An even closer relation can be shown: the longer he has been without food, the hungrier he feels and the more voraciously he eats, the more violently he is attacked, the angrier he feels and the more aggressively he responds; the longer he has gone without reinforcement, the more discouraged or frustrated he feels and the less likely he is to respond at all. But the feelings are at best accompaniments of the behavior, not causes.

We sometimes eat because we are hungry and sometimes to avoid hurting the feelings of the cook. We may eat in the same way in both cases, but we may "feel" differently. It is sometimes argued that we must mention the feelings in order to give an adequate description of the behavior, but what we need to mention are the controlling variables—which also account for the feelings. A distinction is usually made between killing animals for food and killing a rival or predator. There may well be a difference in feeling, but again the main difference is in the controlling variables, which account for both the behavior and the bodily conditions felt.

Blanshard (19) has argued against the behavioristic position on the grounds that it "strictly and literally" follows that "Hitler's hatred of the Jews contributed nothing toward his orders to have them exterminated" or that Newton's ideas of gravitation never affected "in the slightest degree what he said or put down on paper." The implication is that these statements are absurd. But are they? We infer Hitler's hatred from a long series of verbal and physical acts. Hitler himself no doubt had other information, for he must have felt hatred in the form of covert acts of the same sort as well as strong responses of his autonomic nervous system. But no part of this complex was the cause of any other part—unless, indeed, following James' famous dictum, we could say that part of the action caused the feelings. A simpler view is that both the public persecution of the Jews and the private emotional responses were the result of Hitler's environmental history. It is too late to discover enough of that history to make a convincing case, (only historians and psychoanalysts attempt to explain individual behavior on such evidence), but it is important not to overlook its probable relevance. If we want to do anything about genocide, it is to the environment that we must turn. We cannot make men stop killing each other by changing their feelings; we must change the environment. In doing so we may well reduce the "mental tensions" which accompany, and are erroneously said to foster, warlike acts.

And so with Newton. We infer Newton's ideas from the things he said and wrote. Newton himself knew about things he almost said or wrote, as well as things he said or wrote and revoked, but the ideas he did not *quite* express were not the causes of the ideas he expressed. Covert responses are not the causes of overt, both are the products of common variables. It is important to remember this when we try to induce young people to have ideas. For more than two thousand years teachers have been trying to stimulate minds, exercise rational powers, and implant or tease out ideas, and they have very little to show for it. A much more promising program is to construct an educational environment, verbal and nonverbal, in which certain kinds of things, some of them original, will be said and written (152).

Did Shakespeare actually represent Othello as moved to action by feelings of jealousy? We should quite justly complain that he had not motivated his character if he had done so. He paints a detailed picture of jealous behavior ending in the smothering of the innocent Desdemona. Most of that behavior, befitting a play, is verbal. Othello tells us about his actions past, present, and future (in the latter as his "intentions") and about his emotional responses, both public and private. These are all parts of his jealous behavior and no one part is the cause of another. If he had had time, he might have described the wound he inflicts upon himself with his dagger, but the felt pain would have been no more responsible for his death than his feelings of jealousy were responsible for his jealous acts.

Whether feelings are causes may also be asked with respect to external variables. Is massage reinforcing because it *feels* good? Is a child reinforced when spinning around because he *feels* dizzy? Is taking heroin reinforced by feelings of euphoria? Is shock aversive because it feels unpleasant? Do we scratch an itch to make it feel better? Certainly a reinforcer—positive or negative —must be felt in the simple sense in which a picture must be seen or music heard if it is to act as a reinforcer. We intensify the effect through active feeling, as we *listen* to music or *look* at pictures, but it is still possible to distinguish being reinforced from the active or passive feeling of the reinforcer.

We often ask a person how he feels, and we do so to get useful information. His answer to "Are you angry with me?" may help us solve a personal problem. His answer to "Do you feel like going to the movies?" may affect our decision to invite him to go. In telling us about his feelings, he reports information which is useful to us but hitherto available to him alone. Nevertheless, it is not his feelings which are important but the conditions he feels. In the early days of research on LSD, it was seriously argued that all psychiatrists should take the drug in order to see how it feels to be psychotic. We do not ask the dentist to make his own teeth ache, however, or choose a heart specialist only among those who have heart disease. We recognize that what is to be treated is the condition felt and not the feeling. The traditional view that feelings are causes makes it hard to take the same view of psychiatry. The psychiatrist is often regarded as engaged in changing feelings. His goal is to make an adult patient feel less anxious, or a child to feel secure. Even so, he changes what is felt.

Young people are said to get into trouble when they do not "feel wanted," but it is not the lack of a feeling but the lack of the contingencies which would generate it which causes trouble. People who "want" us are people upon whom we have certain kinds of effects. We develop an extensive repertoire of appropriate behavior with respect to them. The repertoire languishes if we break contact. The unwanted person has had no opportunity to acquire such a repertoire, and he can affect people only in other ways. He may resort to extreme, possibly quite violent measures in order to "get through" to people who "do not want him." We can change his behavior by reinforcing him in different ways, by making sure that he gets a response with acceptable means. In doing so, we may make him "feel wanted," but that is a collateral result.

The psychiatrist will not, of course, ignore the patient when he says that he feels like killing himself or, after taking sodium amytal, that he feels sleepy. It does not follow that he kills himself *because* he feels suicidal or goes to sleep *because* he feels sleepy. Nor does it follow that the therapist will reduce the likelihood of suicide or sleep through measures which act directly upon feelings. After therapy or caffeine, a patient may no longer say that he feels suicidal or sleepy, because a change has occurred in what is felt.

The feelings of others.   Do we not admit that feelings are real when we attach importance to the feelings of others? We avoid hurting people because we do not want them to suffer as we should suffer when similarly treated. We enjoy making people "feel good," and we share their pleasure. In this act of showing sympathy and compassion, we exhibit one of the most admirable characteristics of our nature and culture. But here again, what we do or avoid doing concerns the stimuli which are felt. We avoid stimulating others aversively and are reinforced when we reinforce them. We do not need to assume that there are ways in which we directly alter their feelings or, certainly, feel their feelings.

But why should we alter the conditions in others which are felt? And why does this involve our feelings? How are we in turn reinforced when we reinforce others? Some answers may seem cynical. It may be that we feed the hungry not out of compassion, whatever that means, but because they show their gratitude by positively reinforcing us or ceasing to act in aversive ways. Quite apart from whether these reasons are admirable, it may be argued that they are not powerful; but the answer to that is that few people do indeed show sympathy or compassion. Very few people do good to others or avoid being cruel. Many primitive cultures, and current cultures which have not taken this line, seem to show that cruelty and indifference are "human nature." The psychoanalyst claims to have discovered this in the depths of the human mind. The responses of a sexual partner have probably been important to only a small percentage of people. The tenderhearted is atypical. The feelings of animals are usually taken into account very late in the development of a culture; most people avoid hurting only those animals which can hurt them.

In some cultures, nevertheless, it is common for people to rejoice in the pleasure of others and to suffer when they suffer. To understand this, we must look at the techniques with which the culture sets up compassionate behavior of this sort. Men are punished not only by those they punish but by society in general, in its concern for the overall reduction of aversive stimuli. To personal retribution we must add contingencies arranged by the group, similar to the contingencies which support ethical practices. The group also reinforces us when we reinforce others; and these consequences, added to those of gratitude and retribution, not only maintain compassionate behavior but generate some of the conditions which are felt as compassion.

This will not explain the fact that what is felt seems to resemble what is felt by others under the same circumstances, but an additional cultural technique supplies further information. The culture may punish grossly aggressive behavior and reward grossly reinforcing, possibly in terms of topography alone; but more subtle instances call for some attention to independent variables. As a culture develops, it becomes more and more difficult to specify doing good or doing ill in arranging ethical contingencies. A useful solution to the problem is formulated as the Golden Rule. If a man is to avoid hurting others, he can learn that what he does hurts by applying the Golden Rule in its negative form. He is to examine the effect on himself; he is not to do unto others what would be aversive if done by others to him.

It is perhaps significant that the negative form emerged first, but the positive is soon reached. A man who behaves in ways which reinforce others is reinforced in turn by the group as well as by the others. He can discover ways which will have these consequences by asking himself whether he would be reinforced. The ethical contingencies which maintain doing good thus lead to an examination of how one would feel oneself if treated as one proposes to treat someone else. When we say that in a given culture a man refrains from hurting someone because he "knows how it feels to be hurt" we are defining a class of behaviors suppressed by the culture. When we say that he feeds the hungry because he knows "how good food tastes when hungry," we are referring to a class of approved behaviors.

William James raised the question by asking whether one

would make love to an unfeeling person, and we might ask whether a sadist would be cruel to such a person. The answer, as a plain matter of fact, is "Yes": men occasionally make love to and attack unfeeling objects and persons. But when the recipients behave in ways which show feeling, an additional reinforcement is involved. The torturer restores the victim who has fainted before proceeding with his torture, and the schoolboy who is being caned deprives the teacher of part of his reinforcement when he refuses to show that he is hurt. If by making love we mean stimulating a person in a given way, we should not make love to an unfeeling person any more than we would play recorded music to a deaf person or show a blind person beautiful pictures—even though, if we are enthusiastic about music or pictures, we may be aware of a generalized tendency to do so.

Note 8.8   The invasion of privacy

Some recently developed physiological techniques seem to testify to the reality of private experiences. They seem to provide independent evidence of what introspective psychologists have been talking about. Subjective experience has become, so to speak, an objective fact. But the evidence is important for a different reason. If events hitherto classified as private can now be directly observed by the verbal community, the community can arrange better contingencies in teaching its members to talk about them. If an independent indicator of what is felt as anxiety were available, for example, we could teach a person to report its presence or absence and to compare it with other things felt. The new evidence simply points to the fact that what is experienced introspectively is a physical condition of the body, as a behavioristic theory of knowledge has always contended.

Note 8.9   Behavior and performance

Santayana, says David Bakan, put Watson in the position of a spectator at a play. "The inner psychological processes of the actors are, in effect, nonexistent" (9). But what processes are existent, in both actor and spectator?

Puppets and marionettes are effective automata even though the viewer knows about the concealed operator (see Chapter 9). The actor is a puppet and operator in one skin. He uses his body to simulate the behavior of another person, moving it directly rather than by pulling strings. He does so in given ways because, like the puppeteer, he is under the control of special contingencies of reinforcement which shape and maintain his behavior. His speech is simple intraverbal behavior, spoken on cue, and its timing and expression are controlled by contingencies arranged by the director. This is all known to the experienced spectator, who nevertheless enjoys the play.

We are likely to forget how awe-inspiring the speaking of memorized passages must once have been. The Brahmin priest reciting one of the Vedas must have seemed to be speaking for the author, or to be the author. Reading aloud must once have had a similar effect. Though a text may have been visible to the listener, reading was still largely a mystery; the reader spoke the same words as the writer whose transcribed words he was reading. It did not matter to the listener that he was not uttering sentences under the control of more important variables. We listen to a poet reciting or reading a poem of his own even though he has long since ceased to be the man who wrote it and may indeed merely be uttering it as intraverbal behavior, as we listen to those who read the poems of others.

We are not entertained or impressed by puppets, marionettes, actors, or readers simply because of the topography of their behavior. We say that the behavior must have meaning or significance, and we mean that independent variables must be operative in *our* behavior. The child enjoys seeing Punch beat Judy when something Judy has said or done predisposes the child to take similar action. If later parts of a poem are not to some extent controlled by earlier parts, the poem says nothing we ourselves are inclined to say, and we stop listening or reading. We do not watch theatrical representations of purely abstract forms behaving with respect to each other in no way which resembles human conduct, nor do we listen long to speech in an unknown tongue.

Most of the independent variables which induce us to listen and watch a reader or mime or actor have played a part in our own history. When these variables are operative, the psychoanalyst speaks of projection and identification. We understand a poem to the extent that we tend to say it with the poet (141). The simulated behavior of an actor interests us either because we should behave in the same way or because we should be curious or surprised or frightened when someone behaved in that way when we should not. The actor himself is not beyond the reach of variables of this kind. He may enter into his role and respond to other characters and to the setting for reasons other than those established by the playwright or director.

A recitation, reading, or theatrical presentation simulates human behavior, which we as listener, reader, or viewer tend to imitate. It supplies independent variables giving us other reasons for behaving in the same way, and it is particularly enjoyable when it does so. (We ourselves read books under similar conditions, of course.) Simulated topography alone does not reinforce us as we watch or listen. It is quite incorrect therefore to say that Watson or any other behavioral scientist regards "human functioning as one might regard a theatric production" if this means that only topography of response is at issue. It is equally untrue if it means that only the independent variables operative in actor or spectator enter into a scientific analysis of behavior. As we have seen, it is not good scientific practice to explain behavior by appealing to independent variables which have been inferred from the behavior thus explained, although this is commonly done, particularly by psychoanalysts, cognitive theorists, and factor analysts. Nor is it good scientific practice to read into topography of response the variables which might have prompted similar behavior on our own part. This also is characteristic of almost all branches of psychology *except* behaviorism.

The mechanical simulation of behavior raises the same issues in a clearer form, as we shall see in the next chapter. An unusually realistic simulation was achieved at a World's Fair when figures were controlled by a computer which had been programmed by sensing devices attached to the bodies of actors. (Structuralists, by the way, should be particularly interested in this demonstration.) Suppose a figure convincingly acts out "being afraid."

Unless we are alert to the Formalistic Fallacy, we could easily conclude that "fear" is to be found somewhere in the program. There is a good analogy in linguistics. According to some definitions of the field a collection of tape recordings should contain not only a language, but everything needed to account for it. A tape recording is, however, in itself quite meaningless—except to those who speak the language—just as the simulated figure will not appear afraid except to those who have seen similar behavior (perhaps in themselves) under special kinds of circumstances.

Santayana probably meant that Watson was taking no account of the feelings of the actors. Actors differ from real people in the variables which control their behavior, and to the extent that they feel what they are doing and why they are doing it, they have different feelings. A behavioral scientist presumably "regards a theatric production" in a way which depends upon his analysis of the behavior of the actor. When he analyzes real life, he arrives at different independent variables. He then "regards human functioning" in a very different way from that in which he regards a theatrical production.

Note 8.10   The geography of the mind

One of the more absurd things about the world of the mind is the space it occupies. It is an inner world and hence observed through *intro*spection, but one looks at one's thoughts with an as yet unidentified organ. Proprioceptive and interoceptive nerves respond to private stimuli, but they do not seem appropriate to visual, auditory, gustatory, and other kinds of mental events, nor do they seem to be in the right places.

Some thoughts are "superficial"; they come off the top of the head. Others are on the tip of the tongue. An idea may remain at the back of one's mind, but others rise up in consciousness, floating to the surface. William James observed ideas passing through his mind in a steady stream. Unconscious thoughts are out of sight, but they can come into view, possibly in the manner of stimulation as it reaches the conscious level. There are mental effectors as well as receptors, and they operate in the same space.

The cognitive psychologist moves about in his mental world and manipulates the things in it. He searches his storehouse of memory for a forgotten word or face and compares it with a word or face just received from the outside world. He puts ideas aside for the moment or dismisses them from his mind. He pushes some of them down into his unconscious where they will no longer bother him.

A mentalistic psychologist may reply that the geography of the mind is merely a useful metaphor. But why is it useful? What are the facts which need to be thus metaphorically represented? The world of the mind was invented, largely by the Greeks, to bring a person close to the things he sees so that he can know them. The theory worked fairly well in explaining a man's knowledge of the outside world so long as inner copies could be defended. It led to the mental science of Wundt and Titchner who explored the ways in which inner copies of reality were produced. It was the rigorous methodology of introspective psychology which explored the limits of the usefulness of such copies. Gestalt psychologists and others interested in perception rather than sensation built upon its failures—failures which were actually to its credit since they testified to the rigor of introspective methods. The end of the story is the long overdue recognition that what is perceived is after all the external world.

It was the use of the world of the mind to represent activities which were not copies of the external world which raised a special problem. The cognitive and other processes which William James claimed to observe were not copies of external activities and hence their status could not be explored in terms of their representational accuracy. The behavioral processes which are actually at issue are as much inside the organism as any mental life, but we learn to talk about them in ways which are much more devious than those with which we learn to talk about the stimulating environment. It is not surprising, however, that the geography of the mind should be borrowed from the geography of the world or that one should be said to behave mentally in some strange land.

Note 8.11   The death of behaviorism

Sigmund Koch's (83) obsequies show an unseemly haste. Behaviorism, as we know it, will eventually die—not because it is a failure but because it is a success. As a critical philosophy of science, it will necessarily change as a science of behavior changes, and the current issues which define behaviorism may be wholly resolved. The basic question is the usefulness of mentalistic concepts. Efforts have been made to answer it from time to time simply by fiat: we shall not study the nature of the soul but its manifestations, not the essence of mind but the actions of men, as Juan Luis Vives (161) put it more than four hundred years ago and as methodological behaviorists and operational psychologists put it today. Behavior is thus defined as a field which can be successfully analyzed apart from the world of mind, but the existence of another world is admitted, with or without the implication that we can know about it in some other way.

A radical behaviorism denies the existence of a mental world, not because it is contentious or jealous of a rival, but because those who claim to be studying the other world necessarily talk about the world of behavior in ways which conflict with an experimental analysis. No science of mental life stays within the world of the mind. Mentalists do not stay on their side of the fence, and because they have the weight of a long tradition behind them, they are listened to by nonspecialists.

A radical behaviorism attacks dualistic explanations of behavior first of all to clarify its own scientific practices, and it must do so eventually in order to make its contribution to human affairs. As it increases its power, both as basic science and as the source of a technology, an analysis of behavior reduces the scope of dualistic explanations and should eventually dispense with them altogether. Behaviorism, as an -ism, will then have been absorbed by a science of behavior. There may always be room for a logic of science peculiar to such a science, but it will not deal with the issues which define behaviorism today.

Scientific formulations do not change the nature of the things formulated, and a science of behavior neither ignores nor destroys the phenomena associated with introspection or any other form of self-observation. It simply represents them in other ways. J. D. Keehn (79) has denied that behaviorism is dead, particularly in answering Burt (29), arguing that there is a variety of behaviorism "that does *not* deny that men are conscious." He equates consciousness with "private experiences," not as private stimuli in the present sense, but presumably as private responses to private stimuli. This is perhaps an acceptable translation of some uses of "consciousness," but the term is still dangerous unless other traditional associations can be avoided. We can indeed examine the extent to which a verbal community induces the individual to respond to events with which the community is not in contact, and our formulation will clarify many traditional problems in the so-called study of mind, but its principal merit from the present point of view is that it permits an analysis of what has traditionally been regarded as a very different kind of stuff.

9   The inside story

Like what the fellow said—In Italy for thirty years under the Borgias they had warfare, terror, murder, and bloodshed, but they produced Michelangelo, Leonardo da Vinci, and the Renaissance. In Switzerland they had brotherly love. They had five hundred years of democracy and peace, and what did that produce? The cuckoo clock!

Thus speaks Orson Welles in the role of a Fascist black marketeer in *The Third Man*. The passage does not appear in Graham Greene's novel, published after the film, and in a preface Greene says that Welles added it to the script himself. It is neither good history nor good logic, but it is a convenient text because it brings together Michelangelo and the cuckoo clock.

Michelangelo

The "Creation of Adam" in the Sistine Chapel is described by one art historian (52) in this way: "The space [is] divided into two masses . . . Adam . . . is just awakening, still dreamy, but his physical perfection is impregnated with latent physical power. The right shoulder thrust back, the turn of the head, the twist in the torso, and the bent leg indicate capacity for powerful movement. . . . The second group, that of God with his attendant spirits, is full of vigor and movement. These two contrasting masses . . . are unified by the wonderful connecting link of the two hands, each marvelously expressive of the mood of its possessor—Adam's limp and lifeless, God's tense with active power. The touch of finger to finger is the act of creation."

Another interpretation is possible. Michelangelo has portrayed Adam as a cadaver. The body lies against a hillside, the right shoulder shored by the upper half of the right arm. The head tilts backward pulling on the neck tendons. The left foot is wedged under the right leg so that the left knee can support the extended left arm. The hand is indeed "limp and lifeless." Adam's body is complete but not yet alive; it is structure without function. But across the gap between the two fingers will pass the Spark of Life—that mysterious thing which enters the body when a fetus quickens and leaves it when a man dies. When Adam's body receives Life, it will move. It will act without being acted upon; the heart will beat and the lungs will breathe spontaneously.

In the scientific view, nothing crosses the gap. Form does not wait to receive its function. Life on earth began when certain complex molecules came into being. They did not have to be invested with a vital principle or essence; they were alive as soon as they existed. If Adam's body were complete, it would *be* alive. When a fetus quickens or a man dies, the change in function is more conspicuous than any change in structure, but we must suppose that structure changes.

Across the gap also jumps the Spark of Mind, and the living body then not only moves but moves appropriately with respect to the world around it. Mind has a much more complex role to play than Life. It must be more than the function which invests structure because it must reach into the environment if it is to explain the complex adjustment of the organism to contingencies of reinforcement. In early theories, the role was played by another person who was believed to enter the body and take control. This was in line with a primitive notion of causality: things moved because one moved them, and if other things moved, it was because someone else moved them. The gods were personified movers. As a man might blow a feather, so Boreas blew the branches of trees. As a man might make a noise when angry, so an angry Jove made the noise called thunder. Big things called for big movers, but the gods were also credited with lesser happenings: when Apollo threw a quoit and accidentally killed Hyacinthus, it was because a jealous Zephyrus blew the quoit out of its path. It was not necessary to impute motives—a poltergeist could make aimless noises—but the gods who explained the vagaries of human behavior usually acted for human reasons. Two great sets of reasons—good and evil—were particularly important. Some spirits gave a man a chance to do good and even told him what to do. He asked them for guidance, interpreted chance remarks as signs from them, and generated signs through divination. (Primitive man could whirl a rhomb until an unseen spirit spoke to him through its murmuring hum.) Other spirits put temptation in a man's way and told him to be bad, and he resisted by putting them behind him, wrestling with them, or throwing ink pots at them.

Agents of this sort were outside the person they acted upon but, as the metaphor of the Spark Gap suggests, they could go inside. Sometimes they were useful (the poet's Muse helped in the composition of a poem), but more often they caused trouble. The possessing demon was usually a mischief maker. Exorcism is still not uncommon, and a remnant survives when we say "God bless you" to a man who has sneezed. Montaigne said he crossed himself even when he yawned, and other reflex actions, such as hiccupping, vomiting, coughing, and shivering, have suggested alien actors. Possession is a useful theory when the indwelling spirit can be blamed for otherwise punishable behavior. Casanova told of a young girl who malingered as possessed, partly to enjoy the attentions of an attractive young exorcist but partly to do as she pleased, blaming her conduct on the devil within her. Causal agents were said to go inside inanimate things, too; but it was easy for physical science to dispossess them as soon as better explanations were at hand. Alternative explanations of human behavior have not been so successful, in part because what is explained bears a confusing resemblance to what is said to explain it.

When supernatural aspects have been abandoned, the character and role of demon and muse do not differ greatly from those of the man whose behavior they explain. Minor adjustments may need to be made. Behavior may suggest an indwelling animal rather than a man (some outdwelling gods were also therianthropic), and we reverse the relation when we say that some animals are "almost human." A person who behaves in markedly different ways at different times is said to have multiple personalities—one or more of whom, mythology suggests, may be nonhuman. The Freudian Superego, Ego, and Id are multiple Inner Men who struggle with each other, the outcome determining the behavior of the body they inhabit. The Self is a softened version. When a man sets an alarm clock at night to wake himself in the morning, the man who sets the clock differs very little from the man who is awakened, but when a man "struggles to control himself"— say, in anger—we are likely to think of different personalities.

As all these examples show, the Inner Man is most often invoked when the behavior to be explained is unusual, fragmentary, or beyond control—unusual with respect to other parts of a man's behavior, fragmentary with respect to his behavior as a whole, and beyond the control of the rest of him as a person.[1] But the "rest of him" must also be explained, and when all parts have been assembled, the Inner Man behaves very much like the Outer. Nothing has been gained by this animistic practice because the Inner Man still calls for explanation. Indeed, we now face all our original problems in

[1] Or when the rest of him seems wholly inactive. The Goncourt brothers note the behavior of their mistress who has fallen into a drugged sleep but nevertheless starts to talk about her early life. "It is an odd voice arousing a strange emotion, almost fear,—the involuntary voice escaping, word without will . . . a frightening thing, like a cadaver possessed by a dream" (55, entry for 3 September, 1859).

a much more difficult form. It is surprising that psychologists permit their task to be set forth in this troublesome way.

We dispossess the Inner Man by replacing him with genetic and environmental variables. To avoid sneezing we ward off, not a devil, but the pepper. We trace multiple personalities to multiple contingencies of reinforcement (135). We replace the Superego and Id of Freud as well as the Conscience and Old Adam of Judeo-Christian theology with "good" and "evil" phylogenic and ontogenic contingencies. Teachers and therapists do not change personalities, they change the world in which students and patients live. Some problems in the dispossession of the Inner Man deserve a more detailed discussion, however.

Cognitive man

The Inner Man is often said to store and recall memories. His behavior in doing so is much like that of the Outer Man when he makes records and puts them aside to be used at a later date. Primitive man marked locations and paths so that he could later find or follow them. Not-so-primitive man counted things and tallied numbers on clay tablets so that he would not need to count them again. With the invention of the alphabet men could record agreements and contracts so that they could use them in future negotiations, and historical events so that they could read about them later. They set down useful rules and directions to be followed when occasion arose. In doing all this, they created physical objects which could serve as stimuli. They labeled them so that they could find them again and put them aside in a convenient place, and they thus improved the chances that they would later behave in ways which were likely to be reinforced.

If the Outer Man can do all this, why not the Inner? But how can the Inner Man do it? With what organs can he receive stimuli and make copies of them? Of what stuff are the copies made? In what space does he store them? How does he label them so that he can find them again? How does he scan the labels in the storehouse of memory to find a particular copy? (The cognitive metaphor is often felt to be supported by the analogy of the computer, which does indeed receive, store, and retrieve information, but the computer simply does what men used to do much less conveniently with clay tablets, and like them it does it in physical space).

We shall not put Cognitive Man in good order by discovering the space in which he works, for it is the work which is the bad metaphor. A man need not copy the stimulating environment in order to perceive it, and he need not make a copy in order to perceive it in the future. When an organism exposed to a set of contingencies of reinforcement is modified by them and as a result behaves in a different way in the future, we do not need to say that it stores the contingencies. What is "stored" is a modified organism, not a record of the modifying variables.

We learn the name of an object by reading the label attached to it, and we can then name the object when asked to do so. Later we shall have to "recall" the name, perhaps with some difficulty. What we recall or reinstate is a response, not a copy of the label which we then read. The conditions which are said to determine the accessibility of stored memories really determine the accessibility of responses. It is not surprising that common verbal stimuli are more easily recalled than rare (as they are more easily seen in an unclear text) because common responses are more likely to be emitted than rare. Verbal stimuli which are easily recalled because they have been efficiently labeled are responses which are under effective control of the stimuli which are said to prompt their recall. Mnemonic systems and other devices for the efficient storage of experiences simply provide for the acquisition of easily recalled responses.

A rather similar physical analogy underlies the metaphor of memory when we recall things we are not looking for. Just as we construct *memoranda* to improve future contingencies to which we can then respond in practical ways, so we construct *memorials* which remind us of persons or things. A memorial, like a memorandum, is often a rough copy of a stimulus in lieu of which it functions, but when we are reminded of something without the help of a memorial, we have no reason to suppose that we are looking at a mental copy. When we are suddenly reminded of a name, the name does not "pop out" of our memory as a stimulus to which we then respond but as a response similar to the response we once made.

Some activities of Cognitive Man cannot be interpreted as metaphors in this sense because there are no behavioral parallels. When an organism responds differently to two stimuli, we say that it discriminates between them, but "discrimination," often said to be one of the activities of Cognitive Man, is not itself behavior. Generalizing, abstracting, and forming concepts are other things in the cognitive repertoire which must be analyzed in a different way at the level of behavior. A behavioral analysis of thinking never comes very close to cognition. A man may act in a way which suggests that he has had an idea, but the behavior is merely the result of the supposed cognitive activity, not an objective version. Jules Henry has reported (64) that the Kaingang Indians "shout at thunderstorms to make them go away," and he notes that "the continuance of the shouting is guaranteed by the fact that sudden squalls always go away." The contingencies are not unlike those in which a hungry pigeon is given food periodically by a clockwork mechanism. In pigeon and Indian alike, adventitious reinforcements generate ritualistic behavior. (The Indian is more likely to show generalization from other contingencies, since shouting at a thunderstorm resembles shouting at men or animals who do then withdraw.) Henry insists, however, that the *idea* of shouting must have come first. It "was an invention—an idea." This is a gratuitous assumption, and it causes trouble because we cannot explain the invention of a superstitious idea as easily as we explain the appearance of superstitious behavior.

The field of paleobehavior has never been carefully explored, but it is not impossible to imagine natural "programs" which, given a hundred thousand years, could teach early men to dig with a stick, make a fire, and plant and cultivate foods. Comparable programs can be investigated experimentally—for example, in young children. The traditional view that the idea of digging with a stick, or making a fire, or planting and cultivating food must have occurred first offers no comparable opportunity for experimental investigation.

All semblance of an inner *person* is lost when behavior is traced to qualities, traits, essences, virtues, and abilities. A similar practice could survive for a long time in physical science without exciting ridicule. We are still likely to say that a metal can be hammered into shape because it is malleable or possesses the property of malleability. Nevertheless, Newton was aware of the danger: "To tell us that every species of things is endowed with an occult specific quality by which it acts and produces manifest effects is to tell us nothing." The mistake is to take the occult quality seriously. There is no harm in saying that an object floats or sinks because of its specific gravity, so long as we recognize that the term simply refers to certain relations. There is no harm in saying that a student gets high marks because of his intelligence or plays the piano well because of his musical ability, or that a politician takes bribes because of his greed or runs for office because of his ambition, so long as we recognize that we are "explaining" one instance of behavior simply by pointing to other instances presumably traceable to the same, though unidentified, variables. We say that a man is tall and strong and that he possesses height and strength, but we do not then say that he is tall because of his height or strong because of his strength. A trait may be useful in directing our attention to a variable responsible for a class of behaviors, but the variable is the thing to study. A great many traits point to ontogenic contingencies of reinforcement, but phylogenic contingencies are important in "human nature."

The power of the inside story

We could rewrite all these versions of the Inside Story in terms of behavior while confining ourselves to phylogenic and ontogenic contingencies, but it must be admitted that something would be lost. Eric Knight's charming story (82) of a dog's valiant struggle to find her way back to the boy who once owned her would lose a great deal if references to "the time sense" which "drove at [Lassie's] brain and muscles," the "impulse" which "warned her faintly" of danger, or "the desire for her true home" which "began to waken" were deleted. Dostoevski's *Crime and Punishment* or George Eliot's *Middlemarch* could be rewritten without mentioning guilt, ambition, strivings, or fears, but readers would no doubt prefer the original versions. The maxims of La Rochefoucauld can be "translated into behavior," but most of their profundity is lost. Why is the Inside Story so moving, so convincing, and so satisfying?

We look inside the body for something more substantial than "historical" variables. We want to bridge the temporal and spatial gaps between behavior and the variables of which it is a function. When we reinforce an organism on Monday and see the effect on Tuesday, it is reassuring to suppose that Monday's reinforcement produced knowledge which survived until Tuesday or a memory which could be recalled on Tuesday. When we take away all food on Monday and observe voracious eating on Tuesday, it is reassuring to suppose that the deprivation has slowly built up a hunger drive.

It is not just a matter of filling a gap, however. An independent variable never quite seems like a cause; it does not seem to *do* anything. We look for something more energetic.

We tend to speak of variables as *forces*. Phylogenic contingencies seem more substantial if we call them "selection *pressure*." The behavior of a man reinforced on a *drh* schedule seems more convincingly described by saying that he is working under "pressure of time." A variable-ratio schedule, effectively programmed, produces a pathological gambler, but the program passes into history while he is still gambling and we are likely to say that he continues to gamble because of the excitement, or to gain a sense of mastery (when he wins), or to punish himself (when he loses). We also give external variables dynamic touches. *Nolentem fata trahunt, volentem ducunt* ("The fates drag the unwilling and lead the willing"). A translation, which might read, "Reinforcement may be positive or negative and we say that a man behaves willingly under the first and unwillingly under the second," contains no term as forceful as "drag" or "lead."

We also turn to the Inside Story when the Outside Story is incomplete. As we have seen, the cognitive processes supposedly taking place in the "black box" are designed to patch up a defective input-output formulation. Psycholinguists try to justify cognitive theorizing on the grounds that "learning theory" cannot account for the appearance of sentences in the behavior of children.[2] Current analyses of verbal contingencies are no doubt still incomplete, but what is gained by appealing to cognitive processes? If new sentences cannot arise in behavior, how can they arise in the mind? It is no answer to say that they arise when the child applies grammatical or syntactical rules (with what organs, in what space?), because the same rules can be applied to behavior (with known organs, in physical space). Nor can we answer by appealing to the innate structure of the mind, because behavior is also innately structured. The implied answer is much simpler: the very nature of the mind is to do what the body cannot do. The body must obey physical laws and cannot therefore per-

---

[2] The justification requires that the shortcoming be absolute: no learning theory must ever be able to account for the acquisition of speech.

form miracles. The mind has a long animistic tradition of being able to do so.

(The miracle may have theological overtones. A man's hand is moved by a simple physical cause which, said Cardinal Newman [107], may be studied by physics and physiology, but it is merely an assumption that the motive cause is physical. Similarly, ". . . if a people prays, and the wind changes, the rain ceases, the sun shines, and the harvest is safely housed . . . our Professor may . . . consult the barometer, discourse about the atmosphere . . . ; but should he proceed to rest the phenomenon . . . simply upon a physical cause, to the exclusion of a divine . . . I must tell him *Ne sutor ultra crepidam:* he is making his particular craft usurp and occupy the universe. . . . If the creature is ever setting in motion an endless series of physical causes and effects, much more is the Creator.")

Lastly, the Inside Story fascinates just because it is a deep dark secret. Much of the interest in the field of perception, for example, is due to an element of mystery. When stimuli are the same but responses differ, or when stimuli are different but the responses the same, we are likely to feel that something inside is needed to explain the discrepancies. We have exhausted a physical account (provided we have ignored past contingencies of reinforcement) and must therefore turn to a mental account—which is much more intriguing. If we study racial prejudice, for example, by giving a subject pictures of black and white people and comparing the times he spends in looking at them, the result adds to the facts with which we started but would not explain them. If, however, we arrange for our subject to see a picture of a black person with one eye and a picture of a white person with the other and if we compare the times during which each is dominant in retinal rivalry, the result seems closer to the roots of prejudice. It is not for nothing that psychoanalysis is called "depth psychology" or that linguists look for the "deep structure" of a sentence. And it is perhaps inevitable that an analysis of the same behavior in terms of contingencies of reinforcement will seem superficial. But those who believe they are looking into the depths usually try to bring things to the surface, and we can reach the surface most readily by starting there.

The nervous system

Why not simply look inside the organism to discover what is going on when it displays evidences of mind? The introspective philosopher and psychologist claim, of course, to do so, but their "look" has a special meaning. With what organs do they look at themselves, and how much can they see? The techniques of the physiologist seem much more promising. There is no doubt of the existence of sense organs, nerves, and brain, or of their participation in behavior. The organism is neither empty nor inscrutable; let the black box be opened.

The body has always seemed to offer an attractive escape from the problems of mind. La Mettrie saw that his physical condition affected his thinking, and Cabanis and other eighteenth-century materialists discussed the relations between the physical and moral aspects of human behavior. Thought was possibly only one of the workings of the body. Possibly the brain secreted thought as the liver secreted bile. And so, today, when a mentalistic theory grows murky or unconvincing, it is tempting to reflect that it is after all simply a matter of the way in which the brain functions. Freud was free to speculate with great abandon because, as a strict determinist, he believed that a physiological substrate would eventually be discovered. And when mentalism grows politically dangerous because it may be mistaken for idealism, it is reassuring to speak only of "higher nervous activities."

Physiological Man was invoked to explain human behavior long before the functions of organs were correctly identified. Generosity was attributed to a large heart, and depression to an excess of black bile ("melancholia"). Hunger was easily traced to the stomach, but room for speculation remained. In 1668 John Mayow (99) suggested that "if the stomach be quite empty of food, its internal membranes are, as is possible, pinched by the nitroaerial particles, and hunger seems to arise from this." Cervantes contended that Don Quixote's troubles were neurological. His brain was "distempered," "out of order," "turned topsy-turvy," and "dried out." ("By sleeping little and reading much, the moisture of his brain was exhausted to that degree that at last he lost the use of his reason.") His uncle's brains were cracked.

Cervantes may have been poking fun at physiology, but if so, we have not learned the lesson. We still say that we must use our brains to succeed, and we rack our brains (not our minds) for a fresh idea or a forgotten memory. We wonder whether bigger brains might not mean greater intelligence, and we call a stupid man addlebrained or soft in the head. "Nerves" are metaphorical too, but the metaphor is confounded by the fact that νεῦρον meant tendon as well as nerve. When we say that a man's nerves are taut, on edge, strained, or jumpy, we may be talking about his tendons, but we are probably using metaphors when we describe the man as nervous (though he presumably has no more nerves than anyone else) or subject to attacks of nerves, or when we give him credit for living on his nerve or having the nerve to speak up or challenge the world.

Professional theories of the nervous system are restricted in scope by the available facts. We cannot plausibly speak of circuits or centers or cell assemblies which do not conform to observed anatomy, or propose a chemical theory of memory if the required molecules are not to be found in the brain. But room for speculation remains, and it is still tempting to take refuge in an unquestionably physical, if necessarily poorly understood, system. Rather than attack mentalistic concepts by examining the behavior which is said to be explained by them, the physiologist is likely to retain the concepts and search for their physical bases. A recent article in a scientific journal on the visual space sense asserts that "the final event in the chain from the retina to the brain is a psychic experience." Another reports research on "the brain and its contained mind." Another is entitled "Mind and Molecules." A distinguished group of physiologists have participated in a symposium on "Brain and Conscious Experience."

The unhappy result is that physiologists usually look into the black box for the wrong things. The telephone switchboard is no longer in favor, but the computer is more than an adequate replacement. Physiologists follow the stimulus through the body in its various transformations, searching for those inner copies of the world to be equated with experience and those stored copies which are retrieved as memories. They look for patterns in "brain waves" associated with having ideas and making decisions. The physiological activities which account for the functional relations demonstrated in an experimental analysis of behavior tend, therefore, to be neglected.

It would be easiest to see how physiological and behavioral facts are related if we had a complete account of a behaving organism—of both the observable behavior and the physiological processes occurring at the same time. We should then know what it means to say that some part of such an account "explains" another part. (We should not be likely to say that any two parts reveal the "double aspect" of anything.) The organism would be seen to be a unitary system, its behavior clearly part of its physiology. At the moment, however, physiological techniques are limited, and we cannot study everything at once. We can show only that physiological processes observed upon one occasion have properties which plausibly account for behavior observed upon another, possibly in another organism. Hence, we cannot be sure that physiological facts explain behavior until behavior has been exhaustively analyzed. A successful *independent* experimental analysis of behavior is a necessary half of any "physiological explanation."

The requirement is not always recognized by those who try to tell the physiological Inside Story. On the contrary, it is often implied that behavior cannot be adequately described until more is known about the nervous system. A science of behavior is called "highly phenomenological" and is said to show a "studied indifference to brain mechanisms —to what is inside the black box." But we cannot say that what goes on inside is an adequate explanation until we know what the black box does. A behavioral analysis is essentially a statement of the facts to be explained by studying the nervous system. It tells the physiologist what to look for. The converse does not hold. We can predict and control behavior without knowing how our dependent and independent variables are connected. Physiological discoveries cannot disprove an experimental analysis or invalidate its technological advances.

This is not to question the importance of physiology in a science of behavior. In a more advanced account of a behaving organism "historical" variables will be replaced by "causal." When we can observe the momentary state of an organism, we shall be able to use it instead of the history responsible for it in predicting behavior. When we can generate or change a state directly, we shall be able to use it to control behavior. Neither the science nor the technology of behavior will then vanish, however. Physiological manipulations will simply be added to the armamentarium of the behavioral scientist. Pharmacology has already foreshadowed this state of affairs. A drug changes an organism in such a way that it behaves differently. We may have been able to make the same change by manipulating standard environmental variables, but the drug now permits us to circumvent that manipulation. Other drugs may yield entirely new effects. They are used as environmental variables.

The physiological processes which mediate behavior do

not, so far as we know, differ from those involved in other functions of a living organism. The activities which testify to the presence of Mind are simply part of those which testify to the presence of Life.

The cuckoo clock

Can the Inside Story be written in another way? Instead of looking inside to see what crossed the gap when man was created, why not build a machine that behaves like a man and see what must be put into it to make it work? The question brings us back to the cuckoo clock. It is perhaps the most familiar of all automata: as the hour strikes, a door opens and a bird moves into view; it lifts its wings, opens its beak, moves its tongue, bobs rhythmically, and utters an appropriate number of minor thirds. It offers a useful service to those who cannot see the clock and an amusing spectacle to those who can.

As Life explains movement, so movement means Life, and machines which seem alive because they move without being moved have a long history. Early examples were probably invented to mystify or frighten, and even when they came to be designed to amuse, something of the mysterious or frightening may have survived. A wooden pigeon that could fly is said to have been invented as early as 400 B.C., and at the beginning of the Christian era Hero of Alexandria constructed animated theatrical representations. The more complex the behavior, the more impressive the toy. Eighteenth- and nineteenth-century automata included a lady who played the harpsichord, each finger moving independently, and a boy who dipped his pen in ink and wrote "Soyez les bienvenus à Neuchatel" (97). Speech has always seemed peculiarly human. A small reed organ in the belly of a doll says *Ma-ma*, and a device which spoke recognizable words was invented as early as 1791. It has its modern electronic counterparts.

Machines which not only simulate the topography of be-havior but respond appropriately to environmental variables are particularly impressive. A mechanical mouse may frighten or amuse as it runs along the floor, but it is espe-cially fascinating when it turns back from the edge of a table (thanks to an unseen transverse wheel). The hydraulic devices in the Royal Fountains in France which suggested to Descartes the principle of the stimulus were distinguished by the fact that they behaved appropriately. "[The ladies and gentlemen of the court] tred on certain tiles or plates which are so disposed that if they approach a bathing Diana they cause her to hide in the rose bushes, and if they try to follow her they cause a Neptune to come forward to meet them, threatening them with his trident" (see 124). The magnet (which Thales felt must have a soul because it could move iron) is useful in simulating appropriate movement. Rous-seau (118) described a duck floating in a bowl of water which approached when a bit of bread was held toward it. (When the exhibitor allowed Rousseau to hold the bread, the duck went away. Rousseau inferred that a child beneath the table was using another magnet, but the exhibitor may have reversed the poles of the magnet in the bread. Several mechanical puzzles, including a mummy which in the hands of a naive operator refuses to stay in its sarcophagus, are based on that principle.)

Machines which appear to solve problems or think for themselves in other ways are presumably in the forefront of the art. One of the first and possibly the most famous was the chess player invented by von Kempelen in 1770 and later exhibited by Maelzel of metronome fame. Although a human player was suspected, and various theories proposed to ex-plain how he escaped detection when the inner mechanism was exposed to the public, the secret was kept for seventy years (59).

Verisimilitude is not essential. A floating magnet behaves amusingly even when it does not look like a duck. A clock which strikes the hour is useful even when a bellringer is not simulated. The giant crane or earthmover is fascinating even though it does not look like a living thing. In Maelzel's device a figure dressed in the fashionable Turkish style of the day moved the pieces, but a chess-playing computer does not look like a chess player at all. It learns of the moves of its opponent and announces its own moves in its own way, to which its opponent must adjust. Topography of behavior essentially vanishes in the mathematical model, an ideal machine whose behavioral processes are like those of animals and men only in the sense that they can be described with the same equations.

If we disregard verisimilitude, we can say that automata do indeed behave very much like men. They detect, identify, and classify stimuli. They store and retrieve information. They learn and teach. They solve problems and play games. They behave as members of a social system, in which other members may or may not be machines. We treat them as men, "instructing them" and "asking them questions," and we listen to their answers. We even do what they tell us to do. They are certainly *almost* human, and since we know why they behave as they do, do we not know what it means to possess a Mind?

The ghost in the machine

We must first be sure that there is no Little Man inside. A familiar toy pig seems alive because it moves its ears and tail, but it does so thanks to an imprisoned fly. The doors of an ancient Egyptian temple seemed to open by themselves, but they were probably moved by men concealed on a lower level. An early "horseless carriage" had four large spokeless wheels, in each of which a man walked as on a treadmill. (The fraud was exposed by putting pepper in the wheels.) The voice of the oracle of Orpheus on the isle of Lesbos was a human voice delivered through a pipe, and a modern doll says much more than "Ma-ma" thanks to a recording of real speech.

Mechanical simulations remain awesome and mystifying even when the presence of a living operator is known. The dragons which wind through the streets in a festival are obviously moved by men, and so are marionettes and puppets, and they still impress and amuse. But if we wish to argue that a machine genuinely behaves like a man, we must make sure that no man is involved. There was, of course, a human operator in Maelzel's chess player. (The soul of the magnet, incidentally, contributed to his success and proved a formidable obstacle to those who tried to discover the secret. Small magnets in the bases of the chessmen moved tell-tales on the underside of the board to show the concealed player where his opponent has moved.) No man is concealed in a computer when it is playing chess, but important contributions from human players have been stored in it. The computer, even with its great speed, does not have time to test the consequences of every move. It can play chess reasonably well only if it has been programmed to evaluate positions a few moves ahead, and the systems of evaluation it uses "correspond to the various features that chess players assert are important" or "follow the common and tested lore of the chess world."

There is a homunculus in any machine built and instructed by men, and his role throws light on the hypothetical Inner Man of traditional theories. A machine is, by definition, a human product; it is, etymologically, a means to an end. We design machines to work for us, to do what we should otherwise have to do ourselves, and to do it more rapidly and effectively. Some of the conspicuous gains fit a stimulus-response formula. Devices which are sensitive to new kinds or very small amounts of energy or which can respond to large amounts without danger amplify and extend stimulation. Other devices amplify the reach, power, speed, subtlety, and complexity of responses. Human achievements then become possible which are no doubt remarkable, but no particular awe or mystery attaches to them. The radio-telescope is a hand cupped behind the ear; the earthmover is a digging stick.

It is only when machines seem to take over central processes that we grow uneasy. When they select stimuli, identify patterns, convert stimuli into forms more suitable for processing, categorize data, extract concepts, and follow problem-solving strategies, they perform functions which in man are attributed to Mind. And the functions are not trivial. One expert in computer simulation, as Eliot Hearst has pointed out (61), "was at one time so optimistic . . . that he predicted that a digital computer would be world [chess] champion within ten years." But the real question is not whether machines think but whether men do. The mystery which surrounds a thinking machine already surrounds a thinking man. We can dispose of it in both cases by extending our analysis of contingencies of reinforcement. The distinction between rule-governed and contingency-shaped behavior (Chapter 6) is crucial.

Computer simulation is often defended on the ground that it forces the simulator to analyze behavior. If a computer is to engage in trial-and-error learning, it must be programmed to try efficiently. If it is to make decisions, it must be programmed to evaluate outcomes. If it is to play games, it must be programmed to follow useful strategies. The programs are useful to men as well as computers. Newell, Shaw, and Simon (106) have said, for example, that "if one could devise a successful chess machine, one would seem to have penetrated to the core of human intellectual endeavor," but they add that "any information processing system . . . that plays chess successfully will use heuristics generically similar to those used by humans."

All these examples have to do with rule-governed behavior. A problem or game is a set of contingencies of reinforcement, and one way to solve or play it successfully is to extract appropriate rules. It is not the only way, however.

THE INSIDE STORY   289

As Newell, Shaw, and Simon say, "Man can solve problems without knowing how he solves them." In other words, his behavior can be shaped by contingencies which he has not analyzed. When the authors continue, "Let us simply assume that it is good to know how to do mechanically what man can do naturally," we may take natural to mean contingency-shaped and mechanical to mean rule-governed. In other words, it is good to extract rules from contingencies so that we can avoid the possibly prolonged process of being shaped by them.

But rule-governed behavior is not the same as contingency-shaped, even when it is topographically similar and equally successful, and this explains why all the things said to be lacking in problem-solving machines are also said to be lacking in rule-governed behavior in man. A person who solves a problem simply by following algorithmic rules behaves "mechanically"; unlike the "intuitive" thinker he has not been touched by the unanalyzed contingencies. As science becomes more and more rule-governed, the behavior of the scientist loses the personal touch of contingency-shaped behavior, as Polanyi and Bridgman have complained, and may not seem to show the genuine possession of knowledge.

A difference in *purpose* follows (see page 106). As Neisser (105) says, "It is difficult not to be impressed with the 'homing missile,' which pursues its target tenaciously through every evasive action, until it achieves its destructive goal. On the intellectual level, the 'Logic Theorist' of Newell, Simon, and Shaw . . . is just as persistent: determined to prove a theorem, it tries one logical strategy after another until the proof is found or until its resources are exhausted. . . . Machines are evidently *more* purposive than most human beings, most of the time." But there is something wrong with this, and Neisser tries to identify it by saying that machine purpose is "monolithic." But that is not the fault of the machine; machines are usually built and programmed for only one purpose at a time. A child playing checkers may avoid the loss of a piece "by every possible maneuver, including removing it from the board and putting it in his mouth," and he seems more than a monolithic machine because he does; but a checker-playing computer could be programmed to preserve or capture pieces in more than one way—by following the rules of the game or by taking them off the board when the opponent was not looking. It is our monolithic human purpose which explains why a machine plays checkers in only one way at a time.

A real difference in purpose between men and machines resembles one of the differences between rule-governed and contingency-shaped behavior in men. The reinforcers which induce men to follow rules may be quite unrelated to the reinforcers in the contingencies from which the rules are drawn. Compare two men walking from Grand Central Terminal to Central Park, one of whom "knows New York" while the other has never been in New York before and is following a map. Both may take the same route and, apart from the behavior of consulting the map, behave in much the same way—but for different "reasons." Both are perhaps reinforced by the same consequences upon arriving in Central Park, but the events which reinforce their responses at each turn differ. For the man who knows New York, they are conditioned reinforcers derived from the ultimate consequences; he makes a turn and finds himself in a street which is the occasion for further walking toward Central Park. The man who is following a map makes a turn and finds himself in a street which is "right" according to the map; he is reinforced by this because of the instructions or advice which led him to follow it. The distinction is important when the culture reinforces behavior in order to bring remote consequences to bear on its members. We recognize a substantial difference in purpose when a man responds to ethical sanctions or obeys the law simply to escape punitive consequences and when he responds because to some extent he has been affected by the natural advantages of an orderly society. Machines are law-abiding citizens; they always follow rules.

The mistake, as we saw in Chapter 5, is to regard purpose as a characteristic or essence of the topography of behavior rather than as a relation to controlling variables. A similar issue concerns meaning. A machine may behave like a man but its behavior may still be called meaningless. So may that of a man who is mechanically following directions. A machine —say, a tape recorder—does not "mean what it says," but neither does a man who is reciting a passage learned entirely by rote, possibly in a tongue unknown to him. A listener may respond meaningfully to the recording or to the recitation, but only with respect to the original source. A transmitter is limited in important ways and its shortcomings may be resented: "Six to eight inches of snow, according to the telephone weather service. I don't know whether that includes what we have already had, and of course the recorded voice didn't know either." Nor would a living operator who was simply reading or reciting a message from the weather bureau. What is resented is the lack of collateral behavior. A book is a mechanical transmission of verbal behavior, and Socrates objected to it on the same grounds: one cannot ask it questions. But a book does not sound like or look like, and hence does not "pretend to be," a living person; and it cannot therefore be accused of sham or fraud. If the telephone weather service used a code—for example, a sustained tone for fair, a wobbly tone for cloudy, a drum roll for rain—we should accept this as readily as we accept storm warnings along the coast. We accept the word of a simulated cuckoo because we do not interact with cuckoos in other ways, but a clock which intoned, "Nine o'clock and all is well," would be resented.

(Collateral responses are lacking in what may be called receptive automata. Children talk to and play with dolls, and grown men have been known to live with mannikins, but their behavior falls far short of that emitted with respect to real people. The Goncourt brothers reported the arrest of a man who constructed a particularly receptive female "à l'usage des communautés religieuses ou bien des riches navigateurs" (55, entry for 6 May, 1858), a device which recalls William James' question whether we would make love to a nonfeeling person. Except for the extent of the responses they permit, these receptive automata do not differ essentially from portraits or statues, with respect to which we also behave in fragmentary ways appropriate to real people.)

The search for meaning in the structure of behavior and the rejection of simulated topography on the ground that it lacks meaning has a bearing on the issue of reductionism. In a paper called "On Comparing the Brain with Machines" D. M. MacKay (96) argues as follows:

> If I say that an electric advertising sign is "nothing-but" a certain array of lamps and wires, I may mean one of two things: (1) I may mean that an electrician could make a complete catalogue of all that is there, and have nothing left over, without mentioning "the advertisement." This is true. (2) Or I may mean that since there is nothing left over from the electrician's account, there isn't really an advertisement there at all. This is the error of reductionism. It consists in confusing *exhaustiveness* with *exclusiveness*. The electrician's account is *exhaustive*, at least in the sense that a perfect replica could be constructed from it. But the electrician's account and the advertiser's account of "all that is there" are not mutually *exclusive*. The advertisement is not something to be fitted into a gap in the electrician's account. It is something that we find when we start all over again to describe what is there in another complementary language.

The appeal to a "complementary language" savors of the Formalistic Fallacy. A complete acoustical description does not reveal "all that is there" in a verbal response, no matter what language it uses, because other variables must be taken into account. On the side of a verbal stimulus, meaning is not to be found in its acoustic properties but in its effects on a listener. To improve our prediction of its effects, we should learn more about the listener, not about the verbal stimulus. Similarly, an "advertisement" is not a physical property of a sign, and no physical analysis will permit us to predict its effect upon those who see it. Yet it is this effect which makes it an advertisement. To reduce its effects as a stimulus to its physical properties is not reductionism; it is the impossible aspiration of structuralism.

A similar issue concerns originality. A machine which is constructed and instructed to follow rules does not behave in original ways, because its behavior has been specified in the rules. But this is also true of men who behave simply by following rules, since others have behaved in the same way before. It is only behavior which is shaped by contingencies of reinforcement which may be said to appear for the first time.

These distinctions lose their force when the behavior of a machine is shaped by contingencies. Machines have been built which come to respond to one stimulus rather than another when the two have occurred together, as in Pavlovian conditioning. Other machines have been built in which the rate of responding is increased when a response is followed by a certain kind of consequence, as in operant conditioning. The behavior of the latter (1) is related to its consequences in a way traditionally described with the term purpose, (2) has meaning in the sense that we can infer from it something about the environmental contingencies to which it has been exposed, and (3) is original in the sense that the behavior it acquires under some contingencies may not have been foreseen by its designer. It therefore comes close to the contingency-shaped behavior of men. Is there any surviving difference between man and machine?

One difference which will certainly be urged is that such a machine "would not be aware of what it was doing." It would not be "conscious." It would have no "feelings." But, as in asking whether a machine really "thinks," the importance of these distinctions rests upon an analysis of human behavior. What does it mean to say that a man is aware of what he is doing, is conscious, and has feelings?

A man learns to respond to himself and his own behavior as he learns to respond to things in the world around him, although it is hard for the verbal community to teach him to "know himself" in this sense effectively. Machines respond to themselves, to features of their own structure, and to their own behavior. A machine stops or switches to an alternative mechanism when something goes wrong, and "feedback" is often necessary in a delicate operation or when a machine "thinks." Theoretically there is no limit to the extent to which a machine could respond to its own parts and activities. It may still be argued that this is not "real feeling," that no matter how sensitive a machine may be it is still not "conscious." But is this a matter of the behavior with which one responds to oneself or of the self to which one responds? In human behavior the critical issue is not the feeling but what is felt, just as it is not the seeing but what is seen. A machine, no matter how sensitive, can feel only a machine. A machine is all a machine can possibly be conscious of.

This brings us to the one obvious and currently irreducible difference between men and machines. They are built differently. The ultimate difference is in componentry. To have human feelings a machine would have to have human things to feel. To be conscious or aware of itself as a man is conscious or aware of himself a machine would have to be what a man is aware or conscious of. It would have to be built like a man and would, of course, be a man. It would behave like a man and its behavior would include responding to itself in ways which we call being conscious. Once complete, Adam would not only be alive, he would be sentient, intelligent, and capable of becoming aware of himself as Adam.

Man *is* a machine, but he is a very complex one. At present he is far beyond the powers of men to construct—except, of course, in the usual biological way. Only those who be-

lieve that something nonphysical is essential to his functioning are likely to question this. If a science of human behavior
is impossible because man possesses free will, or if behavior
cannot be explained without invoking a miracle-working
mind, then indeed man cannot be simulated. This is, of
course, often argued. Irvine H. Page (109) insists that "the
brain is no more than a physical mechanism which, without
the mind, is not unlike the so-called 'electronic brain' of industry. But without the guiding mind, the brain comes to
little." If we believe with Vannevar Bush that "science is
not enough" (30) and that consciousness and free will have
not been scientifically analyzed, then we may doubt that
man is a machine or that any machine can simulate man.
As our understanding of human behavior increases, however, we appeal less and less to explanatory fictions, and
we can then accept the fact that the essential differences
between machines and men concern componentry. The problem of simulation is the technical problem of working with
the stuff of which the human body is made.

A machine which simulated human behavior in detail
would indeed tell us the "Inside Story." We should have only
to look at the blueprints to see what entered into the creation
of man. Like the Inside Story of physiology, however, it
would tell us nothing new about behavior. Only when we
know what a man actually does can we be sure that we have
simulated his behavior. The Outside Story must be told first.

Man the creator

When machines are designed to extend the range of stimuli
and responses, the man who uses them occupies the place
of the Inner Man of stimulus-response or information theory.
He selectively attends to, detects, identifies, discriminates
among, and stores and retrieves possibly amplified stimuli,
and he makes decisions and initiates possibly amplified action. When machines take over these so-called cognitive

functions, he is no longer needed as part of the current system. But he has played the role of designer, constructor, and programmer, and that is precisely the role of the variables which take over the so-called cognitive functions in an experimental analysis. Phylogenic contingencies are responsible for the fact that men respond to stimuli, act upon the environment, and change their behavior under contingencies of reinforcement. When men make machines which have all these characteristics, they play the role of an evolutionary history. Ontogenic contingencies are responsible for the fact that a man reacts to only some of the stimuli to which he is sensitive, makes only some of the responses of which he is capable, and does so with given probabilities upon given occasions. When men program or instruct machines to behave in similar ways, they play the role of an environmental history.

The time scales differ enormously, of course. The construction of a machine may simulate a million years of evolution, and a brief instruction may simulate a long exposure to contingencies of reinforcement. (It has been argued that machines differ from men because they show no period of "development," but the so-called development of a child's behavior is a mixture of phylogeny and ontogeny. A period of development is needed because of certain biological exigencies in the production of a mature organism. A "mature" machine can be constructed in its entirety before instruction begins.) The evolutionary process may seem inefficient, but the human machine has additional properties—it can use cruder sources of energy, it can reproduce itself, and so on. It also shows a much greater variety. Phylogenic and ontogenic contingencies have built men with more than monolithic purposes.

The machine a man builds and instructs continues to operate when he is no longer in contact with it, but we "give him credit" for what it does. He is responsible for its behavior. Similarly, the phylogenic and ontogenic contingencies of which the behavior of a man is a function pass into history while the man is still behaving, but we must "give them credit" for what he does. They are responsible for his achievements. We do not look for ultimate responsibility in a machine, nor should we look for it in man. And this applies as well to the behavior of building and instructing machines. All human behavior, including the behavior of the machines which man builds to behave in his place, is ultimately to be accounted for in terms of the phylogenic contingencies of survival which have produced man as a species and the ontogenic contingencies of reinforcement which have produced him as an individual.

L'Envoi

To a cynical onlooker, says Sir Cyril Burt (29), it appears that "psychology, having first bargained away its soul and then gone out of its mind, seems now, as it faces an untimely end, to have lost all consciousness." Why is this amusing? It is a pun, of course, and a bitter one. By slightly rephrasing three expressions having to do with the rejection of explanatory fictions, Sir Cyril characterizes a behavioristic psychology as unconscious, insane, and damned. None of these suggests impending death, however, and he has, in fact, put the "untimely end" in the wrong field. It is biology which has lost its Life. And just as biology has never been livelier, so psychology has never been more keenly aware of its problems or of the steps to be taken in finding solutions.

Possibly we have misread Michelangelo and have reversed the roles of creature and creator. Is it not man who has created God? And will Adam not awake at last to an intelligent existence when the soporific virtues of Life and Mind have crossed the gap in the other direction?

References

1. Adams, D. K. Experimental studies of adaptive behavior in cats. *Comp. Psychol. Monogr.*, 1929, **6**, No. 1, Serial No. 27.
2. Adrian, E. D. *The basis of sensations; the action of the sense organs.* New York: W. W. Norton, 1928.
3. Allee, W. C. *Cooperation among animals.* New York: Abelard-Schuman, 1938.
4. Anokhin, P. K. Advances in brain research, Nauka i chelovechestvo [Science and humanity], Znaniye, 1965, 35–47. Reprinted in *Soviet Psychology*, 5, #1.
5. Ardrey, R. *African genesis.* New York: Atheneum, 1961.
6. Ashby, Sir Eric. Can education be machine made? *New Scientist*, February 2, 1967.
7. Ayllon, T. and Haughton, E. Control of the behavior of schizophrenic patients by food. *J. Exp. Anal. Beh.*, 1962, **5**, 343–352.
8. Azrin, N. H., Hutchinson, R. R., and McLaughlin, R. The opportunity for aggression as an operant reinforcer during aversive stimulation. *J. Exp. Anal. Behav.*, 1965, **8**, 171.
9. Bakan, David. Behaviorism and American urbanization. *J. History of Beh. Sciences*, 1966, **2**, 5–28.
10. Bannister, D. Psychology as an exercise in paradox. *Bull. Brit. Psychol. Soc.*, 1966, **19**, No. 63.
11. Bauer, Raymond. *The new man in Soviet psychology. Harvard Univ. Press*, 1952.
12. Beach, F. A. The snark was a boojum. *Amer. Psychol.*, 1950, **5**, 115–124.

13. Bellamy, Edward. *Looking backward*. Boston: Ticknor and Company, 1888.
14. Bellugi, Ursula and Brown, Roger (Eds.). The acquisition of language. (Monographs of the Society for Research in Child Development, Serial No. 92, 29, No. 1, 1964.)
15. Bernatowicz, A. J. Teleology in science teaching. *Science*, 1958, **128**, 1402–1405.
16. Bixenstine, V. Edwin. Empiricism in latter-day behavioral science. *Science*, 1964, **145**, 464–467.
17. Blackman, Allan. Scientism and planning. *Am. Behav. Scientist*, September, 1966.
18. Blanshard, Brand. Critical reflections on behaviorism. *Proc. of the Am. Phil. Soc.*, 1965.
19. Blanshard, Brand and Skinner, B. F. The problem of consciousness—a debate. *Philosophy and Phenomenological Research*, 1967, **27**, 317–337.
20. Bloch, H. D. Learning in some simple nonbiological systems. *Amer. Scientist*, 1965, **53**, 59–79.
21. Bloomfield, L. *Language*. New York: Holt, 1933.
22. Blough, D. S. Dark adaptation in the pigeon. *J. of Comp. and Physiol. Psych.*, 1956, **49**, 425–430.
23. Blough, D. S., and Schirer, A. M. Scotopic spectral sensitivity in the monkey. *Science*, 1963, **139**, 493–494.
24. Borrow, George. *The Romany rye*. London: John Murray, 1857.
25. Boswell, James. *Life of Samuel Johnson*. Constable Ed., 1783, Aet. 74, Vol. VI.
26. Breland, K. and Breland, M. The misbehavior of organisms. *Amer. Psychol.*, 1961, **16**, 681.
27. Bridgman, P. W. *The nature of some of our physical concepts*. New York: Philosophical Library, 1952.
28. Bridgman, P. W. *The way things are*. Cambridge: Harvard University Press, 1959.
29. Burt, C. The concept of consciousness. *Brit. J. Psychol.*, 1962, **53**, 229–242.
30. Bush, Vannevar. *Science is not enough*. New York: Morrow & Co., Inc., 1967.
31. Butler, Samuel. *Notebooks*. New York: Dutton, 1917.

32. Butterfield, H. The origins of modern science. Collier Books edition, 1962.

33. Cabanis, P. J. G. *Rapports du physique et du moral de l'homme*. Paris: Crapart, Caille et Ravier, 1802.

34. Cabet, Etienne. *Voyage en Icarie*. Paris: Bureau du Populaire, 1848.

35. Charlesworth, J. C. (ed.) *The limits of behavioralism in political science*. Philadelphia: American Academy of Political and Social Sciences, 1962.

36. Chomsky, N. Review of Skinner's *Verbal behavior*. In *Language*, 1959, **35**, 26–58.

37. Clark, J. H. Adaptive machines in psychiatry. In Wiener, J. and Schadé, J. P. (Eds.). *Nerve, brain and memory models*. Amsterdam, 1963.

38. Cohen, Harold, Filipczah, James, and Bis, John S. *CASE I: An initial study of contingencies applicable to special education*. Educational Facility Press—IBR, 1967.

39. De Laguna, G. *Speech: its function and development*. New Haven: Yale Univ. Press, 1927.

40. Diderot, D. *Supplement au voyage de Bougainville*. (Written in 1774, published in 1796.)

41. Dubos, R. Humanistic biology. *Amer. Scientist*, 1965, **53**, 4–19.

42. Ekstein, Rudolph and Caruth, Elaine. From Eden to utopia. *American Imago*, 1965, **22**, 128–141.

43. Erlenmeyer-Kimling, E., Hirsch, J., and Weiss, J. M. Studies in experimental behavior genetics: III. Selection and hybridization analyses of individual differences in the sign of geotaxis. *J. Comp. Physiol. Psychol.* 1962, **55**, 722–731.

44. Evans, B. and Evans, C. *A dictionary of contemporary American usage*. New York: Random House, 1957.

45. Ferster, C. B. Arithmetic behavior in chimpanzees. *Scientific American*, May, 1964.

46. Ferster, C. B. and Skinner, B. F. *Schedules of reinforcement*. New York: Appleton-Century-Crofts, 1957.

47. Feuer, L. S. *The scientific intellectual*. New York: Basic Books, 1963.

48. Frankenberger, Z. and Kortlandt, A. On the essential morpho-

logical basis for human culture. *Current Anthropol.*, 1965, **6**, 320.

49. Freud, Sigmund. *The origins of psychoanalysis.* Letters to Wilhelm Fliess, Drafts and notes: 1887-1902. New York: Basic Books, Inc., 1954.

50. Friedmann, H. quoted in article entitled "African honey-guides". *Science*, 1956, **123**, 55.

51. Galton, F. *Inquiries into human faculty and its development.* London: J. M. Dent and Company, 1883.

52. Gardner, H. *Art through the ages.* New York: Harcourt, Brace, 1926.

53. Gibbon, Edward. *The decline and fall of the Roman empire.* Modern Library ed. Vol. 1, p. 238, I. footnote 154 to Chapter 10.

54. Godwin, W. Motto on title page of *Caleb Williams.* Quoted by Arnold Kettle, *An introduction to the English novel.* London: Hutchinson, 1951.

55. Goncourt, Edmond et Jules de. *Journal: Memoires de la vie lettéraire.* L'imprimerie nationale de Monaco, 1956.

56. Goodman, Paul. *Compulsory mis-education.* New York: Horizon Press, 1964.

57. Gray, P. H. The descriptive study of imprinting in birds from 1863 to 1953. *J. Gen. Psychol.*, 1963, **68**, 333–346.

58. Grindley, G. C. The formulation of a simple habit in guinea pigs. *Brit. J. Psychol.*, 1932, **23**, 127–147.

59. Harkness, K. and Battell, J. S. Chess Review, February and March, 1947.

60. Harris, Frank. *Oscar Wilde, his life and confessions.* New York: the author, 1916.

61. Hearst, Eliot. Psychology across the chessboard. *Psychology Today*, June, 1967.

62. Hefferline, R. F., Keenan, B., and Harford, R. A. Escape and avoidance conditioning in human subjects without their observation of the response. *Science*, 1959, **130**, 1338–1339.

63. Henry, Jules. Review of human behavior; an inventory of scientific findings by Bernard Berelson and Gary A. Steiner. In *Scientific American*, July, 1964, Vol. 211.

64. Henry, Jules. Letter to the editor of *Scientific American.* September, 1964.

65. Herrnstein, R. J. Relative and absolute strength of response as a function of frequency of reinforcement. *J. Exp. Anal. Behav.*, 1961, **4**, 267–272.

66. Herrnstein, R. J. and Sommers, P. van. Method for sensory scaling with animals. *Science*, 1962, **135**, 40–41.

67. Hirsch, J. Behavior genetics and individuality understood. *Science*, 1963, **142**, 1436–1442.

68. Hoffman, H. S., Schiff, D., Adams, J., and Serle, J. L. Enhanced distress vocalization through selective reinforcement. *Science*, 1966, **151**, 352–354.

69. Hogben, L. *Statistical theory.* London: George Allen and Unwin, Ltd., 1957.

70. Holt, E. B. *Animal drive and the learning process.* New York: Holt, 1931.

71. Hull, Clark L. *Principles of behavior.* New York: D. Appleton-Century, 1943.

72. Huxley, Aldous. *Brave new world.* Garden City, New York: Doubleday, Doran & Co., Inc., 1932.

73. Huxley, J. Psychometabolism. *Perspectives in biology and medicine*, 1964, **7**, #4.

74. Hyman, Ray and Cohen, Elizabeth G. Water-witching in the United States. *Am. Sociological Review*, 1957, **22**, 719–724.

75. Ivanov-Smolensky, A. G. On methods of examining conditioned food reflexes in children and in mental disorders. *Brain*, 1927, **50**, 138–141.

76. Jones, Ernest. *The life and work of Sigmund Freud.* New York: Basic Books, 1953.

77. Kateb, George. *Utopia and its enemies.* New York: Free Press of Glencoe, 1963.

78. Kavanau, J. L. Behavior: Confinement, adaptation, and compulsory regimes in laboratory studies. *Science*, 1964, **143**, 490.

79. Keehn, J. D. Consciousness and behaviorism. *Brit. J. Psychol.*, 1964, **55**, 89–91.

80. Kelleher, R. T. Variables and behavior. *Amer. Psychologist*, 1962, **17**, 659–660.

81. Kierkegaard, Soren. *Diary of a seducer.* New York: Ungar, 1966.

82. Knight, Eric. *Lassie come home.* New York: Winston, 1940.

83. Koch, Sigmund. Psychology and emerging conceptions of

knowledge as unitary. In T. W. Wann (Ed.). *Behaviorism and Phenomenology.* Univ. of Chicago Press, 1964.

84. Köhler, W. The mentality of apes. Translated from the 2nd rev. ed. by Ella Winter. 2nd ed., revised and reset. New York: Harcourt, Brace & Co., Inc., 1927.

85. Kortlandt, A. (and Frankenberger, Z.) *Current Anthropology,* 1965, **6**, 320.

86. Kortlandt, A. Reported in *Time* magazine, April 21, 1967.

87. Krutch, J. W. *The measure of man.* Indianapolis: Bobbs-Merrill, 1953.

88. Laclos, Choderlos de. *Les liaisons dangereuses.* Paris, 1782.

89. Lévi-Strauss, C. *Structural anthropology.* New York: Basic Books, 1967.

90. Lewis, C. S. *The abolition of man.* New York: Macmillan, 1957.

91. *Life Magazine,* June 28, 1948, page 38.

92. Lindsley, O. R. Direct measurement and prosthesis of retarded behavior. *Journal of Education,* 1964, **147**, 62–81.

93. Lorenz, K. *Evolution and modification of behavior.* Chicago: Univ. of Chicago Press, 1965.

94. Lorenz, K. *On aggression.* New York: Harcourt, Brace & World, 1966, German ed. 1963.

95. Mach, Ernst. *The science of mechanics.* (Translated by T. J. McCormack.) Chicago: The Open Court Publishing Co., 1893.

96. MacKay, D. M. On comparing the brain with machines. *American Scientist,* 1954, **42**, 261–268.

97. Maingot, Eliane. *Les automates.* Paris: Hochette, 1959.

98. Maslow, Abraham. *Toward a psychology of being.* Princeton, New Jersey: Van Nostram, 1962.

99. Mayow, John. *De respiratione.* (1668) Medico-physical Works of John Mayow, Alembic Club Reprints, No. 17, Edinburgh, 1907, p. 207. Quoted by T. S. Patterson, *Isis,* 1931, **15**, 530.

100. Mayr, Ernst. Agassiz, Darwin, and evolution. *Harvard Library Bulletin,* 1959, **13**, #2.

101. Miller, S. and Konorski, J. Sur une forme particulière des réflexes conditionnels. Comples rendus des séances de la

société polonaise de biologie, 1928, **49**, 1155–1157. (Eng. trans.: *J. Exper. Anal. Behavior*, 1969, **12**, 187–189.)

102. Morris, William. *News from nowhere*. Boston: Roberts Brothers, 1890.

103. Morse, W. H. and Skinner, B. F. *J. Comp. Physiol. Psychol.*, 1957, **50**, 279.

104. Negley, G. and Patrick, J. M. *The quest for utopia*. New York: Schuman, 1952.

105. Neisser, Ulric. The imitation of man by machine. *Science*, 1963, **139**, 193–197.

106. Newell, Allen, Shaw, J. C. and Simon, H. A. Chess-playing programs and the problem of complexity. *IBM Journal*, October, 1958.

107. Newman, J. H., Cardinal. *The idea of a university*. Originally published in 1852. London: Longmans, 1923.

108. Orwell, George. *Nineteen eighty four*. London: Secker & Warburg, 1949.

109. Page, Irvine. Chemistry of the brain. *Science*, 1957, **125**, 721–727.

110. Peterson, N. Control of behavior by presentation of an imprinted stimulus. *Science*, 1960, **132**, 1395–1396.

111. Polanyi, Michael. *The study of man*. London: Routledge, 1959. (Lindsay Memorial Lectures, 1958.)

112. Polanyi, Michael. *Personal knowledge*. University of Chicago Press, 1960.

113. Polanyi, Michael. Science and man in the universe. In Harry Woolf (Ed.). *Science as a cultural force*. Baltimore; Johns Hopkins Press, 1964. Quoted by G. C. Amstutz, *Main Currents in Modern Thought*, 1968, **24**, #4.

114. Popper, K. R. *The open society and its enemies*. London: Routledge & Kegan Paul, 1957.

115. Pryor, Karen. Personal communication.

116. Rock, Irvin and Harris, Charles S. Vision and touch. *Scientific American*, 1967, **216**, #5, 96–104.

117. Rogers, Carl. *On becoming a person: a therapist's view of psychotherapy*. Boston: Houghton-Mifflin, 1961.

118. Rousseau, J. J. *Émile ou de l'éducation*. Le Haye: Néaulme, 1762.

119. Salaman, R. A. Tradesmen's tools. In *A History of Technology*, Vol. III, London: Oxford Univ. Press, 1957.

120. Schaffer, H. R. Proximity seeking and proximity avoidance: the basic dimensions of social behavior in infancy. *Bul. Brit. Psychol. Soc.*, 1966, **19**, #65, p. 70.

121. Sebeok, T. A. Animal communication. *Science*, 1965, **147**, 1006–1014.

122. Sidman, M. Avoidance conditioning with brief shock and no exteroceptive warning signal. *Science*, 1953, **118**, 157–158.

123. Sidman, M. *Tactics of scientific research*. New York: Basic Books, 1960.

124. Skinner, B. F. The concept of the reflex in the description of behavior. *J. Gen. Psych.* 1931, **5**, 427–458.*

125. Skinner, B. F. Two types of conditioned reflex and a pseudo-type. *J. Gen. Psych.*, 1935, **12**, 66–77.*

126. Skinner, B. F. The generic nature of the concepts of stimulus and response. *J. of Gen. Psych.* 1935, **12**, 40–65.*

127. Skinner, B. F. The verbal summator and a method for the study of latent speech. *Jour. of Psych.*, 1936, **2**, 71–107.

128. Skinner, B. F. Two types of conditioned reflex: A reply to Konorski and Miller. *J. Gen. Psychol.*, 1937, **16**, 272–279.*

129. Skinner, B. F. *The behavior of organisms*. New York: Appleton-Century, 1938.

130. Skinner, B. F. The operational analysis of psychological terms. *Psych. Rev.*, 1945.*

131. Skinner, B. F. Current trends in experimental psychology. *Current Trends in Psychology*. Pittsburgh Univ. Press, 1947.*

132. Skinner, B. F. "Superstition" in the pigeon. *J. Exp. Psychol.*, 1948, **38**, 168.

133. Skinner, B. F. *Walden Two*. New York: The Macmillan Company, 1948.

134. Skinner, B. F. Are theories of learning necessary? *Psychol. Rev.*, 1950, **57**, 193–216.*

135. Skinner, B. F. *Science and human behavior*. New York: The Macmillan Company, 1953.

136. Skinner, B. F. A critique of psychoanalytic concepts and theories. *Sci. Monthly*, 1954, **79**, 300–305.*

* Reprinted in (144).

137. Skinner, B. F. The control of human behavior. *Transactions of the New York Academy of Sciences*, 1965, Series II, Vol. 17, No. 7.*

138. Skinner, B. F. What is psychotic behavior? Theory and treatment of the psychoses. (Dedication of Renard Hospital, St. Louis), 1955.*

139. Skinner, B. F. Freedom and the control of men. *Amer. Scholar*, 1956, **25**, 47–65.*

140. Skinner, B. F. Some issues concerning the control of human behavior. *Science*, 1956, **124**, 1056–1066.*

141. Skinner, B. F. *Verbal behavior.* New York: Appleton-Century-Crofts, 1957.

142. Skinner, B. F. The flight from the laboratory. *Current trends in psychological theory.* Pittsburgh: University of Pittsburgh Press, 1961.

143. Skinner, B. F. Pigeons in a pelican. *Amer. Psychol.*, 1960, **15**, 28–37.*

144. Skinner, B. F. *Cumulative record:* Revised Edition. New York: Appleton-Century-Crofts, 1961.

145. Skinner, B. F. The design of cultures. *Daedalus*, 1961, 534–546.*

146. Skinner, B. F. Two "synthetic social relations." *J. Exp. Anal. Beh.* 1962, **5**, 531–533.*

147. Skinner, B. F. Behaviorism at fifty. *Science*, 1963, **134**, 566–602.

148. Skinner, B. F. Operant behavior. *Amer. Psych.*, 1963, **18**, 503–515.

149. Skinner, B. F. "Man." *Proc. Amer. Philosophical Society*, December, 1964, **108**, #6, 482–485.

150. Skinner, B. F. An operant analysis of problem-solving. Chapter in *Problem Solving: Research, Method, Teaching.* Ed., Benjamin Kleinmuntz. New York: John Wiley, 1966.

151. Skinner, B. F. Preface to paperback edition of *The behavior of organisms.* New York: Appleton-Century-Crofts, 1966.

152. Skinner, B. F. *The technology of teaching.* New York: Appleton-Century-Crofts, 1968.

153. Skinner, B. F. *Freedom and dignity.* (In preparation.)

* Reprinted in (144).

154. Stevens, S. S. The operational basis of psychology. *Amer. J. of Psych.*, 1935, 47, 323–330.

155. Taube, Mortimer. *Computers and common sense: the myth of thinking machines.* New York: Columbia UP, 1961.

156. Taylor, Charles. *The explanation of behavior.* New York: Humanities Press, 1964.

157. Terrace, H. S. Discrimination learning with and without "errors." *J. Exp. Anal. Behav.*, 1963, 6, 1–27.

158. Thorpe, W. H. The learning abilities of birds. Part I. *Ibis*, 1951, 93, 1–52.

159. Tinbergen, N. *The herring-gull's world.* London: Collins, 1953.

160. Tolman, E. C. and Brunswik, E. The organism and the causal texture of the environment. *Psychol. Rev.*, 1935, 42, 43–77.

161. Vives, Juan Luis. (1492–1540). De anima et vita. See F. Watson, *Vives on education.* Cambridge: Cambridge Univ. Press, 1913.

162. Waddington, C. H. The evolution of adaptations. *Endeavor*, July, 1953, 134–139.

163. Warren, H. C. (Ed.). *Dictionary of psychology.* Boston: Houghton-Mifflin, 1934.

164. Watson, J. B. *Behaviorism.* New York: W. W. Norton, 1924.

165. Westby, G. Psychology today: problems and directions. *Bull. Brit. Psychol. Soc.*, 1966, 19, No. 65.

166. White, R. A. Misperception and the Vietnam War. *Journal of Social Issues*, 1966, 22, #3.

167. Wiggins, David. Quoted in advertisement for *Time* in *Sat. Rev.*, February 5, 1966.

168. Wilson, E. Bright. *An introduction to scientific research.* New York: McGraw-Hill, 1952.

169. Wynne-Edwards, V. C. Self-regulating systems in populations of animals. *Science*, 1965, 147, 1543–1548.

Acknowledgments

Chapter 1 was given as an Annual Lecture at the National Institutes of Health, Bethesda, Maryland, on February 22nd, 1968. A briefer version was read in Paris on March 15th at a Symposium arranged by the International Brain Research Organization. An adapted version was published as "Psychology in the Year 2000" by Wayne State University.

Chapter 2 is based on two talks given on the BBC in the winter of 1966–1967 and published in *The Listener* under the titles "Visions of Utopia" (January 5, 1967) and "Utopia through the Control of Human Behavior" (January 12, 1967). The first of these appears here in a slightly modified version and the second has been extensively revised and enlarged. In essentially its present form the chapter appears as "Utopia and Human Behavior" in *Moral Problems in Contemporary Society*, edited by Paul Kurtz (Englewood Cliffs, N. J.: Prentice-Hall, Inc., 1969) and is reprinted here by permission.

Chapter 3 was given as a lecture at the Walter Reed Army Medical Center under the auspices of the Washington School of Psychiatry on March 26, 1965, and published as "Contingencies of Reinforcement in the Design of a Culture" in *Behavioral Science*, 1966, 11, 159–166. Permission to reprint is gratefully acknowledged.

Chapter 4 was part of a symposium on applications of operant conditioning at a meeting of the American Psychological Association, September 6, 1964. It was published as "What is the Experimental Analysis of Behavior?" in the *Journal of the Experimental Analysis of Behavior*, 1966, 9, 213–218, copyright © 1966 by the Society for the Experimental Analysis of Behavior, and is reprinted by permission.

Chapter 5 is a chapter in *Operant Behavior: Areas of Research and Application,* edited by Werner K. Honig, New York: Appleton-Century-Crofts, 1966. It appeared first as "Operant Behavior" in *American Psychologist,* 1963, **18,** 503–515, and is reprinted here by permission.

Chapter 6 was part of a symposium at the Carnegie Institute of Technology, April, 1965. It was published in *Problem Solving: Research, Method, and Theory,* edited by Benjamin Kleinmuntz (New York: John Wiley & Sons, Inc., 1966), and is reprinted by permission.

Chapter 7 was presented at a symposium at the University of Kentucky in November, 1965, and published in *Science,* 1966, **153,** 1205–1213, copyright 1966 by the American Association for the Advancement of Science. Permission to reprint has been granted.

An early version of Chapter 8 was given as the R. M. Elliot Lecture at the University of Minnesota, December, 1962. The present version was part of a symposium at Rice University. It appears in *Behaviorism and Phenomenology,* edited by T. W. Wann, University of Chicago Press, 1964. It appeared first in *Science,* 1963, **140,** 951–958, copyright 1963 by the American Association for the Advancement of Science, and is reprinted here by permission. Some of the material in the notes following Chapter 8 is taken from a debate with Brand Blanshard entitled "The Problem of Consciousness" and printed in *Philosophy and Phenomenological Research,* March, 1967, **27,** No. 3. It is reprinted with permission.

Chapter 9 is based upon a Herrick Lecture given at Denison University in October, 1960; it was prepublished in *Psychology Today* Magazine, April, 1969. Copyright © Communications/Research/Machines/Inc., and used by permission.

Preparation of the book has been supported by a Career Award from the National Institutes of Mental Health (Grant K6-MH-21, 775-01). I am grateful to Mrs. Alexandra Huebner for her help in the preparation of the manuscript.

Index